MEMORIES OF
THE MODERNS

James Joyce: A Critical Introduction (1941, 1960)

The Overreacher: A Study of Christopher Marlowe (1952)

Contexts of Criticism (1957)

The Power of Blackness: Hawthorne, Poe, Melville (1958)

The Question of Hamlet (1959)

The Gates of Horn: A Study of Five French Realists (1963)

Refractions: Essays in Comparative Literature (1966)

The Myth of the Golden Age in the Renaissance (1969)

Grounds for Comparison (1972)

*Shakespeare and the Revolution of the Times:
Perspectives and Commentaries* (1976)

HARRY LEVIN

MEMORIES OF THE MODERNS

A NEW DIRECTIONS BOOK

Grateful acknowledgment is made to the editors and publishers of the following journals and magazines in which some of these essays first appeared: *Actes de VIIe Congrès de L'Association Internationale de Littérature Comparée* (Stuttgart), *Canto: A Review of the Arts, The Harvard Advocate, The Journal of the History of Ideas, The Kenyon Review, The Massachusetts Review, The Monthly Review, The New Republic,* and *Saturday Review.*

Portions of this book appeared in various periodicals or as separate publications and are reprinted by permission of the publishers: "Rue Lhomond: Francis Ponge" (Copyright © 1974, *Books Abroad,* reprinted by permission of the University of Oklahoma Press); "*The Waste Land:* From *Ur* to *Echt*" (Copyright © 1972 by Harry Levin, reprinted by permission of New Directions); "William Carlos Williams and the Old World" in *A Voyage to Pagany* by William Carlos Williams (Copyright © 1970 by Harry Levin, reprinted by permission of New Directions); "Randall Jarrell's *Faust,*" "In Memoriam: I. A. Richards," "Being Strong: Edmund Wilson's Correspondence," "A Contest Between Conjurors: Nabokov and Wilson," and "The Private Life of F. O. Matthiessen in *The New York Review of Books*" (Copyright © 1976–79 Nyrev, Inc.); "Ezra Pound, T. S. Eliot, and the European Horizon," Taylorian Lecture (Copyright © 1975 by Oxford University Press); "*Ulysses* in Manuscript" (Copyright © 1976, The Rosenbach Museum & Library, Philadelphia; "Edmund Wilson: The Last American Man of Letters" (Copyright © 1974, *The Times Literary Supplement,* reprinted by permission of the Editor, *The Times Literary Supplement* of London).

Manufactured in the United States of America
First published clothbound by New Directions in 1980
Published simultaneously in Canada by George J. McLeod, Ltd., Toronto

Library of Congress Cataloging in Publication Data

Levin, Harry, 1912–
    Memories of the moderns.
    (A New Directions Book)
    Includes index.
        1.   Literature, Modern—History and criticism—
Addresses, essays, lectures.   I.   Title.
PN710.L438   1980   809'.04   80-36827
ISBN 0-8112-9733-1

New Directions Books are published for James Laughlin
by New Directions Publishing Corporation
80 Eighth Avenue, New York 10011

Contents

MEMORIES OF
THE MODERNS

A LETTER
TO JAMES LAUGHLIN

Dear J.:

Let us begin—and I hope the old-fashioned phrase can be supported by the paradoxical quirk of my running title—with a dedicatory epistle. It is by no means difficult to justify a dedication to one's publisher in this particular case, and I have been looking forward to the opportunity. Dedications themselves have become somewhat old-fashioned, and therefore not less in keeping with Modernism insofar as we look back upon it; yet I have always used them as a special linkage between books and friendships, and have felt much pleasure when other writers have offered me links of the same kind. A number of years ago, when an Italian publisher planned to bring together a collection of my articles which had been translated into his language, I planned to dedicate that collection to you; it seemed appropriate not only because of your intercultural perspectives, but more specifically because one of the translations had appeared in a periodical you edited, *Prospetti USA*. As it happened, despite the good offices of our friend Renato Poggioli in finding the publisher and writing a preface, the luckless firm went bankrupt and the projected volume never appeared. Hence I am now fulfilling an obligation which has been prolonged and enlarged meanwhile. Moreover, in returning to a sponsorship which virtually launched my critical work, I feel that I have been rounding a personal cycle.

Today it is almost forty-five years since, while an undergraduate at Harvard College, you founded New Directions: both the *avant-garde* publishing house and the quasi-annual showcase for literary talent, now in its thirty-ninth volume and still pioneering. Though we were slightly acquainted already, and had common friends and interests, I cannot claim to have been very sympathetic or encouraging at what must have been a lonely and daring start. On the contrary. Superciliously and not quite seriously, I reviewed your second volume in *The Nation*, with invidious glances toward *New Signatures, New Writing*, and the new school of British poets that John Lehmann was rounding up during the Thirties. What, I asked, was so novel about contributors

1

like Jean Cocteau and Gertrude Stein, who had been parading their quondam novelties ever since the *Belle Epoque?* Were you not constructing, so to speak, an old actors' home? Your good-natured response to this light-minded teasing was to send me a few of your other publications, sufficient to convince any thoughtful reader of your serious intentions, and graciously inscribed "from the majordomo of the old actors' home." Two years afterward in 1939, when you brought out the fourth *New Directions in Prose and Poetry,* I too—though not yet very old and never much of an actor—had become an inmate and was enjoying your hospitality.

The occasion that brought us together was the publication of *Finnegans Wake*—surely one of the most remarkable innovations in the history of literature, though the direction it indicated was and remains problematic, and may well have heralded the end of its epoch, coinciding with the outbreak of the Second World War. Starting to teach, I had been allowed to offer a course in Comparative Literature on Proust, Joyce, and Mann, not without some head-shaking on the part of senior colleagues, and so it was my duty to come to some sort of terms with that demanding text. John Crowe Ransom had invited me to review it in *The Kenyon Review,* as I did with frustrating succinctness. Having spent most of a summer in scanning those pages, gathering impressions, taking notes, checking allusions, and underlining themes in different colors, I needed the more ample allotment of space that you so opportunely provided. The title of the review-article, "On First Looking into *Finnegans Wake,*" with its Homeric reverberation from Keats and its apologetic implication that I was tentatively viewing the object through a dark Chapmanesque glass, seemed to please James Joyce so much that he amiably overlooked my occasional strictures and wild surmises. It was his postcard of thanks that gave you the idea for my *Critical Introduction* to his works, which I managed to write and you managed to print within the year of his death in 1941.

We were lucky to have seized the moment, as I would hardly have done without your persistence. But the luckiest aspect of the timing, you will remember, was wholly accidental. Though the little book had been scheduled for fall publication, it was delayed in production until Christmas week. Had this study of an author chiefly known to the general public for his difficulty and alleged immorality, written by a newcomer and published by a fledgling press on a narrowly limited budget, been issued according to schedule, it would have been snowed out of notice by the better-sellers of the season. Coming when the reviewers were at loose ends, it was widely noticed: one of the comparatively few among my books to be covered by *Time, The New York,* and the daily *New York Times.* Later, when through T. S. Eliot a British edition was sponsored by Faber and Faber, it was sympathetically recommended by George Orwell, Stephen Spender, and other critics. *The Times Literary Supplement,* then an all but official spokesman for the establishment that Joyce had been undermining, thundered editorially against it (it was amusing to be told that the anonymous editorialist had been that faded romanticist, Charles Morgan). Thomas Mann, on the other hand, publicized a much friendlier reaction in one of his notebooks. Thirty-eight years after writing, nineteen years after revision, paperback copies are still in print, and translations exist in five languages.

I would not be mentioning these circumstances if I did not feel entirely detached from them by the passage of time, and interested in recollecting them merely as the original basis of our working relationship. This might also serve to illustrate, for other and younger readers, how quickly Joyce ceased to be what he himself termed "a banned writer" and became—to modify his own phrasing—a happy hunting-ground for professional researchers. The monument of such scholarly dedication, the most important single work in the field, and one of our most distinguished literary biographies, has been Richard Ellmann's *James Joyce* (1959). If I recall Professor Ellmann's overgenerous acknowledgment, that "Harry Levin . . . laid the foundation of Joyce scholarship," it is not that I would boast. In all candor, though I should be proud to think that I had left something he could use in building his grand structure, I feel rather shamefaced at the thought of contriving to set up an academic industry. Some of the recent interpretation and documentation is sound and illuminating; much of it is redundant, overingenious, or half-baked. Joyce had brought it all upon himself, and would probably have loved the scholastic *brouhaha.* Hoping the outline I sketched may hold some continuing relevance to its subject, I am glad to see it augmented by richer detail and outdated by more extensive research at innumerable points.

At all events, my place on your list has been a marginal one. Though we have maintained the association in various other ways, most of my intervening books have been handled by university presses. You did enable me to edit and introduce a handsomely printed selection from the Earl of Rochester's poems and a corrected version of Flaubert's *Three Tales*. During a period when most of my teaching was taken up with Anglo-American literature, you encouraged me to go on with a protracted book about French literature by publishing two related fascicles: *Toward Stendhal* and *Toward Balzac* (and when a provincial printer garbled the foreign names and quotations, you had him reset a whole chapter). Two brief reappearances under your imprint are reprinted in the present volume. Imaginative writing that "makes it new"—as you must have learned from the precept and example of Ezra Pound—calls for fresh modes of critical explication. It is significant that *The New Criticism* was coupled with New Directions on the title page of John Ransom's historic manifesto. This programmatic slant was carried farther when you undertook responsibility for the American distribution of William Empson's books. But, lest your catholicity be identified with any party line, one may point to your support for Yvor Wintors, who was a traditional poet, an anti-Modernist critic, and an austerely dogmatic figure in both spheres.

You have spoken very openly about your early hopes of becoming a writer. Of course you are one; you give an earnest of it now and then in verse or prose which suggests how well that might have been your full-time vocation. Instead it has functioned more broadly as a touchstone for the recognition of other talents. It was Pound who had exercised this faculty of recruitment for the benefit of a prior generation. Temporarily dropping out of Harvard, you did wisely to seek his tutelage at Rapallo. He, cut off more and more from America and increasingly distracted from literature, gave you wise counsel nonetheless: to go home and become a publisher, starting with William Carlos Williams and presumably himself. They were both over fifty, not exactly young unknowns, but blocked at the established commercial houses in the doldrums of mid-career. As you started your venture from the converted stable of your family estate in rural Connecticut, they must have brought you a sense of continuity with Kensington, the Left Bank, and Greenwich Village during the movements and magazines that flourished just before and after the First World War. With them, with an exceptional few among your official teachers (notably Dudley Fitts at Choate and Theodore Spencer at Harvard), and what with one prospect recommending another, you built up a peculiarly sensitive network of talent scouts.

The real test would be your own record of discovery among our more immediate contemporaries. Henry Miller was a late starter in the Thirties, and *Tropic of Cancer* came under the censor's ban until the Grove Press's litigation in the Sixties. Yet you had, as I recall, shocked some readers of *The Harvard Advocate* with a preview; and, upon his repatriation, Miller became one of your regular authors. He, in turn, persuaded you to publish Hermann Hesse's *Siddhartha*, whose mystical vogue must have done wonders for your treasury. The other Williams, Tennessee, you discovered as a poet and went on to foster as a novelist; the sequence of his plays has been among the outstanding staples on your list. Others whose artistic development has been registered in your successive catalogues include Dylan Thomas, Denise Levertov, and John Hawkes. These diverge from cases where your writers have moved closer to the marketplace, or where you were willing to take a chance on an out-of-the-way manuscript by a well-known writer. Thus you had the satisfaction of giving the world Joyce's *Stephen Hero*, and—as I particularly appreciate—the first English writings of Vladimir Nabokov. Where the big publishers were "not doing their jobs," you discerned your opportunities. When Scribner's allowed *The Great Gatsby* to go out of print, you leased the rights for your New Classics; and when they turned down Scott Fitzgerald's *Crack-Up*, you rescued it.

Some day I hope the full story will be set down, preferably by yourself. *A New Directions Reader* did present a sampler of excerpts and a bibliography up to 1964. To date you must have put your imprimatur on over five hundred titles, allowing a liberal margin for those which would make less of a mark, since it has been your policy to combine bold risk with careful selection. Yet, thumbing through the files of your anthologies, we recognize from subsequent achievement many writers who were scarcely known when you first accepted their contributions: I cite almost haphazardly James Agee, John Ashbery, John Berryman, Paul Bowles, Randall Jarrell, Wright Morris, Howard Nemerov, John Frederick Nims, Karl Shapiro, Eudora Welty. Your importations— including Borges, Brecht, Camus, Eluard, Kafka, Lorca, Mishima, Montale, Neruda, Pasternak, Paz, Queneau, Rilke, Svevo, Ungaretti— have been translated with conscientious empathy, to the extent of providing bilingual texts for poetry. Your literary horizons extended beyond the Americas and Europe to Asia and Africa. You invented an economical means for poetic débuts in the subscription series, Poets of the Month (or Year), which ran to forty-two elegant pamphlets. If I remind you that you once rejected a sheaf of poems submitted by Edmund Wilson, possibly at some cost in future good will, it is to stress the intransigence with which you consistently applied your own individual criteria.

You cannot but have drawn encouragement from the growing appreciation of the intellectual community. Lately this has assumed the public form of honorary degrees and institutional citations. It was indeed a meaningful ceremony in 1977, when the National Academy and Institute of Arts and Letters conferred on you its Award for Distinguished Service in the Arts—the only publisher to receive the award in the course of its thirty-six-year existence. Pound would have rejoiced at this positive consequence of his farsighted advice. Nor would he have failed to draw the negative inferences, if he had survived into an era when big publishers have become the adjuncts of bigger conglomerates, when taste gets promoted by talk-shows, and the American Publishers Association has reduced the National Book Awards to the standing of Hollywood's Oscars. Eliot might have added his stoical testimony that the good fight is no longer for popular victory; it is fundamentally an endeavor to keep certain values alive. It has now been two decades since I ventured to argue, instancing the history of New Directions: "In spite of its vanguard title, it has been primarily engaged in fighting a rear-guard action." I did not mean to question the things you stood for or your whole-hearted commitment to them, but simply to note that they were receding, temporally superseded or sea-changed. When we discussed the point, you did not disagree.

This argument was broached in an article, "What Was Modernism?", which came out in *The Massachusetts Review* (August 1960) and was subsequently republished elsewhere—in my *Refractions* (1966), with an updating headnote that drew some controversial responses. Much of the material had been subsumed from a lecture, which I had been offering and revising intermittently since the late Forties, on the significance of the mid-century as a landmark in literary history. Not long ago my article was credited, by a German scholarly journal, with having introduced the adjective *postmodern* into critical discourse. Far from attempting any coinage, I had acknowledged that my specific applications of the term to literature followed the broad conception adumbrated by Arnold Toynbee in his *Study of History*. *Postmodernism* had previously been current in the terminology of architecture, where Modernism defined itself so concretely, as well as in the literary history of Hispanic cultures. Here the important matter is not priority but consensus: the fact that criticism, from differing viewpoints, was demonstrating a need for the expression. In his book suggestively entitled *Decline of the New* (1970), Irving Howe has republished an essay from 1959, "Mass Society and Postmodern Fiction," tracing certain factors that have altered the moral climate. In a postscript appended after several years, he perceives further "shifts in cultural temper which are hard to explain and certain to occur."

To live through such periods of change is to be confirmed in the realization that the word *contemporary*, in its literal meaning, signifies being temporary together. The present always comes as an aftermath to something else: "After such knowledge what forgiveness?" If we place a high value upon the immediate past, we may be prone to indulge ourselves in nostalgia—the mood that Donald Barthelme mocks in his titular plea, *Come Back, Dr. Caligari.* I have no wish to provoke comparisons where the forerunners hold, over their successors, the unfair advantage of settled scores and clarified contours. The predecessors are bound to stand out, in their very alienations and conflicts, against a more conformable situation eased by grants and merchandised by advertisements. My essay tried to sketch a composite profile, even though its basic stress on individuality meant that no two individuals could fit the same model. They were animated by what I called the metamorphic impetus, the challenge to outdo oneself by continuous transmutation of forms and styles. Equally preoccupied by the heritage of art and its confrontation with science, they oscillated between traditions and experiments. Cosmopolitan, often expatriate, they interlinked and transcended cultures. Conscious intellectuals for the most part, writer's writers all in varying ways, craftsmen bent upon extending their craft, they practised the eclectic cult of the fabulous artificer, *il miglior fabbro.*

Though the metaphorical parallel between poetry and painting is an ancient trope, it remained for certain writers of Flaubert's generation to conceive themselves literally as artists. The critique of Jean-Paul Sartre a century afterward, in recoil from post-Flaubertian mandarinism and engaged by sociopolitical urgencies, propagates and exemplifies the image of the writer as a publicist. An extreme American instance of this trend—from the belletristic to the documentary—is that of Norman Mailer. The trend-setting editor of *Les Temps Modernes* has hardly been a proponent of Modernism in its more strictly artistic connotation. Flaubert figures appropriately on your list, as does Goethe in your Makers of Modern Literature. That series seems to have gathered about a dozen monographs, beginning with my *James Joyce*, and depending largely upon the contributor's choice of Maker, as with Nabokov's *Gogol* and Lionel Trilling's *E. M. Forster*. It could not be usefully contrasted with the far more comprehensive and modish scope of Frank Kermode's Modern Masters, except by remarking that those masters are not necessarily men of letters; many of them are ideologues or prophets, not all of them Modernists. Looking backward toward the last, the contrast that may strike us is with Boni and Liveright's Modern Library, when those alluring leatherette volumes (at ninety-five cents) formed our adolescent tastes in the Twenties by weaning us away from the Genteel Tradition.

Writers first declared themselves as Moderns when they were breaking away from the authority of the Ancients. The ensuing patterns of transmission and renewal, influence and recoil, have been lucidly outlined by W. J. Bate and subjected to cabbalistic elaboration by Harold Bloom. No sharp break has been perceptible recently; *modern* is still regarded, by the majority of readers, as synonymous with *contemporary*. Yet the very similarities and continuities between the two attest a latent difference. What was innovation for the precursors has become convention for the aftercomers. The ironic fate that wafted the books of the *avant-garde* from Bohemia to Academe has installed them within the curriculum, where they are imitated as well as explicated. Your experience has led you to observe that few geniuses are shaped by courses in creative writing. Could you imagine Joyce teaching—let alone taking—such a course? His struggles have made it possible for English Departments to incubate fiction that outrivals his in allusiveness, laboriousness, and subjectivity. But these directions cannot be hailed as new. The Modernists seem to have reached their apogee during the first generation of the twentieth century. The middle generation, our own, has come to stand for continuance, consolidation, and transition. Perhaps the third generation, now approaching its prime and emerging in your catalogue, will project us beyond the modern.

Very lately Stephen Spender, at the age of seventy, has been paying his respects to the innovators with a quip that echoes both Beckett and Eliot: "In their end-games were our game-beginnings." This transitional span could not have been more vividly dramatized than in the poetry and the personality—and can the two have ever coexisted more

actively and intimately?—of Robert Lowell. He has figured only once
among your contributors (in a symposium on John Crowe Ransom);
and I was merely in sporadic touch with him, albeit from his student
days to recent terms as a colleague; but you and I had the privilege of
watching and admiring his memorable career as slightly older contemporaries. In sudden retrospect it seems surprising that he actually lived
into his sixtieth year, considering how dangerously he felt compelled
to live, and that he succeeded in building up so large and authentic
an *oeuvre*, perforce refreshing his own imagination with periodic imitations, free translations, dramatic adaptations, and even self-revisions.
Highly conscious of his own beginnings, most directly the guidance of
Ransom and Allen Tate, he went on to acknowledge with Eliot and
Pound an ever-widening circle of poetic forebears. As he moved from
traditionalism to iconoclasm, from the confessional vein toward the
forensic, from history to modernity and back again, it would be inevitable that at times "the composition was garbled." But the inner
tensions were always respondent to the outer conflicts, with unique
sensitivity.

Among the many reverberations that have so extended his frame of
reference one might serve as a pertinent illustration here. Alan Williamson's perceptive study of Lowell's "political vision" derives its title,
Pity the Monsters, from the poem "Florence" in *For the Union Dead*.
There, amid shades of Browning, Lowell addresses himself to the three
monumental statues in the Piazza della Signoria: Michelangelo's
David, Donatello's *Judith*, and Cellini's *Perseus*. All of them personify
liberation and tyrannicide, and yet we are perversely (Mr. Williamson's word) exhorted to sympathize with the darker forces embodied
in their tyrannical victims:

> Pity the monsters!
> Pity the monsters!
> Perhaps, one always took the wrong side . . .

Lowell's retentive ear must at some point have picked up, and then
half forgotten, the poem in E. E. Cummings' *1 × 1* that begins: "pity
this busy monster,manunkind, / not." That note of appeal was canceled out by the negative enjambment. Monstrosity, for Cummings,
was "the bigness" of unkind mankind's "littleness." What it bespeaks
is satire rather than pathos: why sentimentalize the inhumane or the
unnatural? "Pity poor flesh / and trees,poor stars and stones." Had it

not been for the repeated formulation, we might not have thought of comparing Cummings—one of the first poets to appear in *New Directions*—with Lowell. Insofar as we can do so, we must make due concession to the latter's deeper range and resonance. But if we are speaking of verbal technique or artistic control, it is the former who has been the more original experimentalist, the purer lyricist, the sharper wit, the creator of more incisive lines. Octavio Paz may help us to weather the comparison, when he generalizes: "Negation is no longer creative. I am not saying that we are living at the end of art: we are living at the end of *the idea of modern art*."

The present tendency has been summed up, by the gifted Mexican poet-critic, in the paradox: "a tradition against itself." Processes of revaluation and reversal have accordingly been setting in. Eliot, if not canonized during his lifetime, seems to have been attaining his niche of classical aloofness. Pound, who expired in an anxious welter of unfinished business, has left an estate to be endlessly litigated if ever settled. Ernest Hemingway's stock has dropped spectacularly in a bearish market. Hermann Hesse encountered his most enthusiastic audiences after a generation's lag. It is not my intention to chart such reckonings or indulge in invidious discriminations. Most of these impressions should convey some element of the first-hand, in the sense of confronting materials newly available or of drawing on some snatches of personal reminiscence. Most of these authors I first read when their books emerged, sometimes as a reviewer. Gradually, as I became immersed in my academic studies, usually of more distant periods, I found myself reviewing less currently and more for scholarly than for literary journals. If a reversion has come about latterly, it is because the Modernists have been reappearing as subjects for retrospection and scholarship. Nearly all of those before us are no longer living, some of them having prematurely died. Witness the fact that no less than ten of them now disclose themselves through collected letters.

I, if no one else, must thank you for suggesting this book. Neither of us had any set design for it beyond the chronological orientation, plus the circumstance that all except three of these reviews, essays, lectures, introductions, memoirs, or epistles were written and published during the Nineteen-Seventies. If they show variety, it owes a good deal to the diversity of the initial sponsorship. As it happens, out of the twenty-one figures named in the table of contents (yourself excluded), seventeen have been listed one way or another in your offering. This attests much more about your coverage than about mine, since my subjects were mainly assigned or chosen at random, and since an altogether different sequence might be just as fully matched in your catalogue. Naturally, our common starting-point has been the United States; just as naturally the continued movement has been to-and-from Europe. Two of our American mentors have made expatriation a leading principle; five of our eminent Europeans, differing in degrees of adaptation, have been expatriated to America. The American scene has never been complete without its European horizon. Commitment to the international theme has, in practice, involved us with a concern for intercultural communication, and stylistically with problems of translation. The proper study of our literature must be framed by Comparative Literature—a premise which, as Pound so firmly held, applies generally to twentieth-century literature.

We might well leave the last word of this end-game to Pound, inasmuch as he presided over your game-beginning and other matters I shall be touching on. You knew him long and well, as I did not—nor would have wished to, given the conditions of his developing ideology and my ethnic background. As chance would have it, I saw him intensively for about a single week, when he was staying at Cambridge with Theodore Spencer during the spring of 1939. Ted had a busy teaching schedule, while I had a leisurely fellowship, so that I was informally deputed to keep an eye on the distinguished guest and help him to establish local contacts. Delighted as I was by this prospect of casual association, it ended by baffling us all. Politely but shortly and wearily, he would reply to my literary and esthetic questions. What he really wanted to talk about, it became clear, was Social Credit and the corporate state. It was as if Dr. Johnson had insisted that Boswell limit their conversations to the stamp tax. Pound expressed particular eagerness for an evening's discussion with some of Harvard's foremost economists. Never had Ted or I, who made the arrangements, been more keenly embarrassed by a nonmeeting of minds. It may be that this anticlimax prepared Pound for the greater one he was next to experience as a self-appointed lobbyist in Washington, and consequently for his return to wartime Italy, where he would soon be caught up in his tragic errors.

Although I would never see him again, I was—as you were—a member of the committee that recommended him for the Emerson-Thoreau Medal of the American Academy of Arts and Sciences in 1972. Having been instructed that the award was explicitly for services to letters, and that any ideological considerations would be irrelevant, none of us could imaginably have nominated a better-qualified candidate. Twenty-three years after the controversy over the Bollingen Prize, fourteen years after the twelve-year incarceration at Saint Elizabeth's Hospital, with the octogenarian master back in Italian retirement, and with evidence before us of mental delusion and moral recantation, we had no reason to expect that the Council of the Academy would high-handedly turn that professional judgment down. We refrained from raising the issue publicly because we did not want the moribund poet personally subjected to another rebuff. But it was too late for tact; there were resignations and rumors that crossed the Atlantic. A few months before Pound's death a former student of mine became acquainted in Venice with an artist friend of his. When they met again, she relayed a message from Pound to me. True to the habit of taciturnity that he had been cultivating in his ultimate phase, this consisted of just two words: "It matters." What it was that mattered might be referred back to the substance of your earliest dialogues with him. That had been what always mattered. That was not vanity. Old friend, it has mattered.

As ever,

H.L.

Cambridge, Massachusetts
23 September, 1979

EZRA POUND,
T. S. ELIOT,
AND THE EUROPEAN HORIZON

*These italicized headnotes will allow me to acknowledge, with warm grati-
tude and an occasional afterthought, the original circumstances and sponsors
that prompted the papers in this book. The one that follows was first presented as the Taylorian Special Lecture for 1974 at Oxford University, and
published as a pamphlet by the Clarendon Press in 1975. I am grateful to
the Oxford Faculty of Mediaeval and Modern Languages, and particularly
to Professor I. D. McFarlane, for their gracious invitation and hospitality. I
should add that I have here incorporated most of a shorter paper which I
presented to a conference of the International Comparative Literature Association at Montreal in August 1973 under the title of "Ezra Pound, T. S.
Eliot, and the Idea of Comparative Literature," and which has now been
published in* Actes de VIIe Congrès de L'Association Internationale de Littérature Comparée *(Stuttgart: 1979).*

●

> Pound went gunning for trouble, and got it, for cause;
> Eliot, far more astute, has deserved his applause . . .
> Both of them are book-men, but where Eliot has found
> A horizon in letters, Pound has only found Pound.[1]

The foregoing couplets are quoted from the doggerel survey of contemporary American poets, *A Critical Fable,* published anonymously
in 1922. For that date the double characterization showed a certain
degree of prescience. It had even touched a note of unhappy prophecy
in an earlier line: "Each one is a traitor, but with different treasons."
The interwoven pattern of their respective careers might almost have
been prefigured in the uncritical fable of the hare and the tortoise. By
the three years that marked his seniority, Ezra Pound was the innovator, the instigator, the impresario. His discoveries and manifestoes,
his translations and experiments had placed him at the center of what
was just then coming to be known as "the Modern Movement." Most

of the shorter poems that he would be known by were already in print; but his "poem of some length," the *Cantos,* would be strung along through the next fifty years, and would register his restless drift to the dangerous perimeter of the vortex. T. S. Eliot, however, had just emerged with *The Waste Land* to make his major impact and to take his centripetal position. Nicely, precisely, he would be moving on to become a pillar of the Establishment, in its most strictly Anglican connotation. While he assimilated and consolidated the respectable and slightly clerical role of "Mr. Eliot," the bohemian Pound identified himself with the protean voices of his *personae:* from Propertius to Confucius, from Hugh Selwyn Mauberley to Uncle Ez. The recurrent alienation of the artist from society may have been strained to its widest breach in the later stages of his tragic career: his indictment for treason and his commitment for insanity.

The anonymous critic who supplied my quotation had been recognized at once as Amy Lowell; her satirical pamphlet formed a sequel to the nineteenth-century *Fable for Critics* by her relative, James Russell Lowell. Her critique of Pound may have been exacerbated by their quarrel over the Imagists. His campaign for visual concreteness and verbal clarity, coinciding with that of T. E. Hulme, had briefly converged with it into a new school of Anglo-American poetry. As a sort of international gesture, with a nod to the *Unanimistes,* he had entitled his anthology *Des Imagistes.* Did the indefinite French article imply that there were unincluded others, fellow travelers, *Imagistes avant la lettre* or *Imagistes sans le savoir?* Pound was not categorical at this stage, yet he had come to believe that Miss Lowell was appropriating his term, that Imagism was being transposed into "*Amygism.*" Consequently his next anthology proclaimed itself "Catholic," meaning universal. Amy Lowell's charge that Pound found no one but himself might be supported whenever the *Cantos* move from art to self, as in *Section: Rock-Drill* (LXXXV): "from Τέχνη back to σεαυτόν." Yet, as an exponent of technique or a practiced technician, his influence was virtually unparalleled in his time; he is certainly one of the "donative writers," to use his label for some of his masters; and the record of his perception and generosity, in finding and fostering talents, constitutes a unique chapter in the history of modern literature.[2] Witness his spectacular intervention in helping Eliot to find himself, which the younger poet acknowledged by his dedication of *The Waste Land.* There he calls Pound "*il miglior fabbro*"—what Dante called Arnaut Daniel. But, in pursuing the parallel, we should remember that Dante, after all, was the better craftsman.

As for a horizon in letters, Pound's was undoubtedly more exploratory than Eliot's, though considerably less coherent. Beyond the domain of poetry, their fellow Imagist Richard Aldington noted, Pound's "wide knowledge" was rifted by "strange gaps of ignorance," as contrasted with the intellectual discipline that Eliot had undergone through his philosophical training.[3] Polar differences in temperament are reflected by widely diverging prose styles. Ever the mover and shaker, Pound exclaims, exhorts, and polemicizes; his mode of discourse, reversing Eliot's celebrated refrain, is pitched for "A bang, not a whimper" (Canto LXXIV). Eliot is judicious to the point of being judicial, hedging himself within a network of reservations and qualifications, demurely interspersed with mock-pedantry and ironic self-scrutiny. "Has Eliot or have I wasted the greater number of hours," Pound would ask with characteristic impatience, "he by attending to fools and/or humouring them, and I by alienating imbeciles suddenly?"[4] Eliot, in an early satirical sketch, "Eeldrop and Appleplex," depicted himself and his friend as twentieth-century avatars of Bouvard and Pécuchet. The very complementarity of their individual approaches reinforced their effectiveness in achieving common critical goals. For such purposes, roughly similar backgrounds combined to produce a striking joint impression. Born of old Yankee stock in mid-continental America, the two poets had been educated at Eastern colleges, and had continued into graduate school with the prospect of becoming teachers and scholars. Both had originally crossed the Atlantic for the purpose of completing their academic formations: Pound with a traveling fellowship to prepare a thesis on Lope de Vega, Eliot to study philosophy at the Sorbonne and Oxford—Oxford by an accident of war, since his destination had been Marburg.

Wanderjahre led to expatriation in each case, though the circumstances were bound to differ. Brought together during the First World War, both of them brought into English literary life the special perspective of their American origins and their pedagogical inclinations. Henry James was their link in time and place, of course, though their sense of the past had been augmented by postgraduate studies, and their quest for landmarks and paraphernalia would meet the distracting tensions and complications of the postwar years. Pound could take his stand in a Parthian jingle, *"L'Homme moyen sensuel"*:

> . . . Poe, Whitman, Whistler, men, their recognition
> Was got abroad. What better luck d'you wish'em,
> When writing well has not yet been forgiven
> In Boston, to Henry James, the greatest whom we've seen living?

The "serious artist," for Pound, the young American seeking to become a man of letters, could but follow the Jamesian precedent. "Art," Pound liked to say, "is a matter of capitals," and London was the capital of the world.[5] "London," he wrote back to William Carlos Williams, "deah old Lundon, is the place for poesy."[6] After fourteen years and the war, he followed—or rather, helped to set—the shifting trend of intercultural activity, by living through the next four years in Paris ("the laboratory of ideas").[7] Yet, for all the artistic ferment of the Twenties, he was soon disillusioned there; his praise for Cocteau and Picabia was devalued by his scorn for Claudel and Valéry, not to mention his utter indifference to Proust and Gide. Subsequently he took the centrifugal course of the various English poets who had retreated to Italy. But his two decades at Rapallo ended by consigning him to a much grimmer place of retreat, to his thirteen-year incarceration at Saint Elizabeth's, the government asylum near Washington. In 1972, fourteen years after his release, and eighty-seven years after his birth at Hailey, Idaho, he died and was buried at Venice, where his first volume of poems had been published in 1908.

His continual restlessness, his quasi-Goliardic wandering, his frustrated search for an ideal cultural milieu, was characterized by Eliot as "a kind of resistance against growing into any environment."[8] Eliot's phrasing reveals at least as much about his own assimilation as it does about Pound's deracination. Eliot's development had proceeded, consistently and cyclically, in a single direction: from Saint Louis via ancestral New England to East Coker, the scene of his last *Quartet* and the site of his grave, whence his Puritan ancestors had set forth for the New World. He now has his cenotaph in Westminster Abbey. Consequently it is easier for us to think of him in terms of his latterday establishmentarianism, rather than of that younger iconoclasm which gained for him and Pound such epithets as "drunken helots" and "literary bolsheviks."[9] After his naturalization as a British subject and his entrance into the Anglo-Catholic communion in 1927, he was provoked—as he would recall—by a conversation with his old Harvard master, Irving Babbitt, into the provocative declaration of orthodoxy that prefaced his collection of essays, *For Lancelot Andrewes*.[10] In the pamphlet, *Thoughts after Lambeth,* he proved himself more Catholic than the Archbishop of Canterbury. In *After Strange Gods: A Primer of Modern Heresy,* he pronounced anathema upon some of his chief contemporaries. Those Virginia lectures, ill timed in 1933 and ill placed at the university of Thomas Jefferson, would be quietly dropped from the canon of his writings, as reprinted or listed in the front matter of subsequent volumes. *Notes towards the Definition of Culture* harked back with Arnoldian nostalgia, from the aftermath of the Second World War, to a set of social ideals which had been purified by the self-evident fact of their obsolescence.

His habit of bracketing Pound together with Babbitt may surprise readers who did not know the two men; it is all the more surprising to one who did. Apart from the Europeanism that was the *cachet* of the American intellectual, their principal affinity was the strong influence that each in turn had exerted over Eliot's critical outlook: Babbitt through the history of ideas, Pound through the cultivation of taste. Both, he came to feel, had abetted his traditionalism without committing themselves to religious belief. In his view, the New Humanism of Babbitt needed the moral support of Christianity, while Pound's increasing preoccupation with Social Credit was a cheap substitute for Divine Grace. In one of these cross-references Eliot speculates: "if Pound had stopped at home, . . . he might have become . . . a professor of comparative literature."[11] This might have given him even more difficulty than his abortive term as instructor in languages at Wabash College, since there were few professorships of comparative literature, and Babbitt's chair was nominally in French. Eliot would voice his disapproval of the elective program as introduced at Harvard by his cousin, President Charles W. Eliot, and a solid number of his undergraduate courses had been grounded in the old classical curriculum. Yet the influential course in which Babbitt traced the tangled ills of the modern world to the Romantic Movement laid a framework for Eliot's critical thought, and directed him toward such anti-Romantic French critics as Charles Maurras and Julien Benda. While a student at the Sorbonne he encountered, as visiting professor, the medievalist W. H. Schofield, first chairman of Harvard's Department of Comparative Literature. It might also be noted that the first volume of the Harvard Studies in Comparative Literature, George Santayana's *Three Philosophical Poets,* came out just as Eliot was graduating.

Pound would claim retrospectively that he "began an examination of comparative European literature in or about 1901."[12] That would have been no later than his freshman year at the University of Pennsylvania. Though he had some good instruction in Latin and modern languages, he was on his own as a precocious comparatist, and would complain that his instructors never dared to cross departmental lines.[13] Presumably he would have written his doctoral dissertation under Hugo Rennert, the Hispanist; and he carried on a friendly correspondence with Felix Schelling, the authority on Elizabethan drama, long after taking his master's degree and breaking his other ties with the faculty; but the letters intimate that the break was not of his choosing, and abound in sardonic comments upon the state of the university. Throughout his life he went on "making noises about universities," as Ford Madox Ford would put it, though—unlike that veteran British writer expatriated to America—he resisted a professorship at Olivet College in Michigan.[14] Nevertheless, he could seldom resist assuming the *persona* of an unfrocked professor. At London he had lectured, as did Eliot, to adult education classes, where on one occasion he met his future wife. At intervals he put out prospectuses for super-colleges he wished to found, and scattered syllabuses through his letters, notably the correspondence course on "KOMPLEAT KULTURE" addressed to Iris Barry.[15] In etymological terms, he considered himself to be rather a *dilettante* than a *connoisseur*, placing delight in the subject above mere knowledge.[16] The professorial impulse merged with that of the *cicerone*, happiest when calling the tourist's attention to topographical beauties heretofore unperceived. Young disciples, visiting Rapallo, sat at the feet of its one-man faculty, the "Ezuversity."

Eliot did not have to improvise so much. Taking his historical bearings from Babbitt, he could read Dante with C. H. Grandgent, Chaucer with F. N. Robinson, Shakespeare with G. L. Kittredge, Elizabethan drama with G. P. Baker, Latin poetry with E. K. Rand, and Sanskrit with C. R. Lanman. But it was only when he picked up a copy of Arthur Symons' *Symbolist Movement in Literature*, or was asked to review J. G. Huneker's *Egoists* for a student periodical, that he responded to the living stimulus of continental Europe. Significantly, those intermediaries were freelances rather than academics. Eliot characteristically finished his thesis, and would have taken his doctorate but for the war, whereupon he could easily have become—at an incalculable loss to literature—a Harvard professor. Had he passed through Marburg rather than Oxford, he might have done so. As poet, critic, editor, and laureate, gathering grand prizes and honorary degrees, albeit he was less of a natural pedagogue than the freelancing Pound, he was gradually gathered into the bosom of Academe. Whereas the embattled Ezra, withdrawing from the movements of London and Paris, and from the "little magazines / That died to make verse free," found himself caught up in farther-reaching causes and more problematic controversies.[17] His pretensions to professional scholarship had their tombstone in his translation and edition of Guido Cavalcanti, described by himself as "ill-starred."[18] His act of renunciation, by his account, took place after he was admitted to the reading room of the British Museum. "Calculating the eye-strain and the number of pages per day that a man could read, with deduction for say at least 5% of one man's time for reflection, I decided against it. There must be some other way for a human being to make use of that vast cultural heritage."[19]

Dropping out of formal education at an advanced stage, he managed to wear his *bouquiniste* erudition with all the didacticism of an autodidact. If his Imagism was culturally richer than Futurism or contemporaneous European schools, according to Eugenio Montale, that richness seemed to be somewhat *parvenu*, that "culture was of a crash-course, night-school variety."[20] Gertrude Stein, predictably refusing to be instructed, categorized Pound as "a village explainer, excellent if you were a village, but if you were not, not."[21] He had come a long way from the village of Hailey, Idaho; it was a thankless task, he told H. L. Mencken, to stay at home and "civilize the waste places"; he himself performed his patriotic duties from abroad, facilitating cultural exchanges through his function as foreign correspondent and editorial adviser.[22] Many of his diatribes against the lowbrow public could have been headed, as was one of them, with the Flaubertian axiom: "Provincialism the Enemy." But underneath the many-colored mantle of his cosmopolitanism, his self-vaunting "world citizenship," he remained provincial in many ways.[23] Eliot had put down roots in England, and had acquired a British accent along with a furled umbrella and bowler hat. The longer Pound stayed away from the United States, the more American he considered himself, parodying the rustic stereotypes of his bygone youth, and modeling his epistolary style on the nasal dialect of the crackerbarrel philosopher. Eliot's introductory brochure about Pound's work, anonymously issued by their New York publisher, quoted a jocose paragraph from *Punch* regarding the sensation created in London by Mr. Ezekiel Ton, "by far the newest poet going," whose

poetry was "a blend of the imagery of the unfettered West, the vocabulary of Wardour Street, and the sinister abandon of Borgiac Italy"—
clearly an adumbration of the *Cantos*.[24]

The American Renaissance that he was heralding in *Poetry*, the Chicago magazine, would—wrote Pound to its editor, Harriet Monroe—
"make the Italian Renaissance look like a tempest in a teapot!"[25] Meanwhile, in a sequence of articles for the British readership of *The New
Age*, "Patria Mia," he was arguing somewhat less cavalierly that America had "a chance for Renaissance," but that it was scarcely emergent
from its Dark Ages, and that the coming day would be rather a *Ris-
vegliamento* than a *Risorgimento*, an awakening rather than an up-
rising.[26] Nor should it be too shortsightedly nationalistic. "Are you for
American poetry or for poetry?" he inquired of Miss Monroe, while he
argued in her pages that American poets should know the French and
English models, not in order to imitate but to pass beyond imitation.[27]
He objected, moreover, to the introduction of courses in American
literature: "You might as well give courses in American chemistry,
neglecting all foreign discoveries. This is not patriotism."[28] If England
and France were his continued examples of civilization it was because
they had not "given way to the yelp of 'nationality'" nor indeed, "more
profoundly, . . . to the yelp of 'race.'"[29] Though the example of James
had reaffirmed the continuities of Anglo-American literature, a command of English was not enough for a writer, and he who knew no
other language should be disqualified as a critic of poetry. Pound once
proposed to edit a twelve-volume anthology of the world's great poems,
which would supplant the Victorian insularity of "that doddard Palgrave."[30] Inasmuch as this proposal was put to the firm of Macmillan,
whose fortunes had been largely founded on Palgrave's *Golden Treasury*, it did not get very far. Long afterward it was partially realized
by the collection, edited by Pound with Marcella Spann, *Confucius to
Cummings*.

The ultimate criterion, in Pound's judgment, became an immediate
one: "a universal standard which pays no attention to time or country
—a Weltlitteratur standard"—again he was advising Harriet Monroe.[31]
There was no particular reason why London, any more than Paris or
Prague "or whatever," should be the pacemaker for Chicago or New
York. Elsewhere he insisted in italics that *the English cribbed their
technique from across the channel*."[32] He became less and less in-

terested in English poets since Chaucer, and more and more anxious to
be "free of all Anglo-Saxon connections," as he confided from Paris to
Marianne Moore.[33] Soliciting a contribution from Joyce, he justified
the *Little Review* by declaring that "the Mercure de France is really
too gaga to be left the sole arbiter of weldtlitteratur!!!"[34] It had recently lost its leading critic, Remy de Gourmont, custodian of the
Latin genius and champion of the Symbolist poets. Pound, though he
placed an extraneous *accent aigu* on Gourmont's forename and never
used his surname alone without a capitalized *particule,* had often cited
him as a mentor and offered a moving eulogy. Joyce, who had begun
by saluting Ibsen and attacking the provinciality of the Irish Literary
Theatre, must have appreciated the strategy of Pound's campaigns on
his behalf. *Dubliners* was greeted by comparisons with Strindberg,
Pérez Galdós, Herman Bang, and Francis Jammes among others, above
all with Flaubert—its French antecedent, just as Eliot's was Jules
Laforgue.[35] Flaubert, preceded to some extent by Stendhal, constituted
the final stylistic touchstone, and his name was repeatedly coupled
with Joyce's. In reaction from the smooth suffusions of the Victorian
poets, Pound repeated his dictum—formerly Victor Hugo's—that poetry
should be as well written as prose, and pointed out that much of the
best prose was being written on the other side of the Channel.

When Pound employed the term *comparative literature,* as frequently he did, he does not seem primarily to have meant the field of
scholarly research and historical interpretation, which he criticizes at
one point because it "has seldom if ever aspired to the study of 'comparative values in letters.' "[36] What he seems to have in mind is something like the Goethean conception of world literature, as envisioned
by a highly active participant. In practice, given the nature of his participation, it usually scales down a bit into what he terms "comparative
poesy."[37] This, he contends, has existed "for at least two thousand
years," insofar as the Roman poets knew Greek.[38] Dante, the greatest
exemplar for him and for Eliot, could write in Latin and Provençal as
well as Italian. Emulously, two of Pound's *Cantos* are in unpublished
Italian, while several of Eliot's early poems are in Laforguian French.
As an object lesson, Pound was fond of retelling a high-table anecdote:

I once met a very ancient Oxford 'head,' and in the middle of dinner he
turned to me, saying: 'Ah—um, ah—poet. Ah, some one showed me a new
poem the other day, the—ah—the *Hound of Heaven.*'

I said, 'Well, what did you think of it?' and he answered, 'Couldn't be bothered to stop for every adjective!'

That enlightened opinion was based on a form of comparative literature called 'the classic education.'[39]

Pound's comment was prompted by admiration, not irony, by an orthodox respect for Greek and Latin not simply as cultural substrata but as continuing sources of stylistic guidance. By contrast his American professors had been, in the main, unenlightened: literature had been vaguely appreciated in English departments, philology had been stressed when foreign tongues were involved. At the age of twenty-five in 1910, still close to such involvements and especially to his own extracurricular lectures, he had launched himself as a critic with *The Spirit of Romance*. "This book is not a philological work."[40] So it begins, in a high-sounding *Praefatio ad lectorem electum* which intermingles diffidence with arrogance. "Only by courtesy can it be said to be a study in comparative literature." And on the next page, more specifically, he announces: "What we need is a literary scholarship which will weigh Theocritus and Yeats with one balance . . ." He does not perform that feat of equilibration; rather, he presents a series of lively evocations from late Latinity, the Troubadours, Dante and Lope; and he counterweighs his own values by a trenchant comparison of François Villon with Walt Whitman.

Juxtapositions like these, when aptly chosen and freshly observed, can be reciprocally illuminating. On the other hand, they can become obsessive and arbitrary, as in Pound's shrill inquiry twenty-four years later: ". . . can anyone estimate Donne's best poems save in relation to Cavalcanti?"[41] This reduction is barely saved from absurdity by the implication, strongly believed, that all poets are related to one another through their craft, and that they must be evaluated on the basis of that interrelationship, principally on what they have to teach the aspirant. Each generation must face its task of reviewing and revising "the Tradition," which may involve rediscoveries (such as the Troubadours) or importations (such as the Symbolists). Much discernment is needed for that effort, but possibly even more of a quality which Pound labels "excernment" and Eliot describes as "casting out devils."[42] The devils not infrequently are those which have possessed the previous generation (for example, Swinburne and Francis Thompson), though there are some displacements all along the line, as when Pound exalts Crabbe and Landor at the expense of Wordsworth and Coleridge or prefers Gautier to Mallarmé. "My pantheon is considerable," he protested to Miss Monroe, yet it had no room for Poe or Pindar, while Milton was condemned to its lowest circle. Most of its brightest luminaries seem to have been drawn from the Romanic territories. With the exception of Heine ("one of the lights"), Pound took little interest in the Germanic sphere, and virtually none at all in the Slavic.[43] But these limitations were transcended by that leap of imagination which conveyed him beyond the hemisphere, engaged him in the Western propagation of Oriental culture, and made him—in Eliot's rather equivocal phrase—"the inventor of Chinese poetry for our time."[44]

Eliot, inheriting a concern for Eastern thought from Babbitt, had studied Sanskrit with C. R. Lanman and Indic philosophy with J. H. Woods. But the benediction to *The Waste Land* from the *Upanishads* could be regarded as his farewell to all that. After his conversion he seems to have settled for Kipling's shrug—East is East and West is West. "Just as I do not see how anyone can expect really to understand Kant and Hegel without knowing the German language and without such an understanding of the German people as can only be acquired in the society of living Germans," he asserted in his regressive *After Strange Gods,* "so *a fortiori* I do not see how anyone can understand Confucius without some knowledge of Chinese and a long frequentation of the best Chinese society."[45] He had read his German metaphysics and kept up, as Pound had not, with Rilke and Gottfried Benn. But a slighting reference makes it clear that he was relatively unfamiliar with Heine. "Dr. Sigmund Freud," he tells us ironically, "has reminded us that we should 'leave Heaven to the angels and the sparrows.' "[46] Here Eliot seems to brush aside a quotation which Freud thought obvious enough to forego the attribution:

> Den Himmel überlassen wir
> Den Engeln und den Spatzen.

The intrepid Pound, though he disapproved more and more of the Bible, had not been put off by his distance from the Orient. From his cult of the image it was logical to proceed, via the Japanese *haiku,* to the Chinese ideogram. The circumstance was fortunate that drew him, after the inspired approximations of *Cathay* and the premature death of Ernest Fenollosa, into a kind of posthumous collaboration on the Noh plays and on the written character. Translation had been a major commitment for Pound from the beginning. It was the novitiate that inducted writers into craftsmanship and cultures into renaissances. He was so committed that he occasionally voiced a preference for certain translations over their originals: for Gavin Douglas' *Æneid* over Virgil's and for Arthur Golding's over Ovid's *Metamorphoses*—"the most beautiful book in the language."[47] His essay on the problems of translating Homer is more incisive and more comprehensive than Matthew Arnold's. He took endless pains in corresponding with W. H. D. Rouse about his version of Homer and with Laurence Binyan about his version of Dante. Those who would dismiss Pound as a "hit-and-run translator" fail to recognize the skilled endeavor that has re-created the Old English *Seafarer* or adapted the elegies of Propertius to the rhythms of the twentieth century—not by close translation, to be sure, but by imaginative transposition.[48]

Pound admitted frankly that his prose was "mostly stop-gap," propaganda serving the interests of fellow writers alive and dead, "pawing over the ancients and semi-ancients," together with such professions of modernist faith as "The Serious Artist."[49] He could rationalize about "the method of Luminous Detail," but what it all came down to was a uniquely discerning eye and ear.[50] Shifting his attention from the practicing poet to the educable reader, at the lower stages of the *gradus ad Parnassum,* he expanded his reading lists, worked out exercises for self-cultivation, and "simplified the concept of world literature" in "How to Read," *ABC of Reading,* and *Guide to Kulchur.*[51] These were intended as textbooks, like the manual of Gaston Paris on Old French or the *haute vulgarisation* of Salomon Reinach on art and religion.[52] But, like the *Cantos,* Pound's outlines follow no outline; under the mounting pressures of the Thirties, they broke down into private notebooks, where the stream of consciousness meanders from poetic diction to monetary theory. "His true Penelope was Flaubert," he had said of his Mauberley—and of himself as well. Hence his own prototype was the wayward Odysseus, postponing his homeward journey to dally with the deceptive enchantments of economics and ideology. Flaubert would not be forgotten; and the lapse is trivial when Pound forgets the circumflex in the spelling of *Salammbô;* yet who but he would ever have replaced it with a *tilde?*[53] And what is this pedagogue doing for his pupils' morale when he assigns them "at least a book and half" by Stendhal? Nearing the end of *Guide to Kulchur,* he throws up his hands and applies a line of Byron to himself: "I wish he would explain his explanation."[54] Gertrude Stein to the contrary notwithstanding, he lacked the patience to be a village explainer.

Eliot put his own prose in the same category as Pound's; it was "workshop criticism" with the attendant merits and limits, speaking with conviction as "a by-product of his creative activity," and best understood in the full context of his poetry.[55] "Shyly" in his own case, graciously in Pound's, he linked them both with the proud succession of English poet-critics from Sidney to Arnold, whose authority was derived from their experience as craftsmen, and whose outstanding spokesmen were Dryden, Samuel Johnson, and Coleridge.[56] In this respect, as in all others, he was linking himself more closely with the central body of English literature. Yet his evaluations were invariably subject to invidious glances across the Channel and to a frame of reference set by the classics. Francophile rather than Anglophile, he was not even sure that English literature deserved a place in the curriculum, and he reprimanded Blake for willful eccentricity: "we are not really so remote from the Continent, or from our own past, as to be deprived of the advantages of culture if we wish them."[57] Marvell's wit could hardly be explicated without such recourse. When Eliot discusses the seventeenth-century English divine, John Bramhall, it is unavoidable to compare him with Bossuet; but Mallarmé is his touchstone in dealing with poets as far apart as Milton and Dryden; and Baudelaire is omnipresent both in spirit and letter. A remark of Gide throws light upon Coleridge, and the purism of Racine's *Bérénice* discredits the Elizabethan mishmash of *Hamlet*. "It is a pity that English poetry has remained so incomplete."[58] Eliot's Penelope was Laforgue, "to whom I owe more than to any one poet in any language."[59] Though he did not actually go so far as to deplore the situation, he took satisfaction in pronouncing that English literature had "no classic age, and no classic poet."[60]

Addressing a manifestly unclassical age, he professed himself a classicist. He may well have been in closer touch with the Continent, as an American expatriate, than if he had been a native Englishman. He had earned his livelihood for some years, as had Joyce, by conducting the foreign correspondence of a bank. He was nearly as concerned as Pound with the art of translation, and produced a sensitive rendering of St.-John Perse's challenging *Anabase*. Plato's Greek, Spinoza's Latin, and F. H. Bradley's English had sharpened the theoretical edge of Eliot's style, so that he could articulate his points and conceptualize his positions in neat—and most un-Poundlike—formulation.[61] Like Pound he habitually started from and returned to Dante, both in verse and prose, affirming that more could be learned from him "about how to write poetry . . . than from any English poet."[62] He suspected Pound of sympathizing more fully with Cavalcanti than with Dante, since the former had been more of an individualist.[63] Dante was not only the first of the "great Europeans"; he had the advantage over later writers of being able to speak for a unified European culture.[64] In the face of national differences, whose importance Eliot would not undervalue, he could still maintain: "I do not believe that the cultures of the several peoples of Europe can flourish in isolation from each other."[65] Shortly after the Second World War he addressed three broadcast talks to Germany—an "appeal . . . to the men of letters of Europe"—on the theme of *Die Einheit der Europäischen Kultur*.[66] In a lecture on American literature he advanced the view that a writer could not become universal without first having been local.

> Who could be more Greek than Odysseus? Or more German than Faust? Or more Spanish than Don Quixote? Or more American than Huck Finn? Yet each one of them is a kind of archetype in the mythology of all men everywhere.[67]

Eliot's conception of universals, though concrete, did not extend beyond the Occident. In a footnote on I. A. Richards he alludes to Pound and Babbitt, and characterizes their common interest in Chinese philosophy as "a deracination from the Christian tradition."[68] A letter to Eliot's partner, F. V. Morley—a letter scrawled, ironically enough, in Pound's backwoods idiom—expresses his anxiety that Eliot will not approve of the pagan gods Pound has been straying after: "He won't laaak fer to see no Chinas and blackmen in a bukk about Kulchur. Dat being jess his lowdown Unitarian iggurunce. . . ."[69]

Inevitably, it was Eliot who promulgated a definitive restatement of tradition, even while reconsidering the perennial problem of artistic renewal. Every hundred years or so, as he specially understood, literature had to be reordered by criticism. "The task," as he defined it, "is not one of revolution but of readjustment."[70] Every innovation or restoration affected the whole continuum, whose "simultaneous order" was forever being "modified by the introduction of the new."[71] The essay that formulated this insight, "Tradition and the Individual Talent," occupied less than ten pages and carried enormous weight. Pound would have modified the phraseology by suggesting that it was funereal to talk about monuments, that there ought to have been some more organic term. He would wryly state that concessions to the philistines and a professorial readiness to settle for less than first-rate authors had "contributed enormously to Mr. Eliot's rise to his deserved position as arbiter of British opinion."[72] Eliot was more truly catholic than his colleague in this regard. Pound would not relax his highbrow intransigence, whereas Eliot confessed to a lurking fondness for detective stories and music halls. His pantheon, though it centered on Dante, held important niches for the Elizabethan Playwrights and the Metaphysical Poets, not to mention the *Symbolistes* and selected moderns. Most of these affinities were elective, and—even for writers—ancestry cannot be altogether a matter of personal choice. Pound was also uneasily indebted to Whitman and Browning, as was Eliot to Emerson and Poe. Pound, though he had boiled the pot by reviewing plays, looked down on the crudities of the stage and was bored by much of Shakespeare, to whom he ended by preferring Chaucer.[73] Eliot became increasingly fascinated by the theater, and finally turned to poetic drama as his "ideal medium," for better or for worse.[74]

He was a shrewd speculator on the literary stock market, and his assessments had their programmatic aims. Having, in "the dogmatism of youth," been unwarrantably severe to Milton and Goethe, he could gracefully recant on more mellow occasions.[75] The critical instruments that he recommended were "comparison and analysis"; the occupational pitfalls he warned against were "opinion and fancy"; and he admiringly instanced the scholarship of W. P. Ker, which was likewise admired by Pound, and which was exceptional for its comparative orientation.[76] Eliot himself worked in this vein, when he was knowledgeably analyzing the Elizabethans or the Metaphysicals. His study of "Seneca in Elizabethan Translation" is a masterly exploration of style and thought, which makes Pound's "Notes on Elizabethan Classicists" look both subjective and superficial. But comparison and analysis gave way to opinion and fancy in "Shakespeare and the Stoicism of Seneca," where Eliot summoned Dante and Aquinas to derogate the Stoic code of belief. His lecture at the Library of Congress, "From Poe to Valéry," commented authoritatively on a remarkable chain of literary influences with which he had first-hand connections. A related note, contributed to a *Festschrift* for Mallarmé (and translated by Ramon Fernandez), assumes

l'aspect de littérature comparée—je ne veux pas dire une vaine étude des origines et des influences, mais la définition du type du poète, établie par une comparaison avec d'autres manifestations de ce type dans d'autres langues et à d'autres époques.[77]

In his presidential address to the Virgil Society, pursuing Sainte-Beuve's query, "What is a Classic?," he naturally took the Roman poet as his model for two qualities he had all too rarely discerned in other writers: "maturity of mind" and "consciousness of history."[78] Eliot's school days had confronted him with a massive exercise in comparative literature by assigning the *Iliad* and the *Aeneid* during the same year. Though he had theretofore "found the Greek language a much more exciting study than Latin," he would recollect, ". . . I found myself at ease with Virgil as I was not at ease with Homer."[79] Had he commenced with the *Odyssey*, it might have been otherwise.

The Odyssean Pound, who venerated Homer even in French or Latin translations, derided Virgil as "a second-rater, a Tennysonianized version of Homer."[80] That Pound should have played so Virgilian a part in Eliot's Dantesque pilgrimage is, perhaps, the crowning irony of their fifty-year relationship. Now that both have left the literary scene—Eliot wearing all the available laurels, Pound amidst a controversy over a prize withheld—personalities no longer matter. "What thou lovest well remains." Pound has made his apologia in his most poignant Canto (LXXXI): "To have gathered from the air a live tradition . . ." *Culture* was a word of such faded gentility, so indicative of what seemed lacking to the esthetic and spiritual atmosphere of the United States at the beginning of the century, that he made a little game out of spelling it with a *K*. For his serious uses he borrowed the Greek word *paideuma*, which had taken on anthropological connotations through the writings of Leo Frobenius about primitive Africa. Pound redefined the term as "the complex of ideas which is in a given time germinal."[81] His old rallying cries for a renascence shifted, in mid-career, to the repeated call for "a New Paideuma." As a contributor to that instauration, a pertinacious lobbyist for standards, his life in letters will be seen at its germinal best. America, in spite of his self-exile, figures continuously in the record; but it figures less and less as, in

Mauberley's description, "a half savage country, out of date." The task of bringing the country up to date and civilizing the savages depended, Pound stressed in a letter to R. P. Blackmur, on "communication between the two sides of the Atlantic."[82] And, as Conrad Aiken has testified, "The eagle scream of Rabbi Ben Ezra was audible across the Atlantic at regular intervals."[83] This paideumatic linkage answered another American need: a temporal, as well as a spatial, extension.

Eliot's contributions were nearly as extensive, far more systematic, and devoted to the same end, to those Virgilian virtues which he had preached: intellectual maturity and historical consciousness. Osip Mandelstam once summed up his own poetic creed as "nostalgia for world culture," and there was much of that sentiment in both Eliot and Pound.[84] But if either poet had gone abroad in the nostalgic hope of escaping to a storied past, a picturesque landscape dominated by Jamesian manor houses or Browningesque *palazzi*, he was bound to be disillusioned. Both were confronted with the "tawdry cheapness"—Mauberley again—of the modern metropolis, the *"fourmillante cité"* that Eliot gained the courage to face from Baudelaire and from Dante. London Bridge, as glimpsed in *The Waste Land*, is a gateway to the *Inferno.* "Where are the eagles and the trumpets?," Eliot exclaimed in "A Cooking Egg," on watching "the red-eyed scavengers" creep out of the Underground stations from Kentish Town or Golder's Green. Pound in Paris, "In a Station of the Metro," beheld much the same apparition, and captured it with his most famous distich:

> The apparition of these faces in a crowd;
> Petals on a wet, black bough.

Here, in the *haiku*-like twist that turns the observation into a metaphor, suddenly the urban crowd disappears, magically absorbed into an almost pastoral image. Both poets were adept at the Flaubertian trick of conjuring up a romantic past to comment ironically upon a realistic present. But where the double focus made for sharpness, with Eliot as with Flaubert, it tended to merge and blur with Pound. For all his Confucian talk about making things new, he comes through as more of a romanticist than a realist. He is the arrant modernist who cultivated archaisms, who revived the alba and the sestina, who was accused with some justice of being more at home while translating than while using his own voice, who was saluted by Eliot—in a review of *Quia Pauper Amavi*—for "a unique gift of expression through some phase of past life," and who confessed to Joyce that he himself was "perhaps better at digging up corpses of let us say Li Po, or more lately Sextus Propertius, than in preserving this bitched mess of modernity."[85]

Joyce preserved and controlled the mess in *Ulysses*, as Eliot did in *The Waste Land*. Writing to compliment Eliot for that achievement, which he himself had done so much to foster and indeed to shape, Pound was generously self-critical: "I am wracked by the seven jealousies, and cogitating an excuse for always exuding my deformative secretions in my own stuff, and never getting an outline."[86] He was to lament in his penultimate Canto (and somehow he pushed beyond Dante's hundred to 117): "I cannot make it cohere." His retrospect was "a tangle of works unfinished." Eliot too had lived among the ruins, but had succeeded in shoring up his fragments completed by footnotes; he had rounded his circle and structured his niche. Pound was all along beset with doubts whether or not the *Cantos* were "a rag-bag," into which—echoing a draft of 1912—he was "trying to stuff the modern world."[87] He was happier when he was communing with the Malatestas in Rimini or with Jefferson at Monticello. If the theme was flux, as Yeats suggested hopefully and helpfully, flux was also the process: polyglot echoes, amusing *pastiches*, offensive slogans, *mémoires pour servir*, drafts of drafts, footnotes running wild and overgrowing the text, haunting single lines and purple passages—how could the climactic episode, the imprisonment at Pisa, have been planned when the poet conceived his poem forty years before the event?[88] At a late and penitent moment, he was inclined to write it all off as "a botch."[89] But would it not appropriately serve as a testament for a *Götterdämmerung*, for what was already "a botched civilization" to Mauberley in the apocalyptic aftermath of the First World War? Reconsidering more reflectively his "defects and disadvantages," he could view them as "the defects inherent in a record of struggle."[90] He could look about him and reflect, as he did in the third Pisan Canto (LXXVI): ". . . from the wreckage of Europe, ego scriptor."

Should we then conclude that we have been living through *The Pound Era*—to mention a title from one of the rapidly augmenting studies of his life and work? This is as sweeping as any of his assumptions, and the book itself is pitched to his spasmodic moods and strident mannerisms. A more widely acceptable estimate was registered some years ago, when the last chapter of a one-volume history of English literature was entitled "The Age of T. S. Eliot." The difference between the two designations is much greater than Amy Lowell or anyone could have foreseen, looking ahead from the Twenties rather than back from the Seventies. Eliot adhered to the classic path toward order, precision, and depersonalization that Pound and Hulme and he himself had laid out. Pound, veering toward collapse and recovering fitfully (whether the diagnosis be mental or moral), immersed himself in chaos at first hand. Meanwhile a new generation of poets was appearing, many of whom seemed qualified by the experience of personal breakdown to express the larger desperations of our time—notably the Lowell *de nos jours*, who has been modulating his own cantos into his recent *History*, where along with Robert Lowell himself we can evoke Theodore Roethke, John Berryman, Randall Jarrell, Delmore Schwartz, and Sylvia Plath. All of them, in their dedication to self-exposure, could trace descent from Whitman rather than from his polar opposite among their American ancestors, the arch-formalist Poe. Pound, whose devotion to form was early sealed by his revulsion from Whitman, ended in Walt's camp, after having moved—as Lowell also would—"from Τέχνη back to σεαυτόν." That leaves Pound closer to the immediate urgencies of poetry today than Eliot, who—like his Hippopotamus—has mounted amid the hosannas. Pound remains below, "Wrapped in the old miasmal mist." He was never a safe bet, and he will not cease to be an embattled figure; but, so long as the battles continue, he will stand at a rallying point.

N   O   T   E   S

1 [Amy Lowell,] *A Fable for Critics* (Boston: 1922), p. 91.
2 Ezra Pound, *Selected Prose, 1909-1965* (New York: New Directions, 1973), p. 148. (London: Faber and Faber, 1973.)
3 "A Letter from Richard Aldington," *This Quarter* I, 2 (1925), 312.
4 *Selected Prose*, p. 177.
5 *The Letters of Ezra Pound, 1907-1941*, ed., D. D. Page (New York: Harcourt, Brace, 1950), p. 41n. (London: Faber and Faber, 1951.)
6 Ibid., p. 7.
7 *Selected Prose*, p. 415.
8 T. S. Eliot, "Ezra Pound," *Poetry: A Magazine of Verse*, LXVIII, 6 (September 1946), 327.

9 T. S. Eliot, *The Use of Poetry and the Use of Criticism* (Cambridge, Mass.: Harvard University Press, 1933), p. 62. (London: Faber and Faber, 1933.)

10 T. S. Eliot, *To Criticize the Critic* (New York: Farrar, Straus, 1965), p. 15. (London: Faber and Faber, 1965.)

11 "Ezra Pound," pp. 328, 329.

12 *Literary Essays of Ezra Pound*, ed., T. S. Eliot (London: Faber and Faber, 1954), p. 77.

13 Ibid., p. 16.

14 Noel Stock, *The Life of Ezra Pound* (New York: Pantheon, 1970), p. 348. (London: Routledge & Kegan Paul, 1970.)

15 *Letters*, p. 86.

16 *Literary Essays*, p. 55.

17 Quoted from Keith Preston, *Pot Shots from Pegasus* (New York: 1929), p. 92.

18 *Letters*, p. 72.

19 Ezra Pound, *Guide to Kulchur* (Norfolk, Conn.: New Directions, 1938), p. 53. (London: Faber and Faber, 1938.)

20 Eugenio Montale, "Uncle Ez," *Italian Quarterly*, LVI, 64 (Spring 1973), 25.

21 [Gertrude Stein,] *The Autobiography of Alice B. Toklas* (New York: Random House, 1933), p. 246.

22 *Letters*, p. 146.

23 Ibid., p. 146.

24 [T. S. Eliot,] *Ezra Pound: His Metric and Poetry* (New York: Alfred A. Knopf, 1917), p. 19.

25 *Letters*, p. 10.

26 *Selected Prose*, pp. 2, 111, 128.

27 *Letters*, p. 9; *Literary Essays*, p. 214.

28 Ibid., p. 218.

29 *Selected Prose*, p. 192.

30 *Literary Essays*, p. 56; cf. *Letters*, p. 18.

31 Ibid., pp. 24, 25.

32 *Literary Essays*, p. 92.

33 *Letters*, p. 16.

34 *Pound/Joyce*, ed., Forrest Read (New York: New Directions, 1967), p. 164.

35 Ibid., pp. 29, 89.

36 *Literary Essays*, p. 192.

37 Stock, op. cit., p. 281.

38 *Literary Essays*, p. 214.

39 Ibid., cf. *Selected Prose*, p. 137.

40 Ezra Pound, *The Spirit of Romance* (New York: E. P. Dutton, 1910), pp. 7, 8. (London: J. M. Dent & Sons, 1910.)

41 Ezra Pound, *ABC of Reading* (London: George Routledge & Sons, 1934), p. 73.

42 *Use of Poetry*, p. 77.

43 *Letters,* p. 67.
44 Ezra Pound, *Selected Poems,* ed., T. S. Eliot (London: Faber & Gwyer, 1928), p. 14.
45 T. S. Eliot, *After Strange Gods* (New York: Harcourt, Brace, 1934), p. 43. (London: Faber and Faber, 1933.)
46 T. S. Eliot, *Selected Essays* (New York: Harcourt, Brace, 1932), p. 317. (London: Faber and Faber, 1932.)
47 *Literary Essays,* p. 35; *ABC of Reading,* p. 127.
48 A. S. Amdur, *The Poetry of Ezra Pound* (Cambridge, Mass.: Harvard University Press, 1936), p. 58.
49 Stock, op. cit., p. 292; *Literary Essays,* p. 11.
50 *Selected Prose,* p. 21.
51 *Pound/Joyce,* p. 253.
52 *ABC of Reading,* p. 11.
53 *Literary Essays,* p. 38.
54 *Guide to Kulchur,* p. 295.
55 T. S. Eliot, *On Poetry and Poets* (London: Faber and Faber, 1957), p. 107; *To Criticize the Critic,* p. 13.
56 *On Poetry and Poets,* p. 162.
57 *Use of Poetry,* p. 28; *Selected Essays,* p. 279.
58 *Use of Poetry,* pp. 60, 34.
59 *To Criticize the Critic,* p. 22.
60 *On Poetry and Poets,* p. 59.
61 *To Criticize the Critic,* p. 21.
62 *Selected Essays,* p. 213.
63 *After Strange Gods,* p. 45.
64 *On Poetry and Poets,* p. 212.
65 Ibid., p. 23.
66 T. S. Eliot, *Notes towards a Definition of Culture* (New York: Harcourt, Brace, 1949), p. 127. (London: Faber and Faber, 1948.)
67 *To Criticize the Critic,* p. 56.
68 *Use of Poetry,* p. 124.
69 *Letters,* p. 288.
70 *Use of Poetry,* p. 100.
71 *Selected Essays,* p. 5.
72 *Selected Prose,* p. 390.
73 *Pound/Joyce,* p. 46; *Letters,* p. 306; *ABC of Reading,* pp. 99, 103.
74 *Use of Poetry,* p. 146.
75 *On Poetry and Poets,* p. 48.
76 *Selected Essays,* p. 21.
77 T. S. Eliot, "Note sur Mallarmé et Poe," *Nouvelle Revue Française,* LIV, 158 (November 1926), 524.
78 *On Poetry and Poets,* p. 61.
79 Ibid., p. 124.
80 *Letters,* p. 87.
81 *Selected Prose,* p. 284.
82 *Letters,* p. 198.

83 Conrad Aiken, *Ushant: An Essay* (New York: Oxford University Press, 1971), p. 218.

84 Nadezhda Mandelstam, *Hope against Hope: A Memoir*, tr., Max Hayward (New York: Atheneum, 1970), p. 246.

85 T. S. Eliot, "The Method of Mr. Pound," *Athenaeum*, 4669 (October 24, 1919), 1065; *Pound/Joyce*, p. 148.

86 *Letters*, p. 169.

87 Stock, op. cit., p. 207.

88 *The Oxford Book of Modern Verse, 1892–1935*, ed., W. B. Yeats (Oxford: Oxford University Press, 1936), p. xxiv.

89 Daniel Cory, "Ezra Pound: A Memoir," *Encounter*, XXX, 5 (May 1968), 38.

90 *Guide to Kulchur*, p. 135.

THE WASTE LAND:
FROM *UR* TO *ECHT*

When Eliot's important manuscript found its way into print, I was asked by Octavio Paz to interpret its critical significance for Plural, *his cultural journal published in Mexico City. My initial hesitation proved to be unjustified; his Spanish translator did a precise and sensitive job; and there were presumably many Hispanophone readers who knew the canonical text of the English poem well enough to appreciate the transpositions I pointed out (October 1972). When James Laughlin heard that I still had my own English original in a drawer, he suggested bringing it out in a limited and privately printed edition as a kind of Christmas card for his and my friends and for the clientèle of New Directions (1972). This is the first time it has appeared in a trade publication. I should add the hope that, given the pressures and provocations of several unauthorized biographical studies, Mrs. Eliot—whose collection of her husband's letters should soon be appearing— may be reconsidering the question of an authorized biography.*

•

"The occultation of 'The Waste Land' manuscript (years of waste time, exasperating to its author)," writes Ezra Pound in his preface to the facsimile and transcript of the original drafts, including his own annotations, "is pure Henry James." However, the present mystery has a happier resolution, inasmuch as the Aspern papers were burned in James's tale, whereas these Eliot papers have not only been rediscovered, they have now been painstakingly elucidated and handsomely printed under the editorship of the poet's widow and literary executor, Valerie Eliot. It remains a matter for speculation why the New York Public Library kept this valuable acquisition totally concealed during Eliot's lifetime. But there can be no retrospective doubt that the comparatively modest benefactions of John Quinn—the collector and patron to whom T. S. Eliot had presented the manuscript as a token of gratitude—proved to be a remunerative investment for his heirs. Mrs. Eliot's introduction is all the more poignant because it so objectively limits itself to sorting out the facts and dates and citing the pertinent correspondence. She is expressly enjoined by her husband's will from authorizing any biography. This is unfortunate, for her authority on the subject is more than merely legal or conjugal, and the need is already being exploited by would-be biographers quite lacking in qualifications. Meanwhile Eliot's friends and old admirers will be scrutinizing this *Ur-Waste Land* with feelings profoundly mixed, grateful for so much light on the process that produced such a masterpiece but shaken by the incidental perplexities that all but aborted it.

During the half-century since its publication, the poem has so etched itself into our consciousness that each of its successive episodes has come to seem the inevitable next step. Any alternative seems almost unthinkable. It would be no harder to imagine Chaucer opening *The Canterbury Tales* in some other month than April; and, though the Sanskrit benediction had to be glossed by the most needful of the author's notes, it has become a kind of signature. Many of the earliest readers, to be sure, saw *The Waste Land* as a potpourri of non sequiturs and cross-purposes, and it is true that the technique it introduced calls for a *collage* of surprises and incongruities. But such prearranged discontinuity is more exacting, not less, than a more conventionally linear presentation would have been. Thus Proust, in his essay on Flaubert, singled out for special praise the blank spaces that interrupt the narrative flow of the *Education sentimentale.* Furthermore, the Symbolistic notion that poetic resonance could not be sustained at length had fostered the cultivation of climactic moments, the contrasting vibrations of touchstones, elliptical sequences of epiphanies. To combine diversity of effect with sharpness of definition, it was probably necessary to begin with a miscellaneous accumulation of material, more than twice the amount that could be used, and to proceed by cutting much of it out and tightening the rest of it up. The sculptor, chipping away the crude stone till he unbares the contours of his image, offers no analogy here. More aptly we might think of the shooting and editing of a film, caught at this stage in the cutting-room.

The ultimate *montage* has been so successful that one's initial response to the early version is sheer resistance. It is, at first glance, difficult to see how what was cut could ever have been included or how what was included could ever have been cut. The cuts were not transitions; the juxtapositions are as abrupt as ever in the drafts; further additions might have been distractions. Eliot had thought of using "Gerontion" as a prelude, and Pound wisely advised him against it;

that conjunction would indeed have neutralized the impact of both poems. To the text of the *Ur-Waste Land* are appended ten additional poems, mostly unpublished though gleaned for occasional lines. "One test is whether anything would be lacking," wrote Pound to Eliot, if these "remaining superfluities" were omitted, and very firmly: "I don't think it would." He added that the nineteen pages from "April" to "*Shantih*," as they had just been edited, constituted the longest poem in the English language. "Don't try to bust all records by prolonging it three pages further." And he concluded his letter with an effusion of his own, celebrating his efforts as male midwife with a pun, "Sage Homme."

> If you must needs enquire
> Know diligent Reader
> That on each Occasion
> Ezra performed the Caesarian Operation.

The grateful poet responded by proposing to use this "obstetric effort" as a preface, but later settled for his dedication to Pound, "*il miglior fabbro.*" In his letter presenting the manuscript to Quinn, Eliot declared it "worth preserving in its present form solely for the reason that it is the only evidence of the difference which his criticism has made to this poem." In a recent interview, Mrs. Eliot recalls her husband saying that, if the work-in-progress turned up, it should be published: "It won't do me any good, but I would like people to realize the extent of my debt to Ezra."

The caption that heads the typescript of the first two sections, "He Do the Police in Different Voices," is an affectionate reminiscence from *Our Mutual Friend,* where Sloppy the mangle-boy has a Dickensian talent for dramatizing the crime news as he reads it aloud. This was a facetious working-title, but not without pertinence, since Dickens had been Eliot's greatest predecessor in catching the street-cries—as well as the heart-cries—of London. The operative phrase is "different voices." One of the discarded passages alludes to the "many voices" of the sea, in words which echo Tennyson's "Ulysses" and would find a place in Eliot's "Dry Salvages." *The Waste Land* is an anti-epic in form as well as in purport, since it contains so little in the way of direct narration or description. What it presents is a sequence of many voices, anguished characters speaking for themselves, from the Lithuanian countess at the beginning to the maternal lamentation over the holocaust, from the drinkers in the pub to the crowing cock at the ruined chapel, from the Wagnerian choruses to the Shakespearean ragtime, from the prophecy of the gypsy fortune-teller to the closing *cento* of polyglot quotations. Like Dylan Thomas' *Under Milk Wood,* the poem would adapt itself admirably to choral performance. Pound, when reviewing *Prufrock and Other Observations* on Eliot's debut in 1917, had called attention to "his method of conveying a whole situation and half a character by three words of a quoted phrase." He had also stressed the link—an even stronger one for him—with Browning's dramatic monologues.

The most elaborate and most impressive of Eliot's earlier poems had likewise been monologues: "The Love Song of J. Alfred Prufrock," "Portrait of a Lady," and "Gerontion." Each of them, in a conversational cadence of blank verse, free verse, and irregular rhyme, had projected a self-portrait; and each of those projected selves stood close to the sensibility and outlook of the poet himself. Other and shorter poems—one could scarcely call them lyrics—had taken the shape of jauntily rhyming quatrains, under that same inspiration from Gautier and the *Symbolistes* which brought Pound to "Hugh Selwyn Mauberley." These, as contrasted with the quasi-tragic soliloquies, were predominantly satirical in tone; they seem to have been glimpsed and overheard rather than lived through and deeply voiced. Their characteristic *persona,* antagonist rather than protagonist, is the eternal bounder Sweeney—Sweeney, whose reunion with Mrs. Porter will consummate the *sacre du printemps* of *The Waste Land,* and who will survive to stage his own *agon* or at least a "fragment" of it. Sweeney and his ilk, though they make up the great majority, are coolly viewed from a distance, or else encountered in the street like Stetson. The inner monologue, the central voice of *The Waste Land* is that of Tiresias, "a mere spectator" and blind at that, and yet—as Eliot noted—"the most important personage in the poem, uniting all the rest." And the note cites the relevant passage from Ovid's *Metamorphoses,* where the androgynous prophet must decide between Jupiter and Juno, each maintaining that the other sex gets more pleasure out of copulation.

"What Tiresias *sees,* in fact, is the substance of the poem." He, who has "sat by Thebes below the wall," presides over the clerk's cheap seduction of the typist, and over the whole succession of rapes, revulsions, and loveless couplings; for, as Eliot tells us, just as all the characters blend into one another, so both the sexes merge in Tiresias. Hence, despite his blindness, he can play the passive witness, suffering all if not acting. Though he can be identified with Ezekiel at one point and with Saint Augustine at another, it is interesting that the main interlocutor should be a classical, not a Judeo-Christian, figure. It is particularly significant in this connection that Eliot, at the suggestion of Pound, excised a parenthetical line from the Book of Revelations: "I John saw these things, and heard them." Eliot's apocalypse is syncretic, if not secular; its concluding prayer comes from the *Upanishads;* its principal epiphany occurs not at Emmaus but in the Antarctic; its particular quest for the Holy Grail seems suspended in a universal failure of nerve. Yet the dream-vision of Tiresias takes the course of a Dantesque pilgrimage, which stops at wayside stations for interviews with the *dramatis personae,* traversing Hell and barely reaching Purgatory. The final version substitutes the caged Sybil of the *Satyricon* for an epigraph from Conrad's "Heart of Darkness," but the theme in either case is despair. Mrs. Eliot quotes the poet's response to readers who emphasized the poem's social criticism: "To me it was only the relief of a personal and wholly insignificant grouse against life; it is just a piece of rhythmical grumbling."

Given the ironic deprecation that characterized his later self-criticism, this remark need not be taken too seriously. Certainly he was writing under the most serious personal strain: uncertain health, his father's death, an unhappy first marriage, overwork at a full-time job plus part-time freelancing, financial anxieties which Pound—embarrassingly and vainly—tried to alleviate by raising a fund. Moreover Eliot suffered, as he told Richard Aldington, from "an aboulie and emotional derangement which has been a lifelong affliction." No wonder that the period of gestation culminated with a nervous breakdown and a psychiatric consultation in Switzerland. It was his ensuing lack of confidence, on completing the poem, that referred so many decisions to Pound. But if, as Eliot argued in an essay, Shakespeare's melancholy sought its "objective correlative" in *Hamlet,* and if the anthropologists had shown how malaise could be ritualized into the stuff of poetry, then *The Waste Land* could become a parable of the blight on civilization itself. Intentions are more explicit in the drafts: there the Fisher King for example, though finally tucked away among the notes, appears directly in the pack of cards. More obviously, the appearance of Tiresias was originally preceded by an apostrophe to the city of London, where people are "bound upon the wheel!"—the same Shakespearean metaphor that is employed, in an appended poem, to characterize the inhabitants of Hampstead. The poet seems grimly determined to point a moral:

> London, the swarming life you kill and breed,
> Huddled between the concrete and the sky;
> Responsive to the momentary need,
> Vibrates unconscious to its formal destiny . . .

Not content with slashing out the quatrain here, Pound exploded by writing "B-lls" in the margin. Previously he had indicated his worry lest the street scenes remind the reader too much of Blake. He was clearly justified in his assumption that the "unreal city," as rendered by Eliot, could express itself without being so formally apostrophized in the vocative.

Though the differences between the draft (sometimes reworked and retyped) and the copy-text are far too numerous to be subsumed conveniently in a variorum edition, the familiar words emerge more and more upon a gradual reading. Whereas the end is more or less plain sailing, it is the outset which confronts us—as it did the poet and his editor—with confusion. For the *ur*-text starts, not with the stirring of April and the aristocratic voice of Mitteleuropa, but with fifty-four loose lines about a rowdy evening on the town, the town presumably being South Boston. Eliot was continually fascinated by the vulgarities of metropolitan low-life, in the half-snobbish, half-wistful manner of a Prufrock regarding a Sweeney, and here the binge is led by a namesake, "old Tom, boiled to the eyes." The intonations, reinforced by popular songs and advertisements, are distinctly Irish-American. The problem of diction alone would have been enough for Eliot himself to have scrapped the passage and plunged immediately into April. Despite his fondness for slang, he was never at home in it, and besides the idiom had to be Anglicized. Nonetheless a few Americanisms survived: though the phonograph is an authentic English "gramophone," the narrator goes fishing behind an American "gashouse" instead of a gas-works. Pound had a better ear for the vernacular; he took exception to the fortune-teller's "I look in vain / For the Hanged Man," which Eliot accordingly simplified to "I do not find . . ." And when Eliot groped for a Briticism meaning "Discharge out of the army??," it was Pound who supplied him with the *mot juste*, "demobbed."

This was the word to fit in the cockney dialogue at the pub, which would make the South Boston episode altogether supererogatory.

Eliot's first wife had read and made a few comments on the manu-script, mainly expressions of admiration, occasionally hesitation; but she also furnished a line or two for the repartee of the cockneys, echo-ing the speech of her housemaid. It may be Vivien Eliot's own voice that we hear in the tense ejaculation: "My nerves are bad tonight. Yes, bad. Stay with me . . ." We know it was at her request that Eliot left out a line from his account of the chess-game, which he reinserted in a holograph copy much later: "The ivory men make company between us." The most extensive passage omitted consists of eighty-seven lines beginning the second section, written in imitation of *The Rape of the Lock,* a satire upon a certain Fresca (the modern bluestocking or "can-can salonnière") in her dressing-room. Fortunately Pound managed to convince Eliot that he could not beat Pope at that sort of game; ac-tually, some misogynistic touches seem no less suggestive of Swift; at all events, this portrait of a lady would have been *de trop* after the rococo pastiche of Shakespeare's Cleopatra in the second section. But similar couplets on Fresca, who is mentioned in "Gerontion," reappear in a pseudonymous article contributed to the *Criterion* by Vivien Eliot, where they seem to accord with her impressionistic small-talk about current happenings in the arts. One of her sentences tellingly stands out: "What happy meetings, what luminous conversations in twilight rooms filled with the scent of hyacinths, await me now?"

The ferment of critical interpretation and exegetical argument that has surrounded *The Waste Land* for fifty years has lately been reani-mated by the rediscovery of these prior texts, which may well bring new illumination to some of the poem's vexed questions. Correspon-dents of the *Times Literary Supplement* have been speculating over the identity and even the sex of "the hyacinth girl," whom the inter-locutor encounters early in the story and who returns with him from the hyacinth garden "neither / Living nor dead." Perhaps the best gloss on this personage would be the reference, in "Portrait of a Lady," to

> the smell of hyacinths across the garden
> Recalling things that other people have desired.

Significantly, "the hyacinth garden" recurs in the draft of *The Waste Land*—where it does not in the definitive version—during the whispered colloquy that comes between Cleopatra's levée and the outburst of jazz: it drops out after "I remember," which thus goes on at once to "Those are pearls which were his eyes." This recollection from Ariel's sea-dirge in *The Tempest* was originally followed by "yes!" Pound, who had demurred at the same Shakespearean echo when it had been parenthetically associated with the fatal card of the drowned Phoenician Sailor, had his way in removing the "yes!" His cryptic comment, "Penelope," with "J.J." initialed under it, refers to the conclusion of *Ulysses* and to the note of Joycean affirmation, which might sound inappropriate here. What is more important, the crucial remembrance is no longer the hyacinth garden but "Death by Water," as portended by the Tarot pack and realized in the fourth section. The change signalizes the movement from the dearth and drouth of the poem's title, from the arid plain and the stony places to the rivers and the sea, the hope of rain and promise of fertility, and hence from Death-in-Life to Life-in-Death. On the back of the canceled Fresca typescript, Eliot drafted in pencil his magnificent evocation of the Thames. He would confide to Ford Madox Ford that the twenty-nine good lines of the poem ("The rest is ephemeral") were those of the water-dripping song, the mirage of thirst in the fifth section.

The third of the major excisions comprises seventy-two lines, interweaving the escapades of sailors ashore—in the ribald Sweeney vein—with the haunting narrative of an ill-fated voyage. In the seascape we recognize the Dry Salvages and other memories of Eliot's youthful sailing days at Cape Ann. The literary prototypes are Tennyson's Ulysses and Dante's Ulisse; yet, when the vessel heads toward shipwreck at the Mount of Purgatory, the catastrophic vision of polar whiteness is like the one described by Poe's A. Gordon Pym.

> Something which we knew must be a dawn—
> A different darkness flowed above the clouds,
> And dead ahead we saw, where sky and sea should meet,
> A line, a white line, a long white line,
> A wall, a barrier, toward which we drove.

Pound's immediate reaction to the whole nautical interlude was "Bad," and he ruthlessly scuttled so much of the context that this fine cinquain could hardly have stood by itself. Eliot's discouraged acknowledgment was an offer to scuttle the remainder of the fourth section, which recounts the drowning of Phlebas the Phoenician. Thereupon the integral role of the latter was vigorously insisted upon by Pound: "And he is needed ABSOlootly where he is. Must stay in." Once again a removal leaves a parallel but far superior passage in the text. Consequently all of "Death by Water" is concentrated into just ten lines. These, in turn, are freely translated from the conclusion to one of Eliot's French poems, "Dans le Restaurant." Though the English drops one or two specific details, it is metaphorically more powerful: "Un courant de sous-mer l'emporta très loin" is transposed to "A current under sea / Picked his bones in whispers." The French ending is rather self-consciously matter of fact:

> Figurez-vous donc, c'était un sort pénible;
> Cependant, ce fut jadis un bel homme, de haute taille.

Whereas the English ending brings the sailor's fate home to the reader, universalizing it into an eloquent cenotaph:

> Gentile or Jew
> O you who turn the wheel and look to windward,
> Consider Phlebas, who was once handsome and tall as you.

It seems likely that Eliot had in mind the friend of his Sorbonne period, Jean Verdenal, who had been killed at twenty-six in the Dardanelles campaign and to whose memory *Prufrock* had been dedicated, with an epigraph from Dante about the shades of Virgil and Statius embracing in Purgatory. If we may so conjecture, we may compare the genesis of *The Waste Land* to that of "Lycidas," since it had been the drowning of a fellow student, Edward King, which inspired Milton to compose his pastoral meditation on study and fame, moral corruption and spiritual resurrection. Eliot, unlike Verdenal but like Gerontion, had not been "at the hot gates / Nor fought in the warm rain." Mourning his fallen friend in the aftermath of the First World War, he could find objective correlatives for such elegiac emotions in *The Waste Land*'s vistas of European devastation, attrition, and decay. Cultural transmutation might be said to bring about "a sea-change / Into something rich and strange"; but richness and strangeness have lost their positive meaning, in Eliot's parody of Ariel's dirge, where they stand for all that looks commercial and alien. Their exponent, the man who drowns in the mock-dirge, is Bleistein—"Chicago Semite Viennese" as caricatured by a Saint Louis Yankee Londoner—who had played the interloper among "Time's ruins" in "Burbank with a Baedeker: Bleistein with a Cigar." It is worth noting, in view of Pound's subsequent antisemitic phase, that he opposed the introduction of Bleistein into *The Waste Land*, writing "doubtful" under two emphatic question marks on the fair copy of these additional verses in Eliot's hand.

It is Phlebas, the sacrificial victim, who must prepare the way for renewal and growth, while the oceanic immersion of "Death by Water" stands in contrast to the scorching desiccation of the land in "What the Thunder Said." Stylistically, the striking facts are that the phrasing of the Phlebas episode needed no correction from either Pound or Eliot, that Pound wrote "OK from here on I think" at the beginning of the final section, and that his suggestions and Eliot's changes were thereafter utterly minimal. Having conceived it in a sustained inspiration during his rest-cure at Lausanne, he explained to Bertrand Russell that, though it might not be the best part, it was "the only part that justifies the whole." Probably he had reason to feel more secure at this basic level of seriousness, whereas his ironic and playful divagations raised problems of tone which had to be tested, often retouched or retrenched. Pound's advice was invaluable in condensing the seduction scene, which Eliot had conceived in greater novelistic detail, relying much too heavily on such adjectives as "squalid" and "dirty." Pound also persuaded him to break up his all-too-regular heroic stanzas; too many lines were "Too easy" or "not interesting enough as verse"; and it was Pound's taste which eliminated the farewell distich, after the seducer gropes down the unlit stairs:

> And at the corner where the stable is,
> Delays only to urinate, and spit.

On the other hand, it is just as well that Eliot was not always ready to accept the Poundian preference. That would have deprived us of such incisive epithets as "One of the low on whom assurance sits . . ." Not to mention the loss of the key-word "inviolable" in describing the extreme violation, the rape of Philomel the nightingale: "Filled all the desert with inviolable voice . . ." Pound regarded the rhythm as "too penty," too prone to fall into iambic pentameters, albeit this line happens to be an iambic hexameter, i.e. an alexandrine. Eliot was wise enough to disregard the objection.

Frequently the task of the blue pencil is not so much to prune and polish as to encourage departures from convention. Compression is urged when "rhyme drags it out to diffuseness," variation when cadences sound "too tum-pum at a stretch." Flatness is succinctly damned as "georgian." The precision of the imagists is asserted when Pound twice condemns "perhaps" ("Perhaps be damned") or takes exception to the ambiguousness of the verbal auxiliary "may" ("make up yr. mind"). On another occasion, when a "closed carriage" is called for, he reminds Eliot that they are living in 1922, not 1880. Eliot is willing to modernize "carriage" into "car" but not "taxi," since he has made use of a taxi elsewhere. That taxi would be considered one of the most arresting metaphors of the new Modernism, and Pound did well to disembed it from the rhymed quatrain that had first enclosed it. Any comparison with the published *Waste Land* will show that Eliot made numerous further corrections, most of them small, some in answer to Pound and some on his own. But the interest that attaches to the revisions should not obscure the strategic instances where the poet hit the nail on the head in the first place. How gratifying it must have been to Eliot, and how awesome it is to us, when a first reading won Pound's imprimatur: "O.K.," "STET," or most emphatically "echt," which he defined as "veritable, real." This stamp of authenticity was set on the emergence of Tiresias, and again—after the hothouse atmosphere of the canceled Fresca pages—on the crucial and unchanged stanza beginning: "A rat crept softly through the vegetation . . ."

One deleted allusion to "cautious critics" drew from Pound the bitter sidesweep: "surely as you are writing of London this adj. is tauto." Pound's willingness to brave such tautological caution made him the single critic to whom Eliot could submit his unresolved dilemmas. On the other side, Eliot's originality might have been constrained by his diffidence, had he not been able to count upon such sure and robust support. There are many cases where writers have worked in collaboration, or have had their works completed or adapted by other writers. The relation of contemporary novelists to their agents and editors can become precariously dependent. But the annals of literary maieutics are unlikely to yield so unique and richly documented a record as this. Pound's remarkable insight was matched by his generosity; he was as proud of *The Waste Land* as if he had been the author; it was, he announced to his old professor Felix Schelling, "the justification of the 'movement,' of our modern experiment, since 1900." Given the respective complementarities of their withdrawn and outgoing talents, of concentration as against diffusion, Eliot had fulfilled the aims best formulated by Pound. In summation the former might have been looking back on the integration of his endeavors, when he wrote: "These fragments have been shored against [originally "spelt into"] my ruins."

Pound transposed the pronoun and varied the verb, in ruefully commencing his "Canto VIII": "These fragments you have shored (shelved)." The irony was that he could not do, for his *Cantos* and for his own fragmented career, what only he could do for his illustrious friend.

ULYSSES IN
MANUSCRIPT

Herewith my critical introduction to Ulysses: A Facsimile of the Manuscript,
*edited by Clive Driver and published by Octagon Books (New York) and
the Philip H. and A. S. W. Rosenbach Foundation (Philadelphia) in 1975.
Since I was writing before the valuable third volume of that edition was
ready for press—the collation between the manuscript and the first edition
(Paris: Shakespeare and Company, 1922) checked against the chapters
published in* The Little Review *and Joyce's own errata—I had to do my own
collating. This was largely a matter of spot-checking, although the spots
were chosen with some attention, and the yield was so rich that I had to
limit myself to some of the most striking illustrations. Armed with that third
volume, the reader can take full measure of the course that Joyce was still
to cover. However, I did have access to some of the proof-sheets and even
to a few pages of the typescript. Meanwhile much research has been undertaken on the earlier and intervening stages before publication, which should
culminate with sixteen volumes devoted to* Ulysses *in the promised sixty-
three-volume* James Joyce Archive *and the critical text computerized by the
English Seminar at the University of Munich. The ghost of Joyce, who lived
from pillar to post, and who met with every conceivable impediment in getting his finished works printed and circulated, must be amused if not surprised by the irony. Since the facsimile is paginated by references to the
corresponding pages of three printed editions, my page-references are to the
first edition as reprinted in the third volume.*

•

Almost unbelievably, it is now some fifty-odd years since the publication of *Ulysses* in 1922. That same year also witnessed the publication of *The Waste Land,* whose jubilee has lately been commemorated
by a facsimile edition of its original manuscript. Nothing that has
happened since to English prose or verse can be compared with the
simultaneous impact of these two masterworks. In their turn, and after
a probationary period of shock and incomprehension, they have been
accorded a classic status among the artistic landmarks of our unclassical century. They have indeed been so canonized by criticism and

scholarship that it has become hard for us to recapture a sense of the turmoil that engendered them. But now that we have such printed access as this to the preliminary versions in each case, it becomes possible to follow the intricate processes whereby two of our greatest writers asserted their mastery. They could share certain attitudes and approaches, as Eliot pointed out when he hailed Joyce for containing his amorphous material within the ordered contours of rediscovered myth. It may be significant that neither was an Englishman; for each of them brought to the language a special dedication, as well as a special impatience with facile or flaccid styles. Yet they were widely divergent in native temperament as well as formal intention, and those divergences were mirrored in their respective methods of composition. Eliot's manuscript is twice the length of his poem; Joyce's is considerably shorter than his novel. Final redaction was largely a matter of cutting for Eliot, of amplification for Joyce.

The circumstances attending the present version are well described by Mr. Driver in his editorial introduction. This is—or sets out to be—the author's fair copy, though its increasing burden of afterthoughts, marginalia, interlineations, and corrections indicates that much of the text was still being drafted at first hand. Behind it looms the seven-year labor (closer to eight) of "*Trieste-Zurich-Paris*, 1914–1921": plans and notes and drafts extending through prior stages, thousands of descriptive details and associated ideas sorted out and recombined and interwoven into parallel streams of consciousness. Looking back toward those earlier endeavors, some of them recorded by notebooks in the Lockwood Library at the University of Buffalo, others in the outlines at the British Museum, we are bound to view the pages before us as the critical stage of a tremendous and complicated process of assemblage. But if we look ahead to the published version, we are bound to observe that the actual writing of the book went on continuously until it reached the printing press. Though the printers worked from typescript based in large part on this fair copy, the text would be corrected much further by the author, who supplied other texts for certain chapters published in periodicals and kept on adding and changing through as many as six or seven sets of page-proof. Joseph Prescott's unpublished Harvard dissertation, a careful study of the additions and changes in the galleys (*placards*) now at the Houghton Library, bears the suggestive title, "James Joyce's *Ulysses* as a Work in Progress." Like Balzac, Joyce could not resist the compulsion to rewrite as he read proof, so that the definitive text would only be crystallized with the printer's last deadline.

These proofs afford an eloquent testimonial to the patience of the printer, Maurice Darantière, and the generosity of the publisher, Sylvia Beach. Thus, when at a momentary loss for the *mot juste,* Joyce could simply postpone it until the next proofreading. Into the library episode he inserted a line in which Malachi Mulligan parodies Synge: " 'Twas murmur we did for a gallus potion would rouse a friar, I'm thinking." Whereupon Joyce instructed the compositor in French to leave a space for six or seven additional words. Inspiration came to him succinctly with five words on the subsequent proof, catching both Synge's cadence and Mulligan's scurrility: "and he limp with leching." In such a light as this it is understandable, though still rather awesome, that Joyce could send the body of his work to be set up before he wrote the concluding seven pages of Molly Bloom's soliloquy. He must have had that climax well in mind, but perhaps it was so climactic for him that he did not want others to see it except in print. (Two days before the date of printing, he was still writing it, as proof-sheets now at the University of Texas disclose.) Despite his failing eyesight, he cherished a Mallarméan feeling for the appearance of type upon a page. Those headlines which intersperse the chapter located in a newspaper office were written afterward, and so were the opening paragraphs, as if in conformity with the journalistic procedures they illustrate. Moreover, Joyce transposed italics to Roman capitals, and experimented with the phrasing from proof to proof. "IN THE HEART OF THE METROPOLIS" was brought home by the adjective "HIBERNIAN," while "A STREET PROCESSION" became a more fastidious "CORTEGE."

Ulysses, in the Rosenbach Manuscript, is less interrupted by such devices as headlines, and it stands by itself except for Molly's peroration. To reread the story in Joyce's own hand is to enter his workshop; for, though it neatly subsumes the tangle of earlier recensions, it revises itself as it goes along and gathers codicils in the last two chapters. The peculiar slanting conformation of its margins seems to suggest a restless speeding-up as the lines move down, while the tendency to diminish in size—especially as contrasted with the twenty-one pages copied by Frank Budgen, or even with the larger and more regular holograph of *Stephen Hero* written nearly twenty years before—conveys a costive effect which readily submits itself to Freudian analysis. Joyce's handwriting anonymously submitted, has been analyzed by a student of graphology, Yvonne Skinner, who finds marked expressions of culture, intelligence, and sensitivity in his habits of penmanship. Mental energy, extreme self-consciousness, conscientiousness to the point of fussiness, powers of intense concentration and command of precise detail, musical if not mathematical talents, a rare combination of intuition and logic—these are traits that have imprinted themselves, according to Mrs. Skinner, along with impracticality, obstinacy, irritability, reticence, and occasional brusqueness. This can do no more than confirm what we already know from letters and memoirs, from Richard Ellmann's admirable biography, above all from our own unmediated impressions; but it marks a correlation that Joyce himself might have relished between his substance and his presentation.

There are some points where the manuscript carries more authority than the printed texts, which admitted and persisted in certain errata. Joyce went out of his way to specify that the first syllable of his hero's forename, as shouted and echoed in his first chapter (page 20), should be spelled with twelve *e*'s: "Steeeeeeeeeeeephen!" Both the American and British editions have skimped on this long-drawn-out vocative. Both again have ignored a speech-prefix (occurring in the manuscript on page 517), thereby confusing the song of the moth with the voice of Mr. Bloom's grandfather. A more notable omission takes place at the end of the "Ithaca" chapter, in which the question "Where?" is supposed to be answered by a large period, cryptically symbolizing the world itself as it recedes into space. Recognizing the danger of an oversight here, Joyce was explicit in his instructions to Darantière: *"La réponse à la dernière demande est un point"* (689). This is betokened by a small square in the first edition, and subsequently omitted as often as not. In general, since Joyce worked by accumulation, discarding little while amplifying and embroidering much, few passages appear in the manuscript that do not arrive at the final text in some form or other. An interesting exception crops up during Stephen's morning meditation, when he broods for a moment over "Wilde's love that dare not speak its name" (49). The manuscript continues with four more words, which have been omitted from the book "His arm: Cranly's arm." Stephen, recalling an early friendship signalized in *A Portrait of the Artist as a Young Man,* retrospectively hints that it may have had a homosexual tinge. Joyce evidently decided against that implication, which was scarcely present when the phrase (in reverse) was introduced on page 7.

Stephen returns to youthful memories in eight lines later omitted from his Shakespearean discussion, where his mental comment includes a Latin definition of love from Saint Thomas Aquinas, who will be quoted elsewhere at all events (187f.). Those who are theologically inclined may ponder the significance of the marginal substitution on page 215, when Father Conmee is reading his breviary, wherein one of the displaced quotations seems to relate more directly than the substitute to the business of Bloomsday: "*Notus in Iudaea Deus. . . .*" Alterations of single words are often purely functional. A comparison of the contexts will show why "stretched" was altered to "inclined" (103) or "procuress" to "bawd" (418f.); "ambled" was turned into "slunk" (46) and "dog" into "beagle" (446f.) with a clear gain in expressiveness. Joyce took particular pains to choose proper names that rang with an appropriate resonance. As a language teacher, he quite advisedly replaced Bué's by Chardenal's French primer (241f.). While he was revising his manuscript, he substituted Kino's for Hyam's as a brand-name for trousers (146f., 635f.). Minor personages were rechristened for local reasons when John Murray became Red Murray (112f.), the foreman Castell became Nannetti (113f.), and the Honourable Mrs. Paget Butler became Mrs. Mervyn Talboys (442). Bloom's wife, singing in concerts under her maiden name, Madame Marion Tweedy, seems to have started her professional career as Madame Marie Meagher (102f.). Her manager and lover, the uncouth Boylan, is generally known by his nickname "Blazes"; but he had originally been baptized Edward, which was emended to Hugh E. in the latest proof (683f.).

Simplicity could never be anything more than a relative consideration with Joyce; but, insofar as the manuscript is simpler than its ultimate outgrowth, its story-line is more immediately graspable. Edmund Wilson argued that Joyce had overdone his verbal elaboration of *Finnegans Wake,* that it had proved more effective in the briefer and somewhat less highly wrought extracts published previously as *Work in Progress.* Yet, once a writer ventures so far afield, he transcends the usual norms, and the critic has no basis for imposing limits. There are likewise readers who prefer the more solidly naturalistic texture of *Stephen Hero* to the refined impressionism of the much-rewritten *Portrait of the Artist.* But Joyce's master then had been Flaubert; and he was engaged in reproducing, on a more tentative scale, the efforts of documentation, arrangement, retrenchment, and distillation that had created *Madame Bovary.* Since his maturer aims were encyclopedic, his narrative techniques were—in his own coinage—"allincluding." Since nothing endemic to Dublin was alien to his panorama, there were always posterior touches of urban color to be worked in. The more he developed the minds of his characters, the greater the opportunities they opened up for reminiscence and coincidence, linking themselves with one another and with their environment. All the important connections had been established, and the basic synthesis achieved, by the time the manuscript was written out. But the habit of accretion would continue as long as the pages lay open to correction; as long as the snowball rolled, it would be augmented by fresh layers of observation and insight.

The specific differences that emerge from even the most casual collation of the Rosenbach facsimile with a standard edition of *Ulysses,* accordingly, are touchstones for Joyce's imagination in action. Every chapter, to be sure, presents a different problem, and—at least through the dramatic scenes that have been likened to Goethe's *Walpurgisnacht*—they tend to increase successively in length and complexity. All of them are meaningfully extended here and there, with new sidelights and unexpected linkages, as among the funeral guests in "Hades" or the assortment of pedestrians in "The Wandering Rocks" (it is convenient to make use of Joyce's Homeric terms as phantom chapter-headings). Some episodes, the more technically experimental, had to be carefully elaborated and tightly composed from the outset, and have consequently been less reworked than the others: "The Sirens," to whose musical interplay he had already devoted five months, and "The Oxen of the Sun," where the evolution of English prose style is retraced by the obstetrical narration. Two other episodes, involving parody at a more limited and commonplace level, invited any number of addenda. The diction of "Nausicaa" is that of novelettes and advertisements in sentimental women's magazines, and Joyce could enhance the description of Gerty MacDowell by adding "that tired feeling" to the typescript and "blushing scientifically cured" to the proof. The parlance of "Eumaeus" is a kind of masculine counterpart, the clichés of some long-winded pretender to what he would call *sang froid;* and Joyce took a grim pleasure in piling up such tired foreign phrases as *confrères, hoi polloi,* and *tête-à-tête.*

Both in manner and subject, "The Cyclops" offered many opportunities for substantial interpolation. It is primarily a realistic monologue in a raffish Dublin idiom, with a good deal of barroom conversation;

but its nationalistic and racial argument sets off a series of imaginary projections, both mythological and religious, with Ireland represented by its traditional heroes and the half-Jewish Bloom by the prophet Elijah. Joyce enlarged the easy flow of pub-talk by repeated extensions in the guise of epic catalogues or ecclesiastical litanies: a list of prominent clergymen, a roll-call of the saints, a survey of the natural beauties of Ireland, a fashionable wedding of the trees, a well-attended public execution. To an even greater degree, the section entitled "Ithaca" could be filled in and pieced out with lengthy inserts, since it had the segmented format of a catechism or set of examination questions and answers. Much of the supplementation is in an appended section of the manuscript, notably the sequence of parallels and contrasts between Bloom and Stephen. Still more would be interposed there in the way of material facts: the contents of the kitchen cupboard and of Bloom's desk, including the suicide note of his late father. The intimately personal strain, neutralized by statistical data and large abstractions, would blench before the chill of interplanetary distance. The *Verfremdungseffekt* of the farewell scene has been intensified in revision, when Bloom and Stephen hear the several echoes that have been haunting them all day: for Stephen his mother's funeral Mass, for Bloom the neighborhood churchbells.

"Penelope," the conclusion, is similar to the preceding "Ithaca," having been transcribed in a separate notebook where the opposite pages have ample room for the increment of marginalia, thus giving us the clearest enumeration of Joyce's second thoughts: e.g. the allusion to Rabelais on page 702f. But, along with Molly's powerful valedictory, Joyce had many small particulars to add. His pun on Beerbohm Tree and Trilby's "barebum" adumbrates the sort of wordplay that would soon be engulfing him in *Finnegans Wake*. The keyword *yes* is enumerated more frequently in the definitive version, and the stress on continuity is strengthened by the elimination of introductory capitals and punctuation marks. Probably the focal chapter, certainly the longest, and the one most highly charged with emotions, however, is the expressionistic psychodrama of "Circe." What has gone before builds up to it; what comes later on subsides from it; hence we are not surprised that it should have become what it is by intensive reworking. This gave Bloom more chances to act out his fantasies, such as his elevation and condemnation in the role of Lord Mayor. A curious shift in the speech he makes just after that interlude modulates from "All is

vanity" to "All insanity" (451f.)—conceivably because the message of
Ecclesiastes would be cited and embroidered elsewhere (651f.).
Stephen's epiphany, the apparition of his mother's ghost, had also to be
heightened; and Joyce wrote in—on a page of the typescript subsequently presented by Miss Beach to Theodore Spencer—the most poignant touch, the echo of Mulligan's sneer: "She's beastly dead!"

The fuller treatment of Stephen's streetfight with Private Carr gets
magnified to pageantlike proportions by the hallucinated stage directions involving King Edward VII, with characteristic gestures and responses from dozens of other figures among the audience who have
wandered in from other parts of the story. The blow that lays Stephen
low has been preceded by the reverberation from a black Mass—a reversal of the blasphemous chanting with which Mulligan began the
book. This is spelled out more fully by spelling backward the name
of God and a verse from the liturgy. Bloom rescues Stephen with the
aid of the cheerful undertaker Corny Kelleher, who at various earlier
moments has been heard to hum the amorous refrain: "With my tooraloom tooraloom. . . ." Therefore Joyce took care to write it in on the
occasion of Kelleher's providential reappearance (560f.), and in the
proofs it is used to orchestrate Kelleher's departure, when Bloom
"assuralooms" him and he "reassuralooms" Bloom. What remains behind is the culminating epiphany, Bloom's vision, as he leans down
over the prostrate Stephen, of his lost son Rudy. Here the manuscript
contains the bare core of the human situation, to which it adds one
bathetic detail, the white lambkin. The rich development came at a
late stage in the proofs: the fragments of the Masonic oath with which
Bloom swears himself to secrecy, the sentimentalized lineaments of
the boy that might have been, had he lived to eleven instead of dying
in infancy. And though the manuscript tells us that Rudy is reading,
it is not until the proof that he "reads from right to left," apprising his
wonderstruck father that the book he reads is in Hebrew.

Kelleher's "tooraloom" provides a minor instance of how Joyce asso-
ciates themes, often musical or literary, with moods and characters. He
found many new occasions for introducing and interweaving them
while copying his work and preparing it for the press. Thus the theme
of apocalypse ("shattered glass and toppling masonry") comes into its
own in a stage direction for the midnight hallucination (541f.); but it
first appears, and is slightly amended, as it flashes across Stephen's
mind in the schoolroom (24); and it is interpolated among the musings

of his morning stroll along the beach (43f.). *Agenbite of inwit,* the Middle English locution for remorse of conscience, has come to be regarded as a key to Stephen's character, above all to his relationship with his mother. Yet, having been belatedly superimposed on the text, it is absent from the manuscript. *"Là ci darem la mano,"* the duet from *Don Giovanni,* is Bloom's byword for philandering. It is one of two numbers figuring in Molly's next concert program, the other being "Love's Old Sweet Song." One or the other runs through Bloom's mind all day, a latent reminder of Molly's affair with Boylan. Late at night, during Bloom's subconscious encounter with an old flame, Mrs. Breen, she echoes the Anglo-Irish song: "the dear dead days beyond recall" (421f.). The revised flirtation scene also echoes the repartee of the Mozart duet. Mozart makes a more problematic entrance into the manuscript on the verso of 449, possibly an accidental intrusion in a hand which Mr. Driver has identified as that of Joyce's baritone son Giorgio, a transcription of the High Priest's *"In diesen heiligen Hallen"* from *Die Zauberflöte.* That bass aria has been referred to already under its Italian designation, *"Qui sdegno,"* just before Ben Dollard chooses to sing "The Croppy Boy" (270f.). Why the Temple of the Sun should be invoked, when Bloom is entering a brothel, tempts speculation.

Trains of thematic association help to unify the heterogeneous subject matter after it has been set down and put together. A handbill announcing the modern Elijah, an American evangelist, has been crumpled up by Bloom and dropped into the Liffey. The chapter that chronicles the activities of numerous minor characters, "The Wandering Rocks," has three postscripts that trace this "skiff" as it floats out to sea, incidentally crossing the schooner that is to discharge W. B. Murphy, the nautical spokesman of "Eumaeus" (217f., 230, 239f.). Similarly, the five sandwich-men, advertising H. E. L. Y. 'S. letter by letter, thread their way along the margin (218f., 220). In broaching sexual matters, then so delicate a concern and so much of an obstacle to free expression for Joyce's contemporaries, he became more explicitly candid as he rewrote. Because of Bloom's reluctance to name Boylan, the latter plays an elusive part in the interior monologue. Yet, as a billsticker by profession, he is identified with the observed announcement "POST NO BILLS," while the reconsidered context, by alluding to venereal disease, explains Bloom's secret fear: could his wife be infected through her adultery? The broken queries of the manuscript would scarcely be meaningful without the contextual gloss (146f.). The monosyllabic "Ow!" (356f.) is somewhat better explained by "This wet is very unpleasant," and by the consequent realization that Bloom is feeling the aftereffects of his physical reaction to Gerty MacDowell's exhibitionism. The addendum, "Well the foreskin is not back," not only supplies another gloss; it reveals the ironic fact that the "half and half" Bloom, though victimized by antisemitism, has never been circumcized.

Afterstrokes round out the detailed portraiture, completing the intimacy of our acquaintance with the *dramatis personae*. We might have guessed that Bloom had trouble in throwing a ball at school, or that he once made timid advances to an indignant housemaid. But his underlying humanity emerges from humble acts and compassionate thoughts, as when he helps the blind piano-tuner across the street. In turning from page 172 to page 173 of the manuscript, Joyce recopied and modified the operative sentence, bringing the two men close together physically through the sense of touch. On the margin he subjoined Bloom's psychological impulse: "Say something to him. Better not do the condescending. Something ordinary." Modification in the proof would lead to "a common remark" about the weather, and would indicate that this went characteristically unheeded. It is the proof once more that enables Bloom to probe his motivation in "The Lestrygonians," when he is meditating on his earlier happiness and the breakdown of his conjugal relations with Molly over the past ten years: "Could never like it again after Rudy." Molly herself makes no direct allusion to their dead child; note that her remembrance of having suckled him at her breast gets marginally shifted to their daughter Milly (704f.). Yet, in the course of her egocentric and sensual recollections, she does refer to "knitting that woollen thing"—an aftertouch which relies, for its emotional charge, on a cross-reference to an archaic paragraph in "The Oxen of the Sun," where Bloom recalls her grief over Rudy's death, and her pathetic hope that a little sweater she had knitted might lessen the rigors of winter burial.

The foregoing examples do no more than scratch the surface, though I hope they suggest the unique value and fascinating interest that this facsimile holds for those familiar with *Ulysses*. Most of my illustrations can be pursued much farther, and the practiced reader will have the pleasure of making his own discoveries, as he collates the manuscript with the book itself. He will be privileged to watch the artist at work, now smoothly copying from blotted and interlined drafts, now pausing to reconsider and retouch. Every word has entailed a complex decision. Some of those decisions are visible here in the author's correcting hand; others are to be inferred from the differences between the two redactions. We have become well aware of Joyce's achievement as an incomparable feat of literary organization, according with an elaborately preconceived design. Henceforth we can appreciate more concretely the last-minute insights, the more intuitive flashes of Joyce's artistry. Even Jung, a decade after its first appearance, characterized *Ulysses* as an enigma. To less percipient readers it seemed—as to the great majority of nonreaders—impenetrable. Yet during the last four decades the enigma has been so expounded, the novel has been so accepted, the style has been so scanned by so many admirers, that every phrase has come to seem inevitable. Stasis, the Joycean consummation, has indeed set in. Impressed by a classic, overwhelmed by a monument, we are likely to lose sight of all the problematic and dynamic elements that have gone into its composition. But Joyce had pledged his genius to demonstrating, as well as celebrating, the will to create.

It is something of a paradox that a novelist as committed as he was to the stylistic, esthetic, and formal aspects of his craft should have concentrated as intently on his private experience as he did. This he handled freely, though by no means romantically, since he had subjected it to naturalistic restraints. But his method controverts those critical purists who, in their devotion to the cult of form, would rule out the biographical background of a writer. A well-known formulation in the *Portrait of the Artist,* refining on an even better-known formula of Flaubert, emphasizes a transference from the lyric to the dramatic, from an artist's personality to the impersonality of art. The mean between them is the very act of artistic creation, to which we can bear witness through the document that has been reproduced herewith. It will catch the "fabulous artificer"—and how firmly the epithet is incised into the text (201f.)!—during those mellow hours when he has been putting the finishing touches upon his labyrinth. Not only will the spirit of Daedalus guide us through the maze; he will reveal some secrets of his creative artifice. On the relation of the myth to the novel, for instance: it seems clear that Joyce began by laying down the outline he had somewhat arbitrarily taken from Homer's *Odyssey,* and that he ranged more widely as he proceeded into the latterday welter of Dublin life. Having placed his mythical correspondences where they would serve as guidelines for the adventures of

Bloom and Stephen, he consolidated and animated his picture of the society that would all too briefly interlink and ultimately isolate their lives.

Criticism has followed a parallel path, starting from the authorized commentary of Stuart Gilbert, which dwelled upon the Odyssean scheme as Joyce himself had imparted it, and gradually moving forward toward a broader comprehension of the more literal events of Bloomsday. It was in this connection that the term *exegesis*, hitherto reserved for interpretation of the Scriptures or hieratic books, came to be identified with the analytic reading of difficult secular literature—where it has more recently been reinforced by the adaptation of *hermeneutics*. Joyce, for whom esthetics was a lay religion, would have been pleased by the pious zeal of his exegetes, who have surrounded his works with Scholastic metaphrase and Talmudic conjecture. These are ironic reparations for all the neglect and obstruction and misunderstanding from which he had suffered until he was vindicated by the recognition of *Ulysses*. Once the ban of censorship was lifted, the volume moved quickly through the bookshops and libraries into the academic sphere of study and research. There it faces the hazards of overreading. Joyce's intentions, though sometimes abstruse, were always concrete; his meanings, if recondite, would disclose themselves to perceptive scrutiny. As the mysteries have been unfolded, new interpreters have indulged in mystifications of their own. It is true that, besides the major precedent of Odysseus, Joyce alludes selectively to various other archetypes: Daedalus, Elijah, Don Giovanni, Jesus Christ. But it is either imposture or self-deception to argue, as one recent French commentator has done, that the twelve central chapters are respectively modeled on Suetonius' *Lives of the Caesars*.

Joyce's writing has a tough-minded objectivity which resists such subjective ingenuity and exposes farfetched pretentiousness. The task of his critics has been unduly complicated by their initial need to pave the way for appreciation with an emphasis on disclosure and decoding. As a consequence, we have tended to think about him rather too schematically, and to overlook the more immediate appeal that he can exert on so many other grounds. We have looked for keys, or else clung to vague analogies, rather than approaching him through his boundless particularity. This is understandable enough, since his searching curiosity, his passion for detail, and his exactitude in naming things are not easily blown up into arresting generalizations. Yet his distinguishing quality could be denoted by a favorite concept of his student days: *quiddity,* the whatness of anything or everything, that which makes it so uniquely itself. It was not for nothing that one of his poems got printed in Pound's anthology *Des Imagistes,* for he too professed the aim of the Imagists to behold and convey the object precisely. But he went beyond them in—the novelist's function—showing precisely how the existence of human beings is structured by objects. Whereas the poet could single out a perception and embody it in a poem, Joyce sought out those revealing juxtapositions which he termed epiphanies, and composed a novel by combining them *ad infinitum.* The manuscript of *Ulysses* is a quest for quiddities, a record of such perceptions as synthesized into a profoundly meaningful statement about the world. It is also a manual of style, which permits us line by line to participate in the struggles and share the triumphs.

JOYCE'S LETTERS:
LIFE VERSUS WORK

These self-explanatory comments were printed in The New Republic *(January 17, 1976). Irving Howe, reviewing the same book in another periodical, independently expressed a similar surprise that so much emphasis should now be placed upon the mere restoration of expletives hitherto deleted. Indeed he wrote me that some of his readers had accused him of narrow-mindedness for having raised this point. I have sufficient confidence in his open-mindedness to be reassured by the coincidence. Today there is not, after all, any danger of suppression. Given the radical change in ethical climate, there may be some danger of exploitation—of raising the ghosts of "dirt for dirt's sake," of reinvoking the scandal that Joyce has lived down, of disturbing the balance that he was so careful to set among the daily claims of mind and body.*

•

The first collection of James Joyce's letters, edited in 1957 by his aging friend and authorized commentator, Stuart Gilbert, proved a rather desultory job. Meanwhile Richard Ellmann, in preparation for his masterly biography, had tracked down and sifted out some twice as many more. These—including the notably detailed series addressed to Joyce's closest confidant over the years, his brother Stanislaus—were published as two supplementary volumes in 1966. Some day, Professor Ellmann promises us, there will be a complete edition. What he offers at the moment is a one-volume selection, re-edited when necessary and ordered in duly chronological sequence. We may well regret that, at the present price, we still miss out on the photographs that illuminated his previous volumes.

If these *Selected Letters* add up to somewhat less than a third of Joyce's correspondence already in print, they are interestingly augmented by ten letters hitherto unprinted, as well as by the inclusion of passages deleted from or else modified in earlier transcription. There have been two reasons for these deletions and modifications. Not until

1970 could the British Museum remove its seal from Joyce's original letters to Harriet Weaver, his generous patroness and literary executor. On consulting the texts directly, the editor then discovered that her transcriptions had been shaded by her own modesty and consideration for the family. Several of the new letters will be useful to the elucidators of *Finnegans Wake,* since they undertook to dispel her bewilderment over the project she found herself sponsoring.

The second and more sweeping circumstance, which currently gives us two more of the letters to Joyce's wife and fills in many ellipses among the file, is not so much the passage of time itself as the fact that recent years have lifted most of the taboos on printability. Here we encounter the novel and problematic aspect of the book. Those four-letter words which instigated the early notoriety of *Ulysses* were employed quite sparingly and always in a context where their absence would have been unrealistic. Joyce himself, when speaking, when cursing, even when exchanging stories with fellow males, seems to have demurely avoided such locutions. "You have never heard me, have you, utter an unfit word before others," he wrote to Nora Barnacle.

Yet his letters to her were as dirty and filthy—the adjectives are his— as obsessed carnality could make them. They go far beyond the force of that "heterosexual magnetism" whose salubrious influence was acknowledged by both Leopold Bloom and Stephen Dedalus. Sex is linked with fantasies of sodomy, scatology, fetishism, voyeurism, and sado-masochism. Here are the raw materials for Gerty MacDowall's exhibitionism, Molly Bloom's menstruation, and her husband's cult of lingerie and the lash. But, in Joyce's writing for publication, attitudes and motives are firmly regulated by the fictive situation at hand. It may be the crowning irony of his ironic role that, whereas he was once banned for displaying candor in fiction, posthumous prestige has now stripped away the last vestiges of his personal privacy.

Clearly these once-privileged communications—which zigzag, as the writer freely admits, from the romantic and spiritual to the ugly and bestial—were never meant for other eyes than those of the two impassioned correspondents. Nora, at Joyce's urging, seems to have responded to him in kind, and her responses were evidently destroyed after they had served the obvious purpose of vicarious sexual excitation. Of course it is the biographer's duty to seek out and scrutinize all the available records pertaining to his subject, wherever they lead him, as Mr. Ellmann has faithfully and sensitively done. I for one, however, would be satisfied with his interpretation of the evidence; I find myself gagging when the fetid details are held up to my nose.

At least they might have been left in the archives waiting for the complete edition to set them into perspective, rather than disclosed as the central revelation of a highly selective book documenting Joyce's career for the general reader. The French have a phrase for this: documentation gone wild (*la fureur de l'inédit*). To be sure, it was Joyce himself who initiated the self-exposure, yet he always kept it under the strictest esthetic control. Intimacies can become offensive only when they cease to be intimate, when readers are invited to be voyeurs. What confronts us, though it may seem distasteful, is not abnormal; it seems more embarrassing than shocking; and words have lost the potential shock that they could hold in Joyce's day.

As a writer, Joyce was a past master of the deliberate verbal *frisson*. That effect can hardly be attained in a climate where the use of language is habitually loose and coarse, where the expletives go undeleted. Breathing such an atmosphere, as we do today, it is harder to understand the psychological impetus that had to break through curbs of inhibition by gestures of shamelessness. The testimony that comes through is to Joyce's emotional dependence on this "poor uneducated girl," whose faith in her ever-demanding husband—though not without its trials and tensions—was such that she scarcely bothered to read his writings and would not have understood much of them. His ardent promise that she would share his fame has reached its peculiar fulfillment.

Their elopement was not to become a marriage until they had passed twenty-seven years together and two grown-up children were complicating their lives. Joyce was "not a very domestic animal"—or so he wrote to his Aunt Josephine, even though his many letters to her show an avid interest in family matters. Actually, while he spent his whole adult life moving from town to town and from one address to another, his domestic circle, reinforced by helpful admirers throughout, stabilized his European self-exile. "I loathe Ireland and the Irish," he declared to Nora; elsewhere he evinced his dislike of the French and Italians among whom he lived. Ambivalently, he turned his renunciation of Dublin into the nostalgic theme of his life-work.

Mr. Ellmann speaks aptly of Joyce's "urge to renounce." This could be morally justified by the principle of *non serviam*, not to mention grinding poverty, enervating health, or the obstacles against publication that blocked him through mid-career. The solitary stance he took at nineteen, in his resounding letter to Ibsen, was sustained with admirable resolve—but not without continual demands on many friends, and intermittent suspicions which sometimes approached paranoia. In winnowing the correspondence down to the limits of a single volume, Mr. Ellmann has naturally retained the most autobiographical letters, incidentally leaving out most of the other correspondents. The consequence has been to narrow a narrowing focus, to stretch taut the twisted threads of single-minded endeavor and self-centered complaint.

Readers who look for artistic magnanimity or for curiosity about others had better turn to the epistles of Henry James. Joyce was almost wholly preoccupied with his own work, or with its turbulent fortunes. Consistently and characteristically, he declined Yeats's invitation to join the new Irish Academy; and if he congratulated Shaw on receiving the Nobel Prize, it was as a "fellow townsman." Triumphantly he tells how, at a dinner with Pound and Hemingway, he managed to deflect the conversation to himself. Invariably he declined all such requests as that of *La Revue Nouvelle* to join in a tribute to Hardy. He thanked Sean O'Faolain for an early novel with the chilling statement that he had not read any novels in any language for years.

Indeed, though *Huckleberry Finn* is echoed in *Finnegans Wake*, it now appears that—rather than read Mark Twain—Joyce depended on summaries by his son's American stepson. He did know *The Waste Land* well enough to parody it for Miss Weaver's amusement. But his sole allusion to Proust strikes a petulant note of jealous rivalry. Exceptionally, he did exert himself on behalf of two other writers, each of whom had a special relation to him: Italo Svevo, his pupil in English, and Edouard Dujardin, his forerunner in using internal monologue. Both were older novelists, whose books had been half forgotten. His campaign for the Irish tenor John Sullivan seems associated with his lifelong quest for his own identity, which in turn he identified with Ireland's.

These letters have their moments of Irish banter and, less frequently, Irish charm—particularly the fable devised for his own grandchild, Stephen. But most of his compassion and insight were reserved for his fiction. There his awareness of his own prickly nature emerges when Mulligan, allowed to make a riposte, calls Stephen Dedalus "an impossible person." Since Joyce was committed to an all but impossible task, he must have gloried in the self-impeachment. "The intellect of man is forced to choose," insofar as Yeats defined that choice, "Perfection of the life, or of the work." Joyce was one of the few who opted for, and came very near to achieving, the latter alternative. This testament of human imperfections glows in the brighter light of his achievement.

DIALECTICAL SIBLINGS:
HEINRICH AND THOMAS MANN

It is too bad that this outstanding Brüderpaar *has not yet been the subject of a more incisive and thorough diptych in English than the recent book by Nigel Hamilton,* The Brothers Mann: The Lives of Heinrich and Thomas Mann, 1871–1950, 1875–1955 *(New Haven: Yale University Press), which I reviewed for* The New Republic *(May 19, 1979).*

•

Given the favoring contingencies of heredity and environment, it should not surprise us to encounter more than one established author within the same family, notably the recent Nobel Prize winner and his late brother I. J. Singer. Such a situation may have been sustained by various patterns of interaction, both domestic and professional, as in the mutual supportiveness of the Brontës or the Goncourts. It can also bring out invidious comparisons: the worthy Thomas Corneille was far outdistanced by his illustrious elder, Pierre, even as the easygoing Alec Waugh would be by his crotchety junior, Evelyn. The conjunction that has called forth this dual biography, according to its author, may be regarded as "the most significant literary brotherhood of all time." Nigel Hamilton is not sparing with superlatives, and all time might turn out to be an uncomfortable stretch from the vantage point of mere mortality. Critics are not much accustomed to imagine writers walking in fraternal pairs toward the ark of posthumous fame. Yet, once he has set up his category, Mr. Hamilton has a strong case. As brothers the Manns stand unique in the quality and the individuality of their work, in the depths and heights of their sibling rivalry, and in their respective involvements with the history of our twentieth century.

Materials for a study of this sort have become increasingly abundant, many of them stemming from the Heinrich Mann Archiv in East Berlin or the Thomas Mann Archiv in Zurich. Their correspondence has been duly edited, and they figure vividly in contemporary memoirs ranging from the eulogistic to the polemical. Eloquently and extensively both men have placed their views on public record; both have written fiction which draws deep upon immediate experience; even their nonliterary brother Viktor brought out an informal volume of family history, *Wir waren fünf* (*We Were Five*). Thomas left an autobiographical sketch, and Heinrich a book-length autobiography, as did the precocious and all-too-short-lived son of Thomas, Klaus. Heinrich's friend Alfred Kantorowicz published an impressionistic but documented account of the brothers' relationship a year after Thomas' death. A German monograph on the dialectical interplay of their ideas by André Banuls—more systematic and penetrating than Mr. Hamilton's summaries and quotations—is not listed in the latter's skimpy bibliography, which does include M. Banuls' French dissertation, *Heinrich Mann: Le Poète et la politique*. The title of his monograph suggests the direction a modern Plutarch must take in tracing these parallel lives. In spite of primogeniture, it is called *Thomas Mann und sein Bruder Heinrich*.

Each of them—Heinrich four years ahead of Thomas—lived through just about eight decades. For Thomas, who had not expected to live beyond seventy, those extra ten years were remarkably productive and honorific. Heinrich's last decade, spent unrecognized and unacclimatized in the United States, was unhappy, sickly, and lonely, especially after his second wife's suicide. His voluminous list of publications is longer than that of Thomas, always the more meditative stylist. Yet nearly everything that Thomas wrote was soon translated and widely circulated in the Anglo-American sphere. Heinrich may have belatedly been greeted with a compensatory vogue in Russian translation, but few of his books were made available in English. As chance would have it, his widest impact was indirectly attained when his novel *Professor Unrat* was adapted to the screen twenty-five years after publication; and that smashing film version, *The Blue Angel*, would be associated with him less publicly than with Marlene Dietrich, Emil Jannings, Josef von Sternberg, and Carl Zuckmayer. It was an irony of the doubling circumstances that he had been a thoroughgoing internationalist almost from the beginning, while Thomas had originally been steeped in nationalism, from which he became emancipated gradually and painfully, through historical pressure and following Heinrich's active example.

Thus Heinrich, in a letter to the French interpreter of German literature, Félix Bertaux, disclaimed the quest for "timelessness," which

would be the later course of Thomas. Heinrich's lifelong Francophilia
had prompted him to attempt what he believed was lacking, what
Thomas disclaimed for himself, a timely fictional critique of German
society à la Stendhal or Zola. It was launched in his second novel, *In
Schlaraffenland* (*The Land of Cockaigne*), dealing with the Berlin of
1900, and perhaps most effectively pursued in *Der Untertan* (*Man
of Straw* or, more literally rendered, *The Underling*), a satire on and
an epilogue to the Wilhelminian ideology, which could not have been
released before the collapse of imperial Germany. This will explain
why, though writing in cosmopolitan detachment, he could not so
easily appeal to the non-German reader. Thomas on the other hand,
though by no means uncritical, had started from an intense concern
with his traditional roots. These had been proudly attached to Lübeck,
the free Hanseatic city now decaying, whose leading burgher had been
their senatorial father. Their family's rise and decline provided the
theme of *Buddenbrooks*, which made him famous at twenty-six, one
year after *In Schlaraffenland*, and would win him the Nobel Prize in
1929 (when the citation of the capricious Swedish Academy pointedly
ignored his subsequent accomplishments).

It was followed in 1903 by *Tonio Kröger*, his most popular novella,
which gravitated toward the maternal side of the Manns' heritage. To
the Latin strain in their half-Brazilian mother he attributed a recoil
from ancestral burgherdom and an inclination for the more open and
sensuous purlieus of the arts. Heinrich, the eldest child, had already
rebelled against the mercantile ethic, and the adolescent Thomas had
begun to share his bookish interests, when the Senator died suddenly
in his prime, leaving resigned instructions to liquidate the three-
generation grain firm. The dowager Frau Senator took the significant
step of moving her children from the northern seaport to the warmer
and richer atmosphere of Munich. She continued there as matriarch
for more than thirty years, subsidizing Heinrich's first novel, encouraging Thomas in his vocation for literature, and trying her best to keep
the peace between her "god-gifted boys." She was far less happy with
her two daughters, both of whom—pursuing different paths—were destined for self-destruction. Carla, the younger, who had vainly sought
to succeed as an actress, was particularly close to the bohemian Heinrich. Thomas, writing to him for the family, bitterly and rather unsym-
pathetically, took her death as a betrayal of their common bonds: "I
cannot help feeling that she had no right to leave us."

Meanwhile he had himself become thoroughly committed to domesticity. Except for a crush on a fellow schoolboy (reflected in the Polish youths of *Death in Venice* and *The Magic Mountain*), he did not fall in love until he met the bright and beautiful Katia Pringsheim, only daughter of a Jewish professorial family, whose elegant home was frequently the scene of musicales and intellectual gatherings. After a romantic courtship, she became the most devoted of wives and mothers, graciously stabilizing his existence and that of their six talented children during the years when they would be uprooted and harassed. She had been reluctantly accepted by Thomas' mother; and, though she would succor Heinrich in his old age, their conversation never relaxed from the formal pronoun *Sie*. He, in restless contrast, got little satisfaction from unsettled love affairs and two uncongenial marriages. Thomas composed his lightest novel, *Royal Highness*, as an allegorical celebration of his own princely marriage. He was somewhat loath to see Heinrich read it, since Heinrich too had been assigned a part in the allegory: the part of the Archduke Albrecht, intellectually superior but neurotically shy, who abdicates in favor of his younger brother, Klaus Heinrich. The ascendant Prince, more of an average person, can therefore profess himself ready "to stand at your side and to represent you to the people."

Long afterward, after their ways had parted and come together again, Heinrich could echo that distinction, remarking that Thomas had been born "to represent—not to reject." Accordingly it must have been harder for him to relinquish his Teutonic ideals than it was for Heinrich, that inveterate iconoclast. Temperamentally the brotherly conflict may have been latent from the beginning: in an older child's jealousy of a new baby, in a junior's ambivalent awe of his big brother. Mr. Hamilton points to Heinrich's story about a boy who gives up playing a violin because his little brother has broken one of its strings (Thomas, as a young man, was considered a fairly good violinist). The *Leitmotiv* took responding forms in Thomas' imagination—most expressly, near the outset of the Joseph tetralogy, with the archetypal opposition of the insider Jacob and the outsider Esau. Indeed his magisterial essay on Goethe and Tolstoy, by its hinted self-identification with one or another of its titular figures, implicitly casts Heinrich in the complementary role of Schiller or Dostoevsky. This may be an aggrandizement for Thomas, who tended to look upon himself in an Olympian light; but it is scarcely disparaging to Heinrich, who was habituated to taking a Titanic stance. And the myth has an unclassical sequel when Jove, toppled from his Olympus, joins forces with Prometheus.

Though their destinies were tied together by reciprocal admiration, respect, and often pride, those ties were strained to a breaking point by political divergence. It is characteristic of Heinrich that he passed much of his early career in Italy, where he came to feel more at home than in the fatherland. Thomas had accompanied him there on one or two friendly vacations, but he felt more and more closely identified with Germanic tradition as he conceived it. The *Brüderkrieg* inevitably broke out with the war itself in 1914. Both were heavily engaged in wartime journalism: a more difficult engagement for Heinrich as a pacifist, a liberal turning radical, albeit never a Marxist. Thomas viewed his patriotic function as that of a conservative spokesman. His voice became shriller, his arguments more extreme, with racist overtones and allusions to a "Third Reich," as Germany was moving toward defeat. Frederick the Great was his hero, where Heinrich's was Voltaire. When Heinrich somehow managed to publish his essay on Zola, his own "*J'accuse* against the imperialistic war," Thomas insisted on taking it as a personal affront. There ensued an angry exchange of letters, wherein it must be said that Heinrich—though obviously perplexed and hurt—was seeking some mode of *rapprochement,* while Thomas—possibly because his cause was losing—remained intransigent in his rebuff.

Having earlier been exempted from military service, he offered his contribution to the war effort in *Betrachtungen eines Unpolitischen* (*Reflections of an Unpolitical Man*). Happily, this unwieldy tract has never been translated. It resumes the dialogue with Heinrich in the familiar terms of nationalistic generalizations: artist versus man of letters, music versus rhetoric, German culture versus French civilization. Apologia rather than propaganda, it appeared one month before the Armistice. Retrospectively Thomas admitted his subjective approach: "the problem of the German nation was beyond a doubt my own." On the higher plane of postwar internationalism, debate would be resumed in *The Magic Mountain;* but here the "unpolitical" opinions would be assigned to the reactionary authoritarian Naphta and countered by the rhetorical liberalism of Settembrini, who maintains that "everything is politics"—thereby provoking a lyrical protest from William Butler Yeats. Mr. Hamilton, while reminding us that the ebullient Peeperkorn may have been modeled on Gerhardt Hauptmann, does not indicate that the Jewish Jesuit was inspired by Georg Lukács, or that the Italian humanist might have prefigured Mann's anti-Fascist son-in-law, G. A. Borgese. At all events, the brothers had been reconciled during Heinrich's serious illness, and would embrace in public on the occasion of Thomas' fiftieth birthday.

Henceforth, as Bruno Frank would slyly note, they would pay ceremonial tributes to each other "every ten years." However, in the controversies of the Weimar period, the unpolitical ironist aligned himself with his activist brother. Heinrich was chairman of the literary section of the Berlin Academy until forced to resign. Thomas, after proclaiming acceptance of the republic, pressed beyond social democracy to downright socialism—toward a radicalism, Heinrich would say, more advanced than his own. He castigated the growing Nazi movement with peculiar fervor because it so grotesquely parodied his Germanic loyalties. Immediately after Hitler's appointment as Chancellor in January 1933, Heinrich left Germany. Having burned his bridges spectacularly, as a seasoned expatriate he was conditioned for exile. Thomas, as René Schickele commented, had not been brought up to be a martyr. He had been abroad on a lecture tour, from which he was resting in Switzerland, when his elder children warned him against returning. For three years he waited in silence, largely because of his Jewish publisher's plans for a German edition of *Joseph,* under mounting criticism from other refugees. Yet his farewell lecture on Wagner had been a challenge. Boldly, generously, and effectively he proposed the imprisoned pacifist, Carl von Ossietzsky, for the Nobel Peace Prize in 1936. An open letter defending the Jewish exiles, and identifying himself with their emigration, was answered by the loss of his citizenship.

He could have retorted, like Coriolanus, when the gates of Rome were closed against him: "I banish you!" In effect he did, with *Lotte in Weimar (The Beloved Returns),* through a monologue which imitated Goethe's style and thought so plausibly that it would be quoted as authentic during the Nuremberg trials. Repeatedly he alluded to Heinrich, himself, and the intellectual diaspora as "the real Germany." It was an obligation the brothers fulfilled by completing their most substantial and affirmative works of fiction while in banishment. Heinrich's two-volume historical novel warmly depicted France's Henry IV as a full-bodied model of humane leadership and ecumenical toler-

ance, ultimately victimized in the cross-fire between the Saint Bar-
tholomew massacre and the Edict of Nantes. *Joseph and His Brothers*
traversed a much longer distance, historically and geographically, yet
it came back to immediacies by deriving from Jewish lore and by testing and expanding the concept of brotherhood. The final reconciliation of the estranged brethren all but sets off a chorus in the background, singing Schiller's words to Beethoven's music: *"Alle Menschen
werden Brüder."* Thomas gave a grimmer twist to this pervasive theme
when, rejecting the simplistic notion of good and bad Germans, he entitled an article on Hitler, "This Man Is My Brother." The complexity
of the German problem, in its cultural strengths and social weaknesses,
would be addressed most directly in his testamentary novel, *Doctor
Faustus*.

His depiction of Egypt, in the last of the Joseph novels, was affected
by his sojourn in America; out of his admiration for Franklin D. Roosevelt, he put something of the New Deal into Joseph's economic stew-
ardship. Mr. Hamilton's treatment of his fourteen years in this country, eight of them as a naturalized citizen, seems sketchy and remote.
Heinrich, now a Czech citizen, worked in France as long as possible,
doing much to organize and co-ordinate the protest, recognized among
fellow dissidents as "the uncrowned President of the Fourth Reich."
He became a lost man after he had to flee from the continent. Whereas
the American prestige of Thomas made him a more effective comrade-
in-arms, energetically pamphleteering and broadcasting in the anti-
Nazi cause. His was a notable presence in academic and emigré circles. But with the peace and its subsequent reaction, the Cold War, he
was less and less inclined to stay. Heinrich, had his health permitted,
would have ended his days in East Germany. Two years after his
death, Thomas returned to live out the last three years of his life in
Europe—but not in the fatherland. There he had come under slander-
ous counterattack from newly vocal writers, who glibly accused him
of having escaped from the totalitarianism that they had silently survived. His second exile terminated in neutral Switzerland, whence between the wars he had risen to the cosmopolite overview of his *Magic
Mountain*.

Mr. Hamilton virtually disqualifies himself as a serious critic when
he describes that brooding masterwork as "the European parallel to
Scott Fitzgerald's winsome, supple portrait of the Jazz Age." He
should be informed too that her father's untranslated poem on the

birth of Elisabeth (not Elizabeth) Mann, *Gesang vom Kindchen* (*Song of the Little Child*), was written not in blank verse but dactylic hexameters, the meter of Goethe's *Hermann und Dorothea* and Longfellow's *Evangeline*—not to mention Homer or Virgil. Sometimes his historical details are misleading or mistaken: the expressionistic playwright Ernst Toller, unlike his friend Kurt Eisner, never was Prime Minister of the brief Bavarian Free State. And it is an embarrassment to confuse the apocryphal Erik Erikson, who signed a scurrilous pamphlet against Thomas Mann, with the distinguished psychoanalyst of that name. Since this book first appeared in England a year ago, there can be little excuse for not correcting—at very least—the misprints. The index and the referential notes let the reader down at times, as does the style. Yet the author deserves his meed of credit for bringing together much that has heretofore been separately discussed, thereby adding another dimension to both careers. Above all, he has maintained the balance between them with an even hand; and that has the additional merit of gaining more attention for the neglected Heinrich Mann from the English-reading public.

TRAVELING COMPANIONS:
HERMANN HESSE
AND THOMAS MANN

Though Thomas Mann would seem to have achieved a unique position among German contemporaries, here again he has been highlighted as an object of comparison. Temperamentally, in terms of his early novella, he seems to have had more in common with the stable and sensible Hans Hansen than with the anxious and impulsive Tonio Kröger, who may bear a closer resemblance to Heinrich Mann or to Hermann Hesse. That may help to explain why Hesse, a marginal figure among the Modernists despite Eliot's citation, came to the fore during the problematic years of mid-century. This account of The Hesse/Mann Correspondence: Letters of Hermann Hesse and Thomas Mann, *edited by Anni Carlsson and Volker Michels (New York: Harper and Row), appeared in* The Saturday Review *(June 14, 1975).*

•

The original German edition of this correspondence, which must be ranked among the more significant literary exchanges of our century, was published in 1968. Since then twenty additional letters, filling in the gaps on Hesse's side, have come to light in the Mann Archives, and will take their places in the augmented edition currently being published to celebrate the centennial of Mann's birth (1875). Meanwhile these have been included among the rest in the present volume, along with fuller notes, some expressive photographs, and appended excerpts from related documents. Ralph Manheim can be counted upon, as usual, for a readable and reliable translation. Given two close contemporaries writing in the same language at a high level, the contrast in personalities could hardly have been more striking. And personality means style, of course. This comes through, even in the English version, where an illuminating foreword by Theodore Ziolkowski further highlights the complementarity of the relationship.

Professor Ziolkowski, who is favorably known for his critical study of Hesse, frames the process of comparison with an unavoidable allusion to "the Weimar Dioscuri," Goethe and Schiller. Mann regarded "the *imitatio Goethe*" as a constant model for the writer's career, and his revelatory essay on Goethe and Tolstoy was read by Hesse with particular sympathy. That essay makes its points through a double juxtaposition: if Goethe has his parallel in Tolstoy, then Schiller likewise has one in Dostoevsky. The Olympian Goethe, late in life and long after Schiller's premature death, had contrasted their respective roles in order to exemplify the distinction between classicism and romanticism—and, more broadly, between health and sickness. Mann would argue that disease conferred a special insight, and go on to write *The Magic Mountain*. Hesse expressed an affinity with the sickly Dostoevsky in his little book, *Blick ins Chaos* (*A Glance into Chaos*), which in turn provided inspiration for the apocalyptic vision of Eliot's *Waste Land*.

There was no question as to who represented Goethe/Tolstoy, and who was the modern avatar of Schiller/Dostoevsky. The antithesis began with their backgrounds: Mann, the scion of that proud North German merchant house he depicted in *Buddenbrooks*, versus Hesse, the descendant of Swabian peasants and pietistic missionaries. Mann was, with six children, very much of a paterfamilias; Hesse would be happily married only after two broken marriages and a Jungian psychoanalysis. Hesse looked continually eastward to India; Mann was moving westward, and would live for fourteen years in America. Temperamentally, he was a skeptical rationalist, who became more and more of a public figure, whereas his counterpart was an intuitive mystic, increasingly reclusive. Hesse continued to be an active poet, grounded in romantic and expressionistic modes, whose fiction is described by Mann as "lyrical and idyllic." Mann's own fiction, inheriting from realism and naturalism, is epic in the Tolstoyan sense and dramatic in the Joycean.

But the polarity was not merely external in either case. Hesse peopled his world with opposite numbers: Demian and Emil Sinclair, Narcissus and Goldmund. Mann dramatized his intellectual conflicts through the artist-burgher ambivalence of Tonio Kröger or the grand dialectic of Naphta and Settembrini. He considered himself "a man of balance," as he wrote to Karl Kerényi, inclined to shift his weight to right or left according to the pressure of the waves. His mode was irony, "the pathos of the middle." Though he was seriously concerned with alienation, he was by nature a mandarin, who would have remained a cultural spokesman for the Weimar establishment, if it had not been so conclusively disestablished. Hesse, attracted by extremes, was innately an "outsider"; he uses the English word in *Steppenwolf.* He thought in terms of quests and conversions, monastic orders or utopian communes; but he shied away from society, and from those cults which belatedly sought to turn him into a guru.

The friendship of some fifty years began in 1904, when the two were introduced by their publisher, Samuel Fischer. Mann was not quite thirty, Hesse two years younger, the rising stars of a distinguished list. Hesse wrote a friendly but not uncritical review of Mann's relaxed second novel, *Royal Highness.* Their interchange was politely casual for many years, until both writers were well into middle age. It broke off altogether during the First World War; indeed there seems to have been no written communication for the decade between 1916 and 1926. Hesse, who had spent some years of childhood in Switzerland, had moved there permanently before the war, and would become a Swiss citizen afterward. Above the battle—along with Romain Rolland and other self-exiled writers, among them Mann's brother Heinrich— he took a neutral, pacifist, and humanitarian line. Thomas Mann was performing his "war service" with the untranslated *Reflections of an Unpolitical Man,* a nationalistic defense of Germanic traditions.

The resuming dialogue, which bears mainly on the exchange of publications, was amplified in the early Thirties by Mann's tactful attempts at persuading Hesse to reconsider his resignation from the Prussian Academy. Hesse was characteristically intransigent and individualistic in his "profound distrust of the German Republic" and all its works, particularly its universities. "Since 1914 and 1918 I have not, like the German people, taken a negligible leftward step; no, I have been driven miles to the left," he declared to Mann, adding that he no longer found it possible to read a single German newspaper. The difference between Mann's lingering traditionalism and Hesse's radical critique of values comes out very strongly in a consequent discussion of Wagner, always the ambiguous touchstone of German culture for Mann. Though Hesse too was a lifelong music-lover, the Nazi exploitation of Wagnerian opera justified, to his undisguised satisfaction (his term is *Schadenfreude*), the fact that he had consistently found it unbearable.

These letters can be vividly supplemented by the taped reminiscences of Mann's widow, as transcribed and edited in her ninetieth

year.[1] Katia Mann's *Unwritten Memories* bespeak the charm and
warmth with which she must have softened the formalities and the
angularities of her husband's career. She tells us about Hesse's occasional visits to their hospitable drawing room at Munich, where he introduced them to Ninon Dolbin, who was to be his third wife and
equally their friend. Hesse was a favorite among their literary acquaintance, especially prized by Mann for his conversation, his human
understanding, and his sense of humor. They were brought much
closer by the catastrophic events of Hitler's rise to power in 1933.
Mann, at fifty-eight, was caught in Switzerland on a lecture tour with
his wife, and warned against returning to Germany, where he would
subsequently lose his property and his citizenship. Hesse, at fifty-six,
was comfortably established near Lugano in a villa obtained for him
by a patron.

Thus the roles for which they had seemed cast were reversed by a
paradox of history. The insider became a refugee, an expatriate wandering for the rest of his life, who would poignantly speak—in the Joseph cycle—of the storyteller's nomadic star. The outsider, who had
gained his freedom by his earlier expatriation, was not so brusquely
cut off from his contact with the German public. Retrospectively, in
an open letter to the novelist Walter von Molo, Mann would attest
the strength and comfort he owed to Hesse's companionship during
those critical months, confessing that he had envied Hesse for the farsighted course he had taken. Hesse had consoled Mann by assuring
him that age and circumstance made the later exile a harder one, and
had recommended his own way out: "a way leading from the German
to the European and from the timely to the realm that transcends
time." This was the ideological direction that Mann would follow. The
ban of nationalism led to the welcome of cosmopolitanism.

He must have needed all the cheer and commiseration that Hesse
could offer, including games of *boccia* and the loan of *War and Peace*,
to get through that suspenseful period of doubts and anxieties, while
learning—as Mann would put it in a later expression of gratitude—"to
recognize an interlude as an era (*die Episode als Epoche zu nehmen*)."
With the recognition came the decision that prompted the break with
his country and his commitment to the emigration. This step differ-
entiated his position from Hesse's, which stayed resolutely non-political.
Mutual sincerity bridged the gap, and Hesse, after some hesitation,
contributed to the emigré journal that Mann was then editing, *Mass*

und Wert. The self-styled "unpolitical man" now deeply and polemi-
cally engaged, Mann was moving far beyond his sometime mentor.
Hesse would remain distrustful of what he termed "the politization of
the spirit." But Mann would reaffirm that "everything is politics,"
thereby inspiring Yeats to retort with his amorous lyric.

Mann's departure for the United States in 1938, by putting so vast
a distance between the correspondents, increased the pains they took
in communicating, except for an enforced interval during the Second
World War. Though he had many contacts with fellow emigrés both
at Princeton and in California, the very strangeness of American culture, which he was entering in his seventh decade (and which would
be reflected in *Joseph the Provider*), confirmed the need to keep in
touch with his old and tested friend. Here, where Hesse has no reason to deviate from his settled patterns, Mann's communications vi-
brate with the impact of new encounters, such as his meeting with
Franklin Roosevelt. Mann and Hesse both are watchful over the postwar problems: the Allied Occupation, the Cold War, and—perhaps
most difficult of all—cultural reconciliation with Germany. Mann will
revisit his native land, finally return to Switzerland, and live through
happy reunions with Hesse during Mann's last three years.

With the anticlimaxes of peace, the emphasis shifted back from
politics to the more congenial domain of literature. And, upon the onset of old age, Mann became more interested in recreating the past,
Hesse in speculating about the future. Mann, whose books were far
more widely known, generously paid his moral debt by advancing
Hesse's literary fortunes. Publicly, and somewhat problematically, he
praised *Steppenwolf* for being "in no way inferior to *Ulysses* or *The
Counterfeiters* in experimental daring." He sponsored, with a preface,
an American re-edition of *Demian*. He not only heralded and hailed
that long-awaited testament, *The Glass Bead Game;* he was struck by
a feeling of kinship at its resemblance to the novel he was composing
about the Faust legend. Katia Mann says she cannot see any likeness
between them, while Mann himself—in a more candid letter to his son
Klaus—would confide that Hesse's last novel had mystified him. Possibly the mystery is inherent in the material.

In *Young Joseph* Mann had playfully alluded to Hesse's lycanthro-
pic protagonist, the Steppenwolf. Hesse returned the compliment
rather pointedly in *The Glass Bead Game*. There his personal hero,
who is moreover a culture hero, becomes the *magister ludi,* the hieratic

master of the mysterious game. (*Ludus,* as E. R. Curtius pointed out, means school as well as play, and one might add that *Spiel* has a two-fold meaning.) His predecessor, the previous *magister,* is named Thomas von der Trave (Mann having been a native of Lübeck on the river Trave). Mann jocosely accepted this designation, and signed it to one of his letters. Did he also accept the implication that Hesse had now become his successor? Since his own receipt of the Nobel Prize in 1929, he had generously campaigned on behalf of Hesse, who did not gain the award until 1946. The fact that he had received the Goethe Prize the same year, though Mann did not receive it until 1949, may reflect the shift of reputations in Germany.

The closing years were punctuated by public testimonials. In the *Neue Züricher Zeitung,* on the occasion of Hesse's seventieth birthday, Mann inevitably viewed him—and, by indirection, himself—in the Goethean perspective of world literature. On Mann's seventy-fifth birthday, in *Die Neue Rundschau,* Hesse recalled that each of them, after his own fashion, "had to travel a difficult and dark path from the seeming security of his own national ties through loneliness and ostracism to the clean and rather cold air of a world citizenship." That was in 1950, and dates meant a good deal to both men in different ways. Mann had achieved his worldwide eminence in the Twenties: a solid place in the humanistic, if iconoclastic, sphere of Gide and Joyce. Hesse, though a contemporary of all three, won his widest fame at mid-century. By the Fifties another generation was searching for its identity, contemplating *anomie* with Beckett and the Absurdists, or readier than heretofore to play Hesse's psychic games.

Correspondingly, the esteem for Mann had placed him on so academic a pedestal that he offered less appeal to younger minds. He and Hesse were paired off invidiously as a critical alternative: either/or. All too frequently it was assumed that readers who liked the one could not abide the other, and Mann's traditional qualities gave him no advantage in a conflict of generations. Hesse, in the vogue of nonconformity, loyally refused to be played off against his foil. He defended Mann from his own "young enthusiasts," but could scarcely have deflected their enthusiasm by praising Mann's "Hanseatic virtues" or singling him out as the "legitimate son and heir of German bourgeois culture." If Mann was "too reasonable, too intellectual, and too ironic," then Hesse had grounds for uneasiness. Both were too self-conscious and self-critical ever to view their own works as classics, or—as they agreed near the end of Mann's life—to feel sure they had accomplished "the real thing (*das Eigentlich*)."

Yet each claimed for the other what he disclaimed for himself. Brotherhood was a powerful theme with Hesse, while Mann's relations with his own brother had been at best uneven. Hesse presented himself as a surrogate when he inscribed to Mann his *Collected Poems:* "To the elder brother from the younger." Mann had spoken of them both as "brothers—or at least cousins—in spirit," more formally as confrères, and most appropriately as "traveling companions." Evidently they had never drunk *Brüderschaft* together, for through thick and thin they addressed one another in the formal second-person plural. It was usually "Herr Hesse" and "Herr Mann," occasionally the full name or "Dear friend." Hesse vainly tried to jolt Mann into something more intimate by once using the Russian forename and patronymic: "Dear and esteemed Foma Genrikowitsch." But Mann seems to have been on first-name terms with few Germans, although he came to call his American publisher "Alfred," and the debonaire Mr. Knopf even dared to call him "Tommy."

Fraternal and complementary, Mann and Hesse were well aware they might seem an odd couple—or better, in the mystical phrase that Hesse borrowed from Nicholas of Cusa, a *coincidentia oppositorum*, a pair of coinciding opposites. Literary history can suggest few parallels for their correspondence; Goethe's and Schiller's does not really come close. Probably the closest analogue would be the remarkable sequence of letters that passed between Flaubert and George Sand. In both situations, one of the correspondents was clearly the greater artist, the other a more sympathetic character. However, they communicated as peers, having been drawn together fairly late in their careers, against a background of war and social upheaval. They bore witness to the undermining of the culture that had nourished them, the questioning of all values, the testing of civilization itself. In confronting and surviving those issues, they set examples of good faith and good will, of the strength of mind that sustains itself against odds, and the power of literature to preserve and revitalize.

N O T E

1 Katia Mann, *Unwritten Memories,* Elizabeth von Plessen and Michael Mann, ed., translated from the German by Hunter and Hildegarde Hannum (New York: Alfred A. Knopf) 165 pages. (London: Deutsch, 1976.)

OBSERVATIONS ON THE STYLE
OF ERNEST HEMINGWAY

All of the papers in this volume, with three specified exceptions, were written during the last decade. This one goes back thirty years to a preceding generation for whom Hemingway was very much alive, was indeed synonymous with vitality itself, though arguably past his prime as a writer—an argument which would be sealed by his tragic suicide in 1961. When I included my essay in a collection, Contexts of Criticism *(Cambridge: Harvard University Press, 1957; now published in paperback by Atheneum), I made some mention of his attempted comeback:*

". . . new honors and further adventures have befallen our subject; but if the analysis here submitted is valid, it is supported rather than modified by The Old Man and the Sea *(1952); for in this latest substantial piece of Hemingway's writing, it might be said that he is neither at his best nor at his worst but at his most typical. The tale again is an expanded short story—indeed, to a large extent, a monologue. The situation is ideally calculated to project the actions and sensations of lonely struggle; and though the narrative conveys this excitement with something of the old muscularity, its contours are weakened by adipose passages of conversation and commentary. The hero, described by the author as 'simple,' turns out to be a garrulous character who talks to himself in the Hispanese of* For Whom the Bell Tolls, *translated or explained by Hemingway in a manner which is pedagogical, if not pedantic."*

There are further autobiographical seascapes in the posthumous Islands in the Stream *(1970), and the advance notices of unpublished fiction in the John F. Kennedy Library do not promise a great enrichment of the Hemingway canon. The present observations began as a book review and continued as* explication de texte. *The book involved was one of the earliest in what is now a library of commentary,* Ernest Hemingway: The Man and His Work, *edited by John K. M. McCaffery (Cleveland: World Publishing Company, 1950), together with a side-glance at Hemingway's introduction to* In Sicily, *by Elio Vittorini (New York: New Directions, 1949). The explication had its first hearing from the seminar in literary criticism at the Johns Hopkins University on October 19, 1950. The resulting conflation was published in* The Kenyon Review, *XIII, 4 (Autumn 1951). Though it has been anthologized and translated on various occasions, and briefly plagiarized by* Time *magazine, I republish it here as an effort to recapture that peculiar quality*

*of Hemingway's which has been blurred and softened by more than three
decades of critical discussion and more than five decades of imitation, not
excluding self-imitation: the direct sense of impact. The irony that prompted
my very title, or my technical use of rhetorical terms, could scarcely have existed in an atmosphere which takes it for granted that everything must be
grist for the academic mills. Moreover, a writer might well defy the conventions of his day; but if he enacted the role of "Mr. Papa" and espoused the
counter-conventions of* machismo, *he may well have courted the distrust of a
succeeding generation. Is it still possible to see Hemingway—as he so luminously saw the world for us—plain?*

I

"The most important author living today, the outstanding author
since the death of Shakespeare," is Ernest Hemingway. So we have
lately been assured by John O'Hara in *The New York Times Book
Review*. We should have to know what Mr. O'Hara thinks of the
various intervening authors, of Shakespeare himself, and indeed of literature, in order to get the full benefit of this evaluation. It might be
inferred, from his review of *Across the River and into the Trees*, that
he holds them well on this side of idolatry. Inasmuch as Hemingway's
latest novel tends regrettably to run certain attitudes and mannerisms
to the ground, merely to describe it—if I may use an unsportsmanlike
simile—is like shooting a sitting bird. Mr. O'Hara's gallant way of pro-
tecting this vulnerable target is to charge the air with invidious comparisons. His final encomium should be quoted in full, inasmuch as it
takes no more than two short words, which manage to catch the un-
certainty of the situation as well as the strident unsteadiness of Mr.
O'Hara's tone: "Real class." That interesting phrase, which could be
more appropriately applied to a car or a girl, carries overtones of petty
snobbery; it seems to look up toward an object which, it admits in
wistful awe, transcends such sordid articles of the same commodity as
ordinarily fall within its ken. To whistle after Hemingway in this fashion is doubtless a sincerer form of flattery than tributes which continue to be inhibited by the conventions of literary discourse. Had Mr.
O'Hara been a French Symbolist poet, he might have said: *"Tout le
reste est littérature."*

Yet Hemingway too, one way or another, is literature. If his preoccupation has been mortality, his ambition—spurred perhaps by having
easily won such rewards as contemporaries offer—is nothing less than

immortality. He doesn't speak of building a monument or even burning a candle, but he sometimes refers to playing in the big league or writing something that will not soon go bad. Shakespeare, as Colonel Cantwell acknowledges in *Across the River*, is "the winner and still the undisputed champion." But Mr. O'Hara's build-up seems to suggest that Hemingway is training for the title bout. At least there are confirmatory signs, to state the matter in milder and more bookish terms, that he is becoming a classic in his time. He has just become the subject of "a critical survey" which should be welcomed as the first of its kind, with the expectation that its shortcomings will probably be made good by a long shelf of future volumes devoted to *Hemingwayforschung*. Since the present volume has been pasted together from other publications, it does not pretend to originality; it offers a readable and typical selection of twenty-one reviews and articles. This sort of symposium, especially when it concentrates upon so compact a body of material, is bound to cross and recross familiar territory. It is no discredit to the contributors—in fact, it reinforces their positions—that they do not diverge from one another more variously. However, it raises questions reflecting upon the judgment and knowledge of the anthologist.

He does not seem to have cast a very wide net. Given the scope and impact of his author, we might fairly expect international representation. But, except for one Soviet contribution, the table of contents is one-hundred-percent American, thereby excluding such significant essays as the almost classical polemic of Wyndham Lewis or the more recent appreciation of Claude-Edmonde Magny. Closer to home, it is hard to see how the editor—whose introduction strives to counterbalance the negative emphasis of so much criticism—could have overlooked the handsome tribute and prescient revaluation by Robert Penn Warren in *The Kenyon Review*. Yet sins of omission, with anthologies, should always be considered venial; and we need not question the individual merits of the editor's inclusions. Some of them justify their place by being too little known and not readily accessible: notably Lincoln Kirstein's sensitive review of *Death in the Afternoon* and Edward Fenimore's informative article on the language of *For Whom the Bell Tolls*. But others, though not less notable, are not so readily justified: chapters from volumes still in print by Edmund Wilson, Alfred Kazin, and W. M. Frohock. It should also be pointed out that Malcolm Cowley has published better pieces on

Hemingway than the profile that Mr. McCaffery reprints from *Life*. The editor might have done a more useful job by collecting Hemingway's unreprinted writings. These are not touched upon by the bibliography, which is therefore inadequate; and there are no notes to identify the contributors, though several of them require identification. Since the chronological arrangement is based on dates of books, rather than periodical publication, it is somewhat misleading.

Yet when these cavils have been duly registered, it should be acknowledged that the book remains faithful to its protagonist. Its qualities and defects, like his, are journalistic—and I use that term in no deprecatory spirit, for journalism has more often than not been the school of our ablest writers, from Mark Twain to Hemingway himself. I simply refer to the losing race that fiction runs against fact, the hot pursuit of immediate reality in which the journalist outstrips the novelist, and also the risks—artistic as well as physical—that the imaginative writer takes by competing on the reporter's ground. For one thing, the successful reporter is seldom content to remain a good observer; give him a by-line, and he starts writing about himself; and he ends by making news for his professional colleagues, the gossip columnists. From all accounts, including his own, it would seem that, as a correspondent in the last war, Hemingway saw action in more ways than one. It may be that his refusal to draw a line between actor and spectator is one of the secrets of his vitality. Herein it is reported by John Groth that "Hemingway's jeep driver knew him as Hemingway the guy, rather than Hemingway the famous writer." And John McCaffery devotes his particular enthusiasm to "Hemingway as a man among men." We see him plain; we hear and applaud his feats as soldier, traveler, sportsman, athlete, and playboy; and sooner or later we find ourselves asking why this consummate extrovert should have taken the trouble to become a famous writer.

If he was, as we are informed, "an okay joe" to his comrades in arms, he is something more complex to his fellow writers. Their collected opinions range from grudging admiration to fascinated suspicion. Though most of them make their separate peace with him, they leave a total impression which is fairly consistent and surprisingly hostile. The exception that proves the rule, in this case Elliot Paul, is the warm admirer who demonstrates his loyalty by belaboring Hemingway's critics. Few of them are able to maintain the distinction, premised by Mr. McCaffery's subtitle, between "the man" and "his work."

Curiously enough, the single essay that undertakes to deal with crafts-manship is the one that emanates from Marxist Russia. The rest, though they incidentally contain some illuminating comments on technique, seem more interested in recapitulating the phases of Hemingway's career, in treating him as the spokesman of his generation, or in coming to grips with a natural phenomenon. All this is an impressive testimonial to the force of his personality. Yet what is personality, when it manifests itself in art, if not style? It is not because of the figure he cuts in the rotogravure sections, or for his views on philosophy and politics, that we listen to a leading *Heldentenor*. No contemporary voice has excited more admiration and envy, stimulated more imitation and parody, and had more effect on the rhythms of our speech than Hemingway's has done. Ought we not then, first and last, to be discussing the characteristics of his prose, when we talk about a man who—as Archibald MacLeish has written—"whittled a style for his time"?

II

Mr. Hemingway, in his turn, would hardly be himself—which he is, of course, quite as consciously as any writer could be—if he did not take a dim view of criticism. This is understandable and, as he would say, right: since criticism, ever seeking perspective, moves in the very opposite direction from his object, which has been immediacy. His ardent quest for experience has involved him in a lifelong campaign against everything that tends to get in its way, including those more or less labored efforts to interpret and communicate it which may be regarded—if not disregarded—as academic. Those of us who live in the shelter of the academy will not be put off by his disregard; for most of us have more occasion than he to be repelled by the encrustations of pedantry; and many of us are predisposed to sympathize with him, as well as with ourselves, when he tells us what is lacking in critics and scholars. That he continues to do so is a mark of attention which ought not to go unappreciated. Thus currently, in introducing a brilliant young Italian novelist to American readers, he departs from his subject to drive home a critical contrast:

The Italy that [Elio Vittorini] learned and the America that the American boys learned [writes Ernest Hemingway, making a skillful transition] has little to do with the Academic Italy or America that periodically attacks all writing like a dust storm and is always, until everything shall be completely dry, dispersed by rain.

Since Hemingway is sparing in his use of metaphors, the one he introduces here is significant. "Dryasdust" has long been the layman's stock epithet for the results of scholarly inquiry; while drought, as evoked by T. S. Eliot, has become a basic symbol of modern anxiety. The country that seems to interest Hemingway most, Spain, is in some respects a literal wasteland; and his account of it—memorably his sound track for the Joris Ivens film, *The Spanish Earth*—emphasizes its dryness. Water, the contrasting element, for Hemingway as for his fellow men, symbolizes the purification and renewal of life. Rain beats out a cadence which runs through his work: through *A Farewell to Arms*, for example, where it lays the dust raised by soldiers' boots at the outset, accompanies the retreat from Caporetto, and stays with the hero when the heroine dies—even providing the very last word at the end. It is rain which, in a frequently quoted paragraph, shows up the unreality of "the words sacred, glorious, and sacrifice and the expression in vain." In the present instance, having reduced the contemporary situation to a handful of dust, as it were, Hemingway comes back to that sense of reality which he is willing to share with Vittorini. In the course of a single sentence, utilizing a digressive Ciceronian device, *paralipsis*, he has not only rounded up such writers as he considers academic; he has not only accused them of sterility, by means of that slippery logical shortcut which we professors term an *enthymeme;* but, like the veteran strategist he is, he has also managed to imply that they are the attackers and that he is fighting a strictly defensive action.

The conflict advances into the next paragraph, which opens on the high note that closed the previous one and then drops down again anticlimactically:

Rain to an academician is probably, after the first fall has cleared the air, H_2O with, of course, traces of other things.

Even the ultimate source of nature's vitality is no more than a jejune scientific formula to us, if I may illustrate Hemingway's point by paraphrasing his sentence. Whereas—and for a moment it seems as if the theme of fertility would be sounded soon again—but no, the emphasis waxes increasingly negative:

To a good writer, needing something to bring the dry country alive so that it will not be a desert where only such cactus as New York literary reviews grow dry and sad, inexistent without the watering of their benefactors, feeding on the dried manure of schism and the dusty taste of disputed dialectics, their only flowering a desiccated criticism as alive as stuffed birds, and their steady mulch the dehydrated cuds of fellow critics; . . .

There is more to come, but we had better pause and ruminate upon this particular mouthful. Though we may or may not accept Hemingway's opinion, we must admit that he makes us taste his distaste. Characteristically, he does not countercriticize or state the issue in intellectual terms. Instead he proceeds from agriculture to the dairy, through an atmosphere calculated to make New Yorkers uncomfortable, elaborating his earthy metaphor into a barnyard allegory which culminates in a scatological gesture. The gibe about benefactors is a curious one, since it appears to take commercial success as a literary criterion, and at the same time to identify financial support with spiritual nourishment. The hopeful adjective "alive," repeated in this deadening context, is ironically illustrated by a musty ornithological specimen: so much for criticism! Such a phrase as "disputed dialectics," which is unduly alliterative, slightly tautological, and—like "cactus"—ambiguously singular or plural, touches a sphere where the author seems ill at ease. He seems more sure of his ground when, after this muttered parenthesis, he returns to his starting point, turns the prepositional object into a subject, and sets out again toward his predicate, toward an affirmation of mellow fruitfulness:

. . . such a writer finds rain to be made of knowledge, experience, wine, bread, oil, salt, vinegar, bed, early mornings, nights, days, the sea, men, women, dogs, beloved motor cars, bicycles, hills and valleys, the appearance and disappearance of trains on straight and curved tracks, love, honor and disobey, music, chamber music and chamber pots, negative and positive Wassermanns, the arrival and non-arrival of expected munitions and/or reinforcements, replacements or your brother.

These are the "other things" missed by the academician and discerned by the "good writer"—whether he be Vittorini or Hemingway. It is by no means a casual inventory; each successive item, artfully chosen, has its meaningful place in the author's scheme of things. Knowledge is equated with experience, rendered concrete by the staple fare of existence, and wet down by essential liquids redolent of the Mediterranean; bed, with its double range of elementary associations, initiates a temporal cycle which revolves toward the timeless sea. Men, women, and dogs follow each other in unrelieved sequence; but the term of endearment, "beloved," is reserved for motor cars; while wavering alternatives suggest the movement of other vehicles over the land. Then come the great abstractions, love and honor, which are undercut by a cynical negation of the marriage ceremony, "disobey." Since chamber music sounds highbrow, it must be balanced against the downright vulgarity of chamber pots. The pangs of sex are scientifically neutralized by the reference to Wassermann tests, and the agonies of war are deliberately stated in the cool and/or colorless jargon of military dispatches. The final choice, "replacements or your brother," possibly echoes a twist of continental slang (*et ton frère!*); but, more than that, it suddenly replaces a strategic loss with a personal bereavement.

The sentence, though extended, is not periodic: instead of suspending its burden, it falls back on *anacoluthon,* the rhetoric of the gradual breakdown and the fresh start. Hence, the first half is an uncharacteristic and unsuccessful endeavor to complete an elaborate grammatical structure which soon gets out of control. The second half thereupon brings the subject as quickly and simply as possible to its object, which opens up at once into the familiar Hemingway catalogue, where effects can be gained *seriatim* by order rather than by construction. After the chain of words has reached its climactic phrase, "your brother," it is rounded out by another transitional sentence:

All these are a part of rain to a good writer along with your hated or beloved mother, may she rest in peace or in pieces, porcupine quills, cock grouse drumming on a bass-wood log, the smell of sweetgrass and fresh smoked leather and Sicily.

This time love dares to appear in its primary human connection, but only in ambivalence with hatred, and the hazards of sentimentality are hysterically avoided by a trite pun. And though the final images resolve the paragraph by coming back to the Sicilian locale of Vittorini's novel, they savor more of the northern woods in Hemingway's Upper Peninsula (Michigan). Meanwhile the digression has served its purpose for him and for ourselves; it has given us nothing less than his definition of knowledge—not book-knowledge, of course, but the real thing. Thus Robert Jordan decides to write a book about his adventures in Spain: "But only about the things he knew, truly, and about what he knew." Such a book is Hemingway's novel about him, *For Whom the Bell Tolls;* and what he knew, there put into words, is already one remove away from experience. And when Hemingway writes about Vittorini's novel, unaccustomed though he is to operating on the plane of criticism, he is two removes away from the objects he mentions in his analysis—or should I call it a hydroanalysis? Critics—and I have in mind Wyndham Lewis—have called his writing "the prose of reality." It seems to come closer to life than other prose, possibly too close for Mr. Lewis, yet for better or worse it happens to be literature. Its effectiveness lies in virtually persuading us that it is not writing at all. But though it may feel like walks in the rain or punches in the jaw, to be literal, it consists of words on the page. It is full of half-concealed art and self-revealing artifice. Since Hemingway is endlessly willing to explicate such artful and artificial pursuits as bullfighting and military tactics, he ought not to flinch under technical scrutiny.

III

Hemingway's hatred for the profession of letters stems quite obviously from a lover's quarrel. When Richard Gordon is reviled by his dissatisfied wife in *To Have and Have Not*, her most embittered epithet is "you writer." Yet Hemingway's writing abounds in salutes to various fellow writers, from the waitress' anecdote about Henry James in *The Torrents of Spring* to Colonel Cantwell's spiritual affinity with D'Annunzio. And from Nick Adams, who takes Meredith and Chesterton along on fishing trips, to Hemingway himself, who arranges to be interviewed on American literature in *Green Hills of Africa*, his heroes do not shy away from critical discussion. His titles, so often quoted from books by earlier writers, have been so apt that they have all but established a convention. He shows an almost academic fondness, as well as a remarkable flair, for epigraphs: the Colonel dies with a quotation on his lips. Like all of us, Hemingway has been influenced by T. S. Eliot's taste for Elizabethan drama and metaphysical poetry. Thus Hemingway's title, "In Another Country," is borrowed from a passage he elsewhere cites, which he might have found in Marlowe's *Jew of Malta* or possibly in Eliot's "Portrait of a Lady." A *Farewell to Arms*, which echoes a title from *The Oxford Book of English Verse*, quotes in passing from Marvell's "To His Coy Mistress," echoed more recently by Robert Penn Warren, which is parodied in *Death in the Afternoon*. Hemingway is no exception to the rule that makes parody the starting point for realistic fiction. Just as Fielding took off from Richardson, so Hemingway takes off from Sherwood Anderson—indeed his first novel, *The Torrents of Spring*, which parodies Anderson's *Dark Laughter*, is explicit in its acknowledgments to *Joseph An-*

drews. It has passages, however, which read today like a pastiche of the later Hemingway:

> Yogi was worried. There was something on his mind. It was spring, there was no doubt of that now, and he did not want a woman. He had worried about it a lot lately. There was no question about it. He did not want a woman. He couldn't explain it to himself. He had gone to the Public Library and asked for a book the night before. He looked at the librarian. He did not want her. Somehow she meant nothing to him.

A recoil from bookishness, after a preliminary immersion in it, provided Fielding's master, Cervantes, with the original impetus for the novel. In "A Banal Story" Hemingway provides us with his own variation on the theme of *Don Quixote,* where a writer sits reading about romance in a magazine advertisement, while in far-off Madrid a bullfighter dies and is buried. The ironic contrast—romantic preconception exploded by contact with harsh reality—is basic with Hemingway, as it has been with all novelists who have written effectively about war. The realism of his generation reacted, not only against Wilsonian idealism, but against Wilsonian rhetoric. Hence the famous paragraph from the Caporetto episode describing Frederic Henry's embarrassment before such abstract words as "glory" and "honor," which seem to him obscene beside the concrete names of places and numbers of roads. For a Spaniard, Hemingway notes in *Death in the Afternoon,* the abstraction may still have concreteness: honor may be "as real a thing as water, wine, or olive oil." It is not so for us: "All our words from loose using have lost their edge." And "The Gambler, the Nun, and the Radio" brings forward a clinching example: "Liberty, what we believed in, now the name of a Macfadden publication." That same story trails off in a litany which reduces a Marxist slogan to meaninglessness: "the opium of the people" is everything and nothing. Even more desolating, in "A Clean, Well-Lighted Place," is the reduction of the Lord's prayer to nothingness: "Our nada who art in nada . . ." Since words have become inflated and devalued, Hemingway is willing to recognize no values save those which can be immediately felt and directly pointed out. It is his verbal skepticism which leads toward what some critics have called his moral nihilism. Anything serious had better be said with a smile, stranger. The classic echo, "irony and pity," jingles through *The Sun Also Rises* like a singing commercial.

There is something in common between this attitude and the familiar British habit of understatement. "No pleasure in anything if you mouth it too much," says Wilson, the guide in "The Short, Happy Life of Francis Macomber." Yet Jake, the narrator of *The Sun Also Rises*, protests—in the name of American garrulity—that the English use fewer words than the Eskimos. Spanish, the language of Hemingway's preference, is at once emotive and highly formal. His Spanish, to judge from *Death in the Afternoon*, is just as ungrammatical as his English. In "The Undefeated" his Spanish bullfighters are made to speak the slang of American prizefighters. Americanisms and Hispanisms, archaic and polyglot elements are so intermingled in *For Whom the Bell Tolls* that it calls to mind Spenser's *Faerie Queene* and looks ahead to Nabokov's *Evgeni Onegin*. Hemingway offers a succinct example by translating *"Eras mucho caballo"* as "Thou wert plenty of horse." It is somewhat paradoxical that a writer, having severely cut down his English vocabulary, should augment it by continual importation from other languages, including the Swahili. But this is a facet of the larger paradox that a writer so essentially American should set the bulk of his work against foreign backgrounds. His characters, expatriates for the most part, wander through the ruins of Babel, smattering many tongues and speaking a demotic version of their own. Obscenity presents another linguistic problem, for which Hemingway is not responsible; but his coy ways of circumventing the taboos of censorship are more of a distraction than the conventional blanks. When he does permit himself an expression not usually considered printable, in *Death in the Afternoon*, the context is significant. His interlocutor, the Old Lady, requests a definition and he politely responds: "Madam, we apply the term now to describe unsoundness in abstract conversation or, indeed, any overmetaphysical tendency in speech."

For language, as for literature, his feeling is strongly ambivalent. Perhaps it could be summed up by Pascal's maxim: "True eloquence makes fun of eloquence." Like the notorious General Cambronne, Hemingway feels that one short spontaneous vulgarism is more honest than all those grandiloquent slogans which rhetoricians dream up long after the battle. The disparity between rhetoric and experience, which became so evident during the First World War, prompted the Twenties to repudiate the genteel stylistic tradition and to accept the American vernacular as our norm of literary discourse. "Literary" is a contradiction in terms, for the resultant style is basically oral; and when the semiliterate speaker takes pen in hand, as Hemingway demonstrates in

"One Reader Writes"—as H. L. Mencken demonstrated in "A Short View of Gamalielese"—the result is even more artificial than if it had been written by a writer. A page is always flat, and we need perspective to make it convey the illusion of life in the round. Yet the very fact that words mean so much less to us than the things they represent in our lives is a stimulus to our imaginations. In "Fathers and Sons" young Nick Adams reads that Caruso has been arrested for "mashing," and asks his father the meaning of that expression.

"It is one of the most heinous of crimes," his father answered. Nick's imagination pictured the great tenor doing something strange, bizarre, and heinous with a potato masher to a beautiful lady who looked like the pictures of Anna Held on the inside of cigar boxes. He resolved, with considerable horror, that when he was old enough he would try mashing at least once.

The tone of this passage is not altogether typical of Hemingway. Rather, as the point of view detaches itself affectionately and ironically from the youth, it approximates the early Joyce. This may help to explain why it suggests a more optimistic approach to language than the presumption that, since phrases can be snares and delusions, their scope should be limited to straight denotation. The powers of connotation, the possibilities of oblique suggestion and semantic association, are actually grasped by Hemingway as well as any writer of our time. Thus he can retrospectively endow a cheap and faded term like "mashing" with all the promise and poetry of awakening manhood. When Nick grows up, foreign terms will hold out the same allure to him; like Frederic Henry, he will seek the actuality that resides behind the names of places; and Robert Jordan will first be attracted to Spain as a professional philologist. But none of them will find an equivalence between the word and the thing; and Hemingway, at the end of *Death in the Afternoon*, laments that no book is big enough to do final justice to its living subject. "There was so much to write," the dying writer realizes in "The Snows of Kilimanjaro," and his last thoughts are moving and memorable recollections of some of the many things that will now go unwritten. Walt Whitman stated this challenge and this dilemma, for all good writers, when he spoke of expressing the inexpressible.

IV

The inevitable compromise, for Hemingway, is best expressed by his account of Romero's bullfighting style: "the holding of his purity of line through the maximum of exposure." The maximum of exposure—this throws much light upon the restlessness of Hemingway's career, but here we are primarily concerned with the holding of his purity of line. It had to be the simplest and most flexible of lines in order to accommodate itself to his desperate pursuit of material. His purgation of language has aptly been compared, by Robert Penn Warren, to the revival of diction that Wordsworth accomplished with *Lyrical Ballads*. Indeed the question that Coleridge afterward raised might once again be asked: why should the speech of some men be more real than that of others? Today this question restates itself in ideological terms: whether respect for the common man necessitates the adoption of a commonplace standard. Everyone who writes faces the same old problems, and the original writers—like Wordsworth or Hemingway—are those who develop new ways of meeting them. The case of Wordsworth would show us, if that of Hemingway did not, that those who break down conventions tend to substitute conventions of their own. Hemingway's prose is not without precedents; it is interesting to recall that his maiden effort, published by *The Double Dealer* in 1922, parodied the King James Bible. He has his forerunners in American fiction, from Cooper to Jack London, whose conspicuous lack was a style as dynamic as their subject matter. The ring-tailed roarers of the frontier, such as Davy Crockett, were Colonel Cantwell's brothers under the skin; but as contrasted with the latter's tragic conception of himself, they were mock-heroic and serio-comic figures, who recommend themselves to the reader's condescension. Mark Twain has been the most genuine influence, and Hemingway has acknowledged this by declaring—with sweeping generosity—that *Huckleberry Finn* is the source of all modern American literature.

But Mark Twain was conducting a monologue, a virtual *tour de force* of impersonation, and he ordinarily kept a certain distance between his narrative role and his characters. And among Hemingway's elder contemporaries, Ring Lardner was a kind of ventriloquist, who made devastating use of the vernacular to satirize the vulgarity and stupidity of his dummies. It remained for Hemingway—along with Anderson—to identify himself wholly with the lives he wrote about, not so much entering into them as allowing them to take possession of him, and accepting—along with their sensibilities and perceptions—the limitations of their point of view and the limits of their range of expression. We need make no word-count to be sure that his literary vocabulary, with foreign and technical exceptions, consists of relatively few and short words. The corollary, of course, is that every word sees a good deal of hard use. Furthermore, his syntax is informal to the point of fluidity, simplifying as far as possible the already simple system of English inflections. Thus "who" is normally substituted for "whom," presumably to avoid schoolmarmish correctness; and "that," doing duty for "which," seems somehow less prophetic of complexity. Personal pronouns frequently get involved in what is stigmatized, by teachers of freshman composition, as faulty reference; there are sentences in which it is hard to tell the hunter from his quarry or the bullfighter from the bull. "When his father died he was only a kid and his manager buried him perpetually." So begins, rather confusingly, "The Mother of a Queen." Sometimes it seems as if Hemingway were taking pains to be ungrammatical, as do many educated people out of a twisted sense of *noblesse oblige*. Yet when he comes closest to pronouncing a moral, the last words of Harry Morgan—the analphabetic hero of *To Have and Have Not*—seem to be half-consciously fumbling toward some grammatical resolution: "A man . . . ain't got no hasn't got any can't really isn't any way out . . ."

The effectiveness of Hemingway's method depends very largely upon his keen ear for speech. His conversations are vivid, often dramatic, although he comes to depend too heavily upon them and to scant the other obligations of the novelist. Many of his wisecracks are quotable out of context, but as Gertrude Stein warned him: "Remarks are not literature." He can get his story told, and still be as conversational as he pleases, by telling it in the first person. "Brother, that was some storm," says the narrator, and the reader hears the very tone of his voice. In one of Hemingway's critical digressions, he declares that he has always sought "the real thing, the sequence of motion and fact which [*sic*] made the emotion . . ." This seems to imply the clear-cut mechanism of verbal stimulus and psychological response that Eliot formulates in his theory of the objective correlative. In practice, however, Hemingway is no more of a behaviorist than Eliot, and the sharp distinction between motion and emotion is soon blurred. Consider his restricted choice of adjectives, and the heavy load of subjective implication carried by such uncertain monosyllables as "fine" and "nice." From examples on nearly every page, we are struck by one which helps to set the scene for *A Farewell to Arms:* "The town was very nice and our house was very fine." Such descriptions—if we may consider them descriptions—are obviously not designed for pictorial effect. When the Colonel is tempted to call some fishing-boats picturesque, he corrects himself: "The hell with picturesque. They are just damned beautiful." Where "picturesque" might sound arty and hence artificial, "beautiful"—with "damned" to take off the curse—is permissible because Hemingway has packed it with his own emotional charge. He even uses it in *For Whom the Bell Tolls* to express his esthetic appreciation of gunfire. Like "fine" and "nice," or "good" and "lovely," it does not describe; it evaluates. It is not a stimulus but a projected response, a projection of the narrator's euphoria in a given situation. Hemingway, in effect, is saying to the reader: *Having wonderful time. Wish you were here.*

In short, he is communicating excitement; and if this communication is received, it establishes a uniquely personal relationship; but when it goes astray, the diction goes flat and vague. Hemingway manages to sustain his reputation for concreteness by an exploring eye for the incidental detail. The one typescript of his that I have seen, his carbon copy of "The Killers" now in the Harvard College Library, would indicate that the arc-light and the tipped-back derby hat were later observations than the rest. Precision at times becomes so arithmetical that, in "The Light of the World," it lines up his characters like a drill sergeant: "Down at the station there were five whores waiting for the train to come in, and six white men and four Indians." Numbers enlarge the irony that concludes the opening chapter of *A Farewell to Arms* when, after a far from epic invocation, a casual introduction to the landscape, and a dusty record of troops falling back through the autumn, rain brings the cholera that kills "only seven thousand." A trick of multiplication, which Hemingway may have picked up from Gertrude Stein, is to generalize the specific episode: "They always picked the finest places to have the quarrels." When he offers this general view of a restaurant—"It was full of smoke and drinking and singing"—he is an impressionist if not an abstractionist. Thence to expressionism is an easy step: ". . . . the room whirled." It happens that, under pressure from his first American publishers, the author was compelled to modify the phrasing of "Mr. and Mrs. Elliott." In the original version, subsequently restored, the title characters "try to have a baby." In the modified version they "think of having a baby." It could be argued that, in characterizing this rather tepid couple, the later verb is more expressive and no more euphemistic than the earlier one; that "think," at any rate, is not less precise or effectual than "try." But, whereas the sense of effort came naturally, the cerebration was an afterthought.

If we regard the adjective as a luxury, decorative more often than functional, we can well understand why Hemingway doesn't cultivate it. But, assuming that the sentence derives its energy from the verb, we are in for a shock if we expect his verbs to be numerous or varied or emphatic. His usage supports C. K. Ogden's argument that verb-forms are disappearing from English grammar. Without much self-deprivation, Hemingway could get along on the so-called "operators" of Basic English, the sixteen monosyllabic verbs that stem from movements of the body. The substantive verb *to be* is predominant, characteristically introduced by an expletive. Thus the first story of *In Our Time* begins, and the last one ends, with the storyteller's gambit: "there was," "there were." In the first two pages of *A Farewell to Arms* nearly every other sentence is of this type, and the third page employs the awkward construction "there being." There is—I find the habit contagious—a tendency to immobilize verbs by transposing them into gerunds. Instead of writing *they fought* or *we did not feel*, Hemingway writes "there was fighting" and "there was not the feeling of a storm coming." The subject does little more than point impersonally at its predicate: an object, a situation, an emotion. Yet the idiom, like the French *il y a*, is ambiguous; inversion can turn the gesture of pointing into a physical act; and the indefinite adverb can indicate, if not specify, a definite place. Contrast, with the opening of *A Farewell to Arms*, that of "In Another Country": "In the fall the war was always there, but we did not go to it any more." The negative is even more striking, when Frederic Henry has registered the sensations of his wound, and dares to look at it for the first time, and notes: "My knee wasn't there." The adverb is *there* rather than *here*, the verb is *was* rather than *is*, because we—the readers—are separated from the event in space and time. But the narrator has lived through it, like the Ancient Mariner, and now he chooses his words to grip and transfix us. *Lo!* he says. *Look! I was there.*

V

Granted, then, that Hemingway's diction is thin; that, in the technical sense, his syntax is weak; and that he would rather be caught dead than seeking the *mot juste* or the balanced phrase. Granted that his adjectives are not colorful and his verbs not particularly energetic. Granted that he commits as many literary offenses as Mark Twain brought to book with Fenimore Cooper. What is behind his indubitable punch, the unexampled dynamics of Hemingway's style? How does he manage, as he does, to animate this characteristic sentence from "After the Storm"?

I said "Who killed him?" and he said "I don't know who killed him but he's dead all right," and it was dark and there was water standing in the street and no lights and windows broke and boats all up in the town and trees blown down and everything all blown and I got a skiff and went out and found my boat where I had her inside of Mango Key and she was all right only she was full of water.

Here is a good example of Hemingway's "sequence of motion and fact." It starts from dialogue and leads into first-person action; but the central description is a single clause, where the expletive takes the place of the observer and his observations are registered one by one. Hence, for the reader, it lives up to Robert Jordan's intention: "you . . . feel that all that happened to you." Hemingway puts his emphasis on nouns because, among parts of speech, they come closest to things. Stringing them along by means of conjunctions, he approximates the actual flow of experience. For him, as for Marion Tweedy Bloom, the key word is *and*, with its renewable promise of continuity, occasionally varied by *then* and *so*. The rhetorical scheme is *polysyndeton*—a large name for the childishly simple habit of linking sentences together. The subject, when it is not taken for granted, merely puts us in touch with the predicate: the series of objects that Hemingway wants to point out. Even a preposition can turn this trick as "with" does in this account of El Sordo waiting to see the whites of his enemy's eyes:

Come on, Comrade Voyager . . . Keep on coming with your eyes forward . . . Look. With a red face and blond hair and blue eyes. With no cap on and his moustache is yellow. With blue eyes. With pale blue eyes. With pale blue eyes with something wrong with them. With pale blue eyes that don't focus. Close enough. Too close. Yes, Comrade Voyager. Take it, Comrade Voyager.

Prose gets as near as it can to physical conflict here. The figure enlarges as it advances, the quickening impression grows clear and sharp and almost unbearable, whereupon it is blackened out by El Sordo's rifle. Each clipped sentence, each prepositional phrase, is like a new frame in a strip of film; indeed the whole passage, like so many others, might have been filmed by the camera and projected on the screen. The course of Harry Morgan's launch speeding through the Gulf Stream, or of Frederic Henry's fantasy ascending the elevator with Catherine Barkley, is given this cinematographic presentation. *Green Hills of Africa* voices the long-range ambition of obtaining a fourth and fifth dimension in prose. Yet if the subordinate clause and the complex sentence are the usual ways for writers to obtain a third dimension, Hemingway keeps his writing on a linear plane. He holds the purity of his line by moving in one direction, ignoring sidetracks and avoiding structural complications. By presenting a succession of images, each of which has its brief moment when it commands the reader's undivided attention, he achieves his special vividness and fluidity. For what he lacks in structure he makes up in sequence, carefully ordering visual impressions as he sets them down and ironically juxtaposing the various items on his lists and inventories. "A Way You'll Never Be" opens with a close-up showing the debris on a battlefield, variously specifying munitions, medicaments, and leftovers from a field kitchen, then closing in on the scattered papers with this striking montage-effect: ". . . group postcards showing the machine-gun unit standing in ranked and ruddy cheerfulness as in a football picture for a college annual; now they were humped and swollen in the grass. . . ." It is not surprising that Hemingway's verse, published by *Poetry* in 1923, is recognizably imagistic in character—and perhaps his later heroics are foreshadowed by the subject of one of those poems, Theodore Roosevelt.

In her observant book, *L'Age du roman américain*, Claude-Edmonde Magny stresses Hemingway's "exaltation of the instant." We can note how this emphasis is reflected in his timing, which—after his placing has bridged the distance from *there* to *here*—strives to close the gap between *then* and *now*. Where Baudelaire's clock said "remember" in many languages, Robert Jordan's memory says: "Now, *ahora, maintenant, heute.*" When death interrupts a dream, in "The Snows of Kilimanjaro," the ultimate reality is heralded by a rising insistence upon the word "now." It is not for nothing that Hemingway is the younger contemporary of Proust and Joyce. Though his time is neither *le temps perdu* nor the past nostalgically recaptured, he spends it gathering roses while he can, to the ever accelerating rhythm of headlines and telegrams and loud-speakers. The act, no sooner done than said, becomes simultaneous with the word, no sooner said than felt. Hemingway goes so far, in "Fathers and Sons," as to render a sexual embrace by an onomatopoetic sequence of adverbs. But unlike Damon Runyon and Dickens, he seldom narrates in the present tense, except in such sporting events as "Fifty Grand." Rather, his timeliness expresses itself in continuous forms of the verb and in his fondness for all kinds of participial constructions. These, compounded and multiplied, create an ambiance of overwhelming activity, and the epithets shift from El Sordo's harassed feelings to the impact of the reiterated bullets, as Hemingway recounts "the last lung-aching, leg-dead, mouth-dry, bullet-spatting, bullet-cracking, bullet-singing run up the final slope of the hill." More often the meaning takes the opposite turn, and moves from the external plane into the range of a character's senses, proceeding serially from the visual to the tactile, as it does when the "Wine of Wyoming" is sampled: "It was very light and clear and good and still tasted of the grapes."

When Nick Adams goes fishing, the temperature is very tangibly indicated: "It was getting hot, the sun hot on the back of his neck." The remark about the weather is thereby extended in two directions, toward the distant source of the heat and toward its immediate perception. Again in "Big Two-Hearted River," Nick's fatigue is measured by the weight of his pack: ". . . it was heavy. It was much too heavy." As in the movies, the illusion of movement is produced by repeating the same shot with further modification every time. Whenever a new clause takes more than one step ahead, a subsequent clause repeats it in order to catch up. Repetition, as in "Up in Michigan," brings the advancing narrative back to an initial point of reference. "Liz liked Jim very much. She liked it the way he walked over from the shop and often went to the kitchen door to watch him start down the road. She liked it about his moustache. She liked it about how white his teeth were when he smiled." The opaque verb "like," made increasingly transparent, is utilized five more times in this paragraph; and the fumbling preposition "about" may be an acknowledgment of Hemingway's early debt to Gertrude Stein. The situation is located somewhere between a subjective Liz and an objective Jim. The theme of love is always a test of Hemingway's objectivity. When Frederic kisses Catherine, her responses are not less moving because they are presented through his reflexes; but it is her sentimental conversation which leaves him free to ask himself: "What the hell?" At first glance, in a behavioristic formula which elsewhere recurs, Colonel Cantwell seems so hard-boiled that motions are his only emotions: "He saw that his hand was trembling." But his vision is blurred by conventionally romantic tenderness when he contemplates a heroine whose profile "could break your . . . or anyone else's heart." Hemingway's heroines, when they aren't bitches, are fantasies—or rather, the masculine reader is invited to supply his own, as with the weather in Mark Twain's *American Claimant*. They are pin-up girls.

If beauty lies in the eye of the beholder, Hemingway's purpose is to make his readers beholders. This is easily done when the narration is conducted in the first person; we can sit down and drink, with Jake Barnes, and watch Paris walk by. The interpolated chapters of *In Our Time*, most of them reminiscences from the army, employ the collective *we;* but, except for "My Old Man," the stories themselves are told in the third person. Sometimes, to strengthen the sense of identification, they make direct appeal to the second person; the protagonist of "Soldier's home" is "you" as well as "he"—and, more generally, "a fellow." With the exception of Jake's confessions, that is to say *The Sun Also Rises,* all of Hemingway's novels are written in the *style indirect libre*—indirect discourse which more or less closely follows the consciousness of a central character. An increasing tendency for the author to intrude, commenting in his own person, is one of the weaknesses of *Across the River.* He derives his strength from a power to visualize episodes through the eyes of those most directly involved; for a page, in "The Short, Happy Life of Francis Macomber," the hunt is actually seen from the beast's point of view. Hemingway's use of interior monologue is effective when sensations from the outer world are entering the stream of a character's consciousness, as they do with such a rush at El Sordo's last stand. But introspection is not Hemingway's genre, and the night-thoughts of *To Have and Have Not* are among his least successful episodes. His best are events, which are never far to seek; things are constantly happening in his world; his leg-man, Nick Adams, happens to be the eyewitness of "The Killers." The state of mind that Hemingway communicates to us is the thrill that Nick got from skiing in "Cross Country Snow," which "plucked Nick's mind out and left him only the wonderful, flying, dropping sensation of his body."

VI

If psychological theories could be proved by works of fiction, Hemingway would lend his authority to the long contested formula of William James, which equates emotion with bodily sensation. Most other serious writers, however, would bear witness to deeper ranges of sensibility and more complex processes of motivation than those he sees fit to describe. Some of them have accused Hemingway of aggressive anti-intellectualism: I am thinking particularly of Aldous Huxley. But Huxley's own work is so pure an example of all that Hemingway has recoiled from, so intellectual in the airiest sense, and so unsupported by felt experience, that the argument has played into Hemingway's hands. We have seen enough of the latter to know that he doesn't really hate books—himself having written a dozen or more, several of which are, and will remain, the best of their kind. As for his refusal to behave like a man of letters, he reminds us of Hotspur, who professes to be a laconic philistine and turns out—with no little grandiloquence—to be the most poetic character in Shakespeare's play. Furthermore, it is not Hemingway, but the slogan-mongers of his epoch, who have debased the language; he has been attempting to restore some decent degree of correspondence between words and things; and the task of verification is a heavy one, which throws the individual back on his personal resources of awareness. That he has succeeded within limits, and with considerable strain, is less important than that he has succeeded, that a few more aspects of life have been captured for literature. Meanwhile the word continues to dematerialize, and has to be made flesh all over again; the firsthand perception, once it gets written down, becomes the secondhand notation; and the writer, who attains his individuality by repudiating literary affectation, ends by finding that he has struck a new pose and founded another school.

It is understandable why no critique of Hemingway, including this one, can speak for long of the style without speaking of the man. Improving on Buffon, Mark Schorer has written: "[Hemingway's] style is not only his subject, it is his view of life." It could also be called his way of life, his *Lebenstil*. It has led him to live his books, to brave the maximum of exposure, to tour the world in an endless search for wars and their moral equivalents. It has cast him in the special role of our agent, our plenipotentiary, our roving correspondent on whom we depend for news from the fighting fronts of modern consciousness. Here he is, the man who was there. His writing seems so intent upon the actual, so impersonal in its surfaces, that it momentarily prompts us to overlook the personality behind them. That would be a serious mistake; for the point of view, though brilliantly intense, is narrowly focused and obliquely angled. We must ask: who is this guide to whom we have entrusted ourselves on intimate terms in dangerous places? Where are his limitations? What are his values? We may well discover that they differ from our assumptions, when he shows us a photograph of a bullfighter close to a bull, and comments: "If there is no blood on his belly afterwards you ought to get your money back." We may be ungrateful to question such curiosity, when we are indebted to it for many enlargements of our vicarious knowledge; and it may well spring from the callowness of the tourist rather than the morbidity of the *voyeur*, from the American zest of the fan who pays his money to reckon the carnage. When Spain's great poet, García Lorca, celebrated the very same theme, averting his gaze from the spilling of the blood, his refrain was "*Que no quiero verla!*" ("I do not want to see it!").

Yet Hemingway wants to see everything—or possibly he wants to be in a position to tell us that he has seen everything. While the boy Nick, his seeing eye, eagerly watches a Caesarian childbirth in "Indian Camp," the far from impassive husband turns away; and it is later discovered that he has killed himself. "He couldn't stand things . . ." so runs the diagnosis of Nick's father, the doctor. This, for Nick, is an initiation to suffering and death; but with the sunrise, shortly afterward, youth and well-being reassert themselves; and the end of the story reaffirms the generalization that Hazlitt once drew: "No young man ever thinks he shall die." It is easy enough for such a young man to stand things, for he is not yet painfully involved in them; he is not a sufferer but a wide-eyed onlooker, to whom the word "mashing" holds out mysterious enticements. Hemingway's projection of this attitude has given his best work perennial youthfulness; it has also armed his critics with the accusation that, like his Robert Cohen, he is "a case of arrested development." If this be so, his plight is generalized by the Englishman Wilson, who observes that "Americans stay little boys . . . all their lives." And the object of Wilson's observation, Francis Macomber, would furnish a classic case history for Adler, if not for Freud—the masculine sense of inferiority which seeks to overcome itself by acts of prowess, both sanguinary and sexual. Despite these two sources of excitement, the story is a plaintive modulation of two rather dissonant themes: *None but the brave deserves the fair* and *The female of the species is more deadly than the male*. After Francis Macomber has demonstrated his manhood, the next step is death. The world that remains most alive to Hemingway is that stretch between puberty and maturity which is strictly governed by the ephebic code: a world of mixed apprehension and bravado before the rite of passage, the baptism of fire, the introduction to sex.

Afterward comes the boasting, along with such surviving ideals as Hemingway subsumes in the word *cojones*—the English equivalent sounds more skeptical. But for Jake Barnes, all passion spent in the First World War, or for Colonel Cantwell, tired and disgruntled by the Second, the aftermath can only be elegiac. The weather-beaten hero of *Across the River*, which came out in 1950, is fifty years old and uneasily conscious of that fact; whereas "the childish, drunken heroics" of *The Sun Also Rises* took place just about twenty-five years before. From his spectacular arrival in the Twenties, Hemingway's course has paralleled that of our century; and at its midpoint he balks like the rest of us before the responsibilities of middle age. When, if ever, does the *enfant du siècle*, that *enfant terrible*, grow up? (Not necessarily when he grows a beard and calls himself "Mr. Papa.") Frederic Henry plunges into the Po much as Huck Finn dived into the Mississippi, but emerges to remind us even more pointedly of Fabrice del Dongo in Stendhal's *Chartreuse de Parme*, and of our great contemporary shift from transatlantic innocence to old-world experience. Certain intimations of later years are present in Hemingway's earlier stories, typically Ad Francis, the slap-happy ex-champ in "The Battler." Even in "Fifty Grand," his most contrived tale, the beat-up prizefighter suffers more than he acts and wins by losing—a situation which has its corollary in the title of Hemingway's third collection, *Winner Take Nothing*. The ultimate article of his credo, which he shares with Malraux and Sartre, is the good fight for the lost cause. And the ultimate protagonist is Jesus in "Today Is Friday," whose crucifixion is treated like an athletic feat, and whose capacity for taking punishment rouses a fellow-feeling in the Roman soldiers. The stoic or masochistic determination to take it brings us back from Hemingway to his medium, which—although it eschews the passive voice—

is essentially a receiving instrument, especially sensitized for recording a series of violent shocks.

The paradox of toughness and sensitivity is resolved, and the qualities and defects of his writing are reconciled, if we merely remember that he was—and still is—a poet. That he is not a novelist by vocation, if it were not revealed by his books, could be inferred from his well-known retort to F. Scott Fitzgerald. For Fitzgerald the rich were different—not quantitatively, because they had more money, but qualitatively, because he had a novelistic interest in manners and morals. Again, when we read André Gide's reports from the Congo, we realize what *Green Hills of Africa* lacks in the way of social or psychological insight. As W. M. Frohock has perceived, Hemingway is less concerned with human relations than with his own relationship to the universe—a concern which might have spontaneously flowered into poetry. His talents come out most fully in the texture of his work, whereas the structure tends to be episodic and uncontrived to the point of formlessness. *For Whom the Bell Tolls,* the only one of his six novels that has been carefully constructed, is in some respects an overexpanded short story. Editors rejected his earliest stories on the grounds that they were nothing but sketches and anecdotes, thereby paying incidental tribute to his sense of reality. Fragments of truth, after all, are the best that a writer can offer; and, as Hemingway has said, ". . . Any part you make will represent the whole if it's made truly." In periods as confusing as the present, when broader and maturer representations are likely to falsify, we are fortunate if we can find authenticity in the lyric cry, the adolescent mood, the tangible feeling, the trigger response. If we think of Hemingway's temperamental kinship with E. E. Cummings, and of Cummings' "Buffalo Bill" or "Olaf glad and big," it is easy to think of Hemingway as a poet. After the attractions and distractions of timeliness have been outdated, together with categorical distinctions between the rich and the poor, perhaps he will be remembered for a poetic vision which renews our interrupted contact with the timeless elements of man's existence: bread, wine, bed, music, and just a few more of the concrete universals. When El Sordo raises his glance from the battlefield, he looks up at the identical patch of blue sky that Henry Fleming saw in *The Red Badge of Courage* and that looked down on Prince Andrey in *War and Peace.*

REVISITING
DOS PASSOS' *U.S.A.*

No American writer of his generation can have gone through such vicissitudes in critical esteem as John Dos Passos. It may well be that his later writing, viewed as a mechanical and reactionary sequel to the books that gained him his reputation, has blurred our appreciation of their genuine merits. Thus I recall an embarrassing session with him on an educational radio program sponsored by the University of Massachusetts (Amherst). We had been slightly acquainted through summers at Cape Cod, and that acquaintance would be strengthened by a ride back to Cambridge and a dinner together, where he was wholly sympathetic, open, warm. The difficulty with the program had been that both the third participant—his skillful and perceptive French translator, Maurice-Edgar Coindreau—and I had tried to center the discussion on what we considered his major achievement, U.S.A. But authors understandably tend to harbor a special affection for their latest-born, and the situation had been further complicated by his ideological change of heart. I was moved to think again about Dos Passos at another bidding from the University of Massachusetts, an issue of The Massachusetts Review *honoring my former Ph.D. student, Sidney Kaplan, who has been a pioneer in Afro-American and related studies (October 1979).*

•

John Dos Passos' reputation reached its highest point in 1938, when Jean-Paul Sartre—reviewing the French translation of *Nineteen Nineteen*—proclaimed him without reservation "the greatest writer of our time." Sartre's critical attitudes have always been dictated by the personal or dialectical use he could make of his subjects, and he went on to imitate Dos Passos' method in his own unfinished tetralogy, *Les Chemins de la liberté.* He might not have considered that method so uniquely experimental, if he had any firsthand acquaintance with *Ulysses* (and Joyce was then still alive). But much of *Nineteen Nineteen* had the advantage, from Sartre's point of view, of being set in France. Insofar as he was interested in the larger patterns of interrelated lives, of course he could have found a precedent within that strong tradition of French fiction which had its fountainhead in the

Comédie humaine and its contemporary manifestation in Jules Romains' *roman-fleuve*. And, as Claude-Edmonde Magny would be pointing out in *L'Age du roman américain* (which in turn would influence the emergent *nouveau roman*), the novel had to register the impact of the cinema. Yet *Nineteen Nineteen,* doubtless because of its sharp confrontations between history and consciousness, fitted in particularly well with Sartre's existentialist position.

Born and nurtured as a romantic individualist, Dos Passos had to work his way toward facing the problems of modern collectivity. His development can be traced from his poems, plays, and travelogues through his two early war novels to his fictional encounters with the city in *Streets of Night* and *Manhattan Transfer,* which Lionel Trilling would hail as perhaps "the most important novel of the decade." When we recall that *An American Tragedy* and *The Great Gatsby* were also published in that same year, or that the decade had already produced *The Age of Innocence* and *Main Street* and would soon be producing *A Farewell to Arms* and *The Sound and the Fury,* we need make no further comment on the vicissitudes of taste. But it was probably *Manhattan Transfer* that went farthest to shock the traditionalists, provoking Paul Elmer More to dismiss it as "an explosion in a cesspool." The more salubrious reaction of Sinclair Lewis may help us to recapture the sense of novelty that it conveyed to sensibilities yet unblurred by nearly a century of metropolitan fiction. Here was, according to Lewis, "the first book to catch Manhattan . . . Here is the city, the smell of it, the sound of it, the harsh and shining sight of it." After all, *The New Yorker* likewise made its first appearance in that *annus mirabilis,* 1925.

Sartre would set his seal of world acclaim on the middle volume of *U.S.A.,* and Dos Passos would win the Feltrinelli if not the Nobel Prize, which has been awarded to many a lesser figure. His decline in standing, during the latter part of his career, was dramatically paralleled by the 180-degree shift in his political orientation. He could scarcely be blamed for sometimes feeling that critics, most of them still more or less liberal, were penalizing him for his congealing conservatism. He rationalized his claims to consistency by restudying Jefferson and the civic fathers in such books as *The Ground We Stand On.* But, as F. O. Matthiessen was able to retort: "They are the ground we stood on a long time ago, before the industrial transformation of our modern world." Moreover, the actual effects of that transformation had been the primary themes of Dos Passos as a novelist. Certain resources of novelistic compassion seem to have withered away, in the process that turned a young man arrested for protesting the Sacco-Vanzetti decision into an old man condoning the Kent State shootings. His second trilogy, *District of Columbia,* is at best a dim sequel to the first; and although *Mid-Century* returns to the documentaries and biographies of *U.S.A.,* significantly it omits the lyrical self-intimations.

Yet there had to be some continuity in which *U.S.A.* was pivotal, if only because it had been poised at a turning point between idealism and disillusionment. The expressionistic play that he wrote in college, *The Moon is a Gong,* was retitled *The Garbage Man* for its off-Broadway production. Edmund Wilson's novel, *I Thought of Daisy,* sketches out a sympathetic portrait of Dos Passos in his Greenwich Village days: earnest, honest, shy, myopic, dedicated, self-denying, a poetic esthete by temperament, willing himself by force of conscience to be a radical activist. His period of active radicalism started with the trial of Sacco and Vanzetti and terminated with the defeat of the Loyalists in the Spanish Civil War, which for him was history's wrong turn, exacerbated by the Soviet betrayal of Marxist principles. That was precisely the interval that witnessed the writing of *U.S.A.* As late as 1939 he answered a questionnaire with this credo: "My sympathies lie with the private in the front line against the brass hat; with the hod-carrier against the straw-boss, or the walking delegate for that matter; with the laboratory worker against the stuffed shirt in a mortarboard; with the criminal against the cop." *The 42nd Parallel* contains a vignette from his Harvard days, contrasting the gentlemanly conformities with a millworkers' strike at Lawrence, Massachusetts.

He never strayed very far from such temperamental alignments, though his hatred of the bureaucracy would complicate them by making a bugbear out of the New Deal. Internal conflicts were bound to be reinforced by his mixed ancestry, his illegitimate birth, his upper-class education—not to mention his exposure to war. He had taken his first public stand in 1916 at the age of twenty, with an article for *The New Republic* entitled "Against American Literature." Characteristically it was the establishment that he opposed, in this case the Genteel Tradition, counterposing to it the modernist stance of Walt Whitman. "Our only substitute for dependence on the past is dependence on the future," declared the youthful Dos Passos. "Here our only poet found his true greatness." Forty years later, after reading an issue of *Les Temps modernes,* he commented to Wilson: "In that connection I read over half of *Democratic Vistas* last night and found it much more based on realities than Sartre." The irony was that, when the future toward which Whitman had looked—"Years of the Modern!"—arrived with the twentieth century, Dos Passos found it harder to contemplate than did his admirer, Sartre. To an inquiring student Dos Passos replied that the original slant of his work was "more likely to stem from Whitman (and perhaps Veblen) than from Marx."

Leaving Marx aside as a marginal though by no means irrelevant interest, we proceed through *U.S.A.* from the tutelage of Whitman to that of Thorstein Veblen. The prologue spelling out the title, added after these three novels were conjoined to form a trilogy, moves from the lonely mind of a young man walking "the night streets" to a collective memory of images and echoes: "But mostly U. S. A. is the speech of the people." This passage turns out to be nothing less than a poem in Whitman's magniloquent vein; and there are many other such fragments of poetry, notably the composite portrait of the Unknown Soldier that concludes the second volume, "The Body of an American." Dos Passos' democratic conception is rooted in a Whitmanesque unanimism, in the prefatory assumption of *Leaves of Grass* that the United States itself is potentially a great poem, worthy of "gigantic and generous treatment" within the total ambience of its immediate present. *Manhattan Transfer* had comprised a kind of urban kaleidoscope. Now the panoramic subject matter, to be treated on a scale of 1500 pages, was a cross-section of the entire country during the first three decades of the twentieth century. Modestly conceiving himself as "a second-class historian," the author claimed firsthand access to his age through its language, and asked no more than that his novels be read as "contemporary chronicles."

One of his strengths was his keen reportorial talent for taking in and getting down a locale. Novelists do not have to be circumscribed by a single region, but most of them stick to certain particular backgrounds. Even Balzac hardly covered his lavishly chosen ground in such full detail and over so wide an area as Dos Passos did with his material. At an ever accelerating pace he zigzags across the continent, with a dip into Mexico and Cuba and a fling at Europe. On the make, his personages gravitate toward a series of capitals, each of them a center for the powers that control American values, all of them described with atmospheric precision: finance (New York), politics (Washington), industry (Detroit), entertainment (Hollywood), recreation (Miami Beach). As with *Manhattan Transfer,* the titles are large connective symbols. *The 42nd Parallel* roughly runs through Chicago, where Dos Passos was fortuitously born, eastward to Provincetown, where he did much of his writing, and westward to the Oregon forest, which flashes by in a last reminiscence of his Unknown Soldier. *Nineteen Nineteen* shifts the titular emphasis from a spatial latitude to a temporal axis. And climactically *The Big Money,* as a central metaphor, universalizes the profit motive and tightens the network of human relations through the cash nexus itself.

The 42nd Parallel begins, in a flush of expectation, by celebrating the turn of the century, and ends with the embarkation of troops for the First World War in 1917. *Nineteen Nineteen,* as the date suggests, is less preoccupied with the war itself (previously and more closely rendered in *One Man's Initiation* and *Three Soldiers*) than with its side-effects and disillusioning aftermath, signalized by the Disarmament Conference at Versailles. *The Big Money* deals with the following decade, the razzle-dazzle of the Twenties, the perturbation beneath the debonaire surfaces of the so-called Jazz Age, ending with the Wall Street crash of 1929, and portending the strikes and breadlines of the Depression. Hence "this lousy superannuated hypertrophied hellinvented novel," as Dos Passos deprecated it in a letter to Ernest Hemingway, was put together just a few years after the incidents it chronicles. Yet it was conceived and executed as a historical novel, bearing witness to its epoch. Like its greatest prototype in that mode, Tolstoy's *War and Peace, U.S.A.* is concerned with the interweaving and shaping of private existences by public events. Like Tolstoy, Dos Passos shows great respect for history, which is conscientiously presented—and unlike E. L. Doctorow in *Ragtime,* who introduces historical figures and then irresponsibly casts them in fictitious roles.

Dos Passos' historicism sets up its social framework through a sequence of biographical sketches. Symmetrically spaced, there are nine of these in each volume, twenty-seven in all, related thematically as well as synchronically to the matter at hand. This assortment of highly typical and widely varied Americans ranges from international bankers (J. P. Morgan) to intransigent radicals (Eugene Debs), from prolific inventors (Thomas Edison) to eccentric artists (Isadora Duncan), from critical thinkers (Randolph Bourne) to film stars (Rudolph Valentino). Technological development has its outstanding proponents: the Wright brothers at Kitty Hawk, the efficiency expert F. W. Taylor, an ambivalent Henry Ford between his "tin lizzie" and his antique collection. Journalism has its playboy in John Reed and its bullyboy in William Randolph Hearst. (Dos Passos' characterization of the latter, "Poor Little Rich Boy," clearly lent inspiration to *Citizen Kane*.) Two presidents are represented: a mock-heroic Theodore Roosevelt and a Woodrow Wilson who comes near to being the arch-villain. "Meester Veelson"—the European accent reflects the hopes for a just peace that he betrayed, after betraying his promise of keeping America out of the war. Dos Passos felt peculiarly embittered, as did Hemingway, because that betrayal debased the language, reducing trusted ideals to rhetorical slogans.

U.S.A. is further structured by two formalized devices: the "Newsreel" and "The Camera Eye." Sixty-eight intermittent Newsreels (modeled on a medium then vital but soon obsolescent) frame the time-scheme objectively with reverberating quotations from subtitles, headlines, and popular songs. At the opposite extreme, the fifty-one Camera Eyes are candidly subjective and autobiographical, revealing the mind of the author himself at the moment of his narration. Though the term sounds mechanical, the textures can be rhapsodic; taken together, these passages might constitute Dos Passos' "Song of Myself." James T. Farrell preferred them to all the others, whereas Hemingway's preference was for the portraits from life. The striking—and slightly dampening—implication is that, between the detailed reportage on the one hand and the introspective evocation on the other, the middle territory of sheer fiction seems less arresting or memorable. One wonders how much force it would have carried if the narrative had been straight, without the interventions of *collage* or *montage*. Through the trilogy Dos Passos has dispersed a dozen imaginary case histories, five in each volume: six men, six women. The numerical disparity is accounted for by the fact that some drop out, while others enter late. Yet those who cease to be protagonists have walk-on parts in other episodes, so that their life stories are continued from other viewpoints than their own.

Novels are invariably progressions from innocence to experience, and not less so when—with Proust—they span decades and volumes. Born on the fourth of July in the century's dewy youth, J. Ward Morehouse is originally viewed through his own eyes as an idealistic high-school debater. Step by step, we watch him from the outside, as he climbs the careerist's ladder: helping to break the Homestead Strike, profiteering as a Dollar-a-Year-Man, pompously and smugly manipu-lating the wiles of public relations. In a parallel movement Janey, whom we meet as a lively tomboy, subsequently crushed by the loss of a boyfriend, will reappear as Miss Williams, a colorless old maid and perfect secretary to the important Mr. Morehouse. Mobility goes downward for her brother Joe, who, after wartime adventures with the navy and the merchant marine, is ironically killed in a tavern brawl on Armistice night. Fainy McCreary, the likeable Irish-American printer's devil, is radicalized on his trek to San Francisco, but some-how makes his Mexican peace and disappears from the cycle. Two aspiring girls from different backgrounds in Chicago, Eleanor Stod-dard and Eveline Hutchins, pass on from the local Art Institute via an interior-decorating studio to intrigues in New York and Paris. Though they get harder and harder to tell apart, one is destined to marry a Russian prince and the other to commit suicide.

The most poignant of these character sketches, which might stand by itself as a novella, comprises the two sections entitled "Daughter." Anne Elizabeth Trent, a headstrong Texas belle, conscience-stricken after her brother's death as a pilot in training, gets into social work and goes abroad as a postwar Red Cross aide. Made pregnant by an American officer, who temporizes because of other ambitions than marriage, she wildly persuades a half-drunk French aviator into loop-ing the loop with her at night, and loses not her baby but her life. A single section is devoted to the radicalization of Ben Compton, a Jew-ish law student from Brooklyn, who goes to jail for his pacifist con-victions. Incidental glimpses afterward reveal him as a loyal member of the Communist Party who is ultimately expelled in a doctrinal purge. The comparable case of Mary French, who briefly takes up with Ben Compton at one point, is more fully developed. Ill at ease with the pretentious gentility of her mother, she drops out of Vassar to nurse her beloved doctor-father, who dies of influenza contracted from his patients. After an apprenticeship among the poor at Hull House, she drifts farther leftward: to radical journalism in Pittsburgh, labor organization in Washington, party work as a fellow traveler. Having rejected her family background and been rejected by her Communist lover, she is left to carry on alone.

If the book has any heroine, it is this committed fighter for losing causes, and much of the Sacco-Vanzetti agitation is witnessed from Mary's standpoint. Her opposite number, who also makes her début in the third volume, is indeed a mock-heroine, a movie queen: the hard-boiled and easygoing Margo Dowling. Sex provides her sordid education; but she learns to use it; and she manages to rise through vaudeville, chorus lines, and night clubs to the precarious heights of Hollywood stardom. On her way up, she has good-naturedly tried to alleviate the fate of Charley Anderson, which dominates *The Big Money*. That stalwart mechanic from North Dakota was left boarding a troopship at the conclusion of *The 42nd Parallel*. He does not appear in *Nineteen Nineteen* at all; he is too busy fighting and learning all about airplanes. Disembarking at the outset of *The Big Money*, he is now a veteran, a war hero, an ace from the Lafayette Escadrille, trying to realize that the war is over. Demobilization means demoralization for a while. Basically skilled and hard-working, however, he invents a new airplane motor. But an invention must not only be patented; it must be exploited, promoted, and capitalized; stock must be issued, and companies formed. Charley's mechanical knowhow would be wasted without the entrepreneurial intercession of shrewd financiers and savvy lobbyists.

His own function, supervising production, inevitably takes him to Detroit, where he is taken up by the country club set. He makes a sort of allegorical choice, when he throws over the engineer's to marry the banker's daughter. He is still most comfortable when tinkering, in his overalls, along with his foreman Bill Cermak. But Bill is killed and Charley is badly injured, when their plane crashes in taking off for a trial flight. That crash on the runway is emblematic, not merely of Charley's anticlimactic fortunes, but of what will be happening in the stockmarket and throughout the business world. Things fall apart for Charley; his hollow marriage is wrecked; he himself becomes a human wreck, increasingly alcoholic and self-destructive. Drifting down to Florida, where Margo moves in and out of his careening existence, he is fatally injured in a drunken automobile accident, and rival claimants beleaguer his hospital bed as his internal monologue tapers off. In five years, he has promised his assistant, they would be "in the big money"— as everyone has promised everyone else. Unpeeling a roll of fresh hundred-dollar bills, he was tempted to kiss them. "Gosh," he had

said to himself at one moment, "money's a great thing." At another
he had wished that "he didn't have to worry about money all the
time," that instead "he was still tinkerin' with that damn motor."

As Margo Dowling had an opposite number in Mary French, so
Charley Anderson has an antiheroic foil in Richard Ellsworth Savage.
He has begun as a well-connected poor relation, a sensitive Harvard
poet, who graduates into the war and gets attached to the brass. After
a number of safe and easy assignments behind the lines, he goes
through the peace negotiations as aide-de-camp to that ever-hustling
arch-operator, J. Ward Morehouse, now in charge of opinion-molding
for the postwar American public. Through that connection Dick is assured of a future, if not as a man of letters, then as heir apparent to a
high-powered advertising agency, as a highly paid apologist for the
ensuing materialistic boom. The moral crisis is underlined by his affair
with Anne Elizabeth ("Daughter"); when he jilts her, his good faith
lies among the casualties. When we take leave of him, in a cynical
miasma of worldly success and self-hate, he is suffering the grimmest
of hangovers, after a homosexual escapade in Harlem. Dos Passos'
classmate, the poet Robert Hillyer, who actually returned to an academic post and took a narrowly traditional line, objected seriously to
this character as a caricature of himself. Dos Passos responded, with
the usual embarrassment prompted by such identifications *à clef*, that
he had simply borrowed certain military associations, along with a few
details from their common undergraduate memories.

We might come closer to the significance of Richard Ellsworth
Savage if we consider him as an imaginary projection of Dos Passos
himself—Dos Passos as he might have become, had he followed the
code of snobbery and careerism, had his talent and integrity been
compromised by the seductions of the big money, the acquisitive society, and the military-industrial complex. Edmund Wilson remarked
that "humanity generally comes off badly" in *Manhattan Transfer*, and
it would be hard to gainsay such an impression of *U.S.A.* All too many
of its *dramatis personae* wind up as sellouts or losers, just as the war
is sold out and the peace is lost. Sartre would interpret this permuta-
tion in Marxist terms: "In capitalist society, men do not have lives,
they have only destinies." That is why these people seem shallow or
two-dimensional, even when contrasted with their historic role-models.
And, though we are not given profiles of Sacco or Vanzetti, we hear

their voices out of the depths—quoted directly from their correspondence and, most powerfully, from the famous response of Bartolomeo Vanzetti to the death sentence. Two Camera Eyes record Dos Passos' own emotions before and after the execution. In one he walks through Plymouth, where Vanzetti had worked, and likens those Italian immigrants to the earliest Pilgrim settlers. In the other, he angrily reacts to the defeat of justice: "all right we are two nations."

On a previous page a Camera Eye has recorded his insomniac misgivings, "peeling the speculative onion of doubt," as Peer Gynt did from layer to layer ("topdog? underdog?"). Against the natural grain of skeptical diffidence, "the internal agitator crazy to succeed" had forced Dos Passos to make a soapbox speech in Union Square. Painfully mulling it over, he confesses, "I go home after a drink and a hot meal and read (with some difficulty in the Loeb Library trot) the epigrams of Martial and ponder the course of history and what leverage might pry the owners loose from power and bring back (I too Walt Whitman) our storybook democracy." Here is a pungent contrast: from Whitman to Martial, whom Dos Passos coupled in a letter with Juvenal, read in the same bilingual edition. Both of those Roman poets attest the decline from the virtues of the old Republic to the corruptions of their present Empire. The nostalgia for Whitman's vistas completes the American analogy. His impetus toward panegyric and rhapsody has been transposed into epigram and satire. The keen attraction that this last form held for Dos Passos made itself felt in his introduction to a portfolio of drawings by Georg Grosz, "Satire as a Way of Seeing," where he equated the satirist with the moralist. He identified his own outlook when he accepted the Gold Medal for Fiction from the National Institute of Arts and Letters in 1957, responding to William Faulkner's citation:

I wonder if any of you have ever noticed that it is sometimes those who find most pleasure and amusement in their fellow man, and have most hope in his goodness, who get the reputation of being his most carping critics. Maybe it is that the satirist is so full of the possibilities of humankind in general, that he tends to draw a dark and garish picture when he tries to depict people as they are at any particular moment. The satirist is usually a pretty unpopular fellow. The only time he attains even fleeting popularity is when his works can be used by some particular faction as a stick to beat the brains out of their opponents. Satirical writing is by definition unpopular writing. Its aim is to prod people into thinking. Thinking hurts.

Dreiser called his most portentous novel *An American Tragedy,* and I suppose that title might subsume many of the destinies—not to say the lives—interwoven through *U.S.A.* Yet it might raise classical questions regarding the stature of the protagonist, since the characters so often seem to be dwarfed by their very multiplicity, if not by the Swiftian perspectives of the author. "We're living in one of the damndest tragic moments in history," he wrote to F. Scott Fitzgerald at about the time he was completing this trilogy. Its tragedy is that of America, and of the world itself. But there are times, he would have read in Juvenal, if he had not felt it in his bones, when it is difficult not to write satire. If the latterday imperialism could not evoke the verse of a Juvenal or a Martial, then it needed something like the prose of a Petronius or a Tacitus. Given the extraordinary scope of *U.S.A.,* there is an additional temptation—which Alfred Kazin has not resisted—to designate it as "a national epic." But critics should be able to discriminate, better than Hollywood press agents, among the fitting literary genres. We might well claim *Moby-Dick* as a national epic, or conceivably the *Leatherstocking* romances. Other and later American novelists, sometimes rather self-consciously, have touched upon the heroic vein: Frank Norris, Theodore Dreiser, Willa Cather.

Not that *U.S.A.* is lacking in heroes, the underdogs to whom Dos Passos professed his own allegiance, and those who fought and spoke on their behalf: the Unknown Soldier, the legendary Joe Hill, the socialist Debs, the progressive Senator LaFollette, Big Bill Hayward of the I.W.W., Sacco, Vanzetti, and most incisively Veblen, who gradually becomes the presiding spirit. In a letter to Edmund Wilson, written during the composition of *The Big Money,* Dos Passos speaks of gathering ammunition from Veblen's socio-economic analyses. As the ideologist of the fable, he had been situated to understand—much more comprehensively than Marx—the uses and abuses of technology, its relationship to human factors, and its vulnerability to sabotage at every level. His will included a caveat against any posthumous memoir, which Dos Passos has flouted in a brilliantly satirical psychograph, "The Bitter Drink." That beverage is the hemlock of Socrates, though it has been sipped in small doses and in sporadic classrooms by this twentieth-century gadfly. As a Norwegian-American compatriot of Ibsen, he has not only peeled the onion of doubt; he has slashed out against a shapeless and all-enveloping monster, the Boyg—

which Georg Brandes interpreted as the Spirit of Compromise. As a congenital nay-sayer, who "suffered from a constitutional inability to say yes," Veblen has his place with Hawthorne and Melville among the iconoclasts of American culture.

Coming closer to the United States than the Marxian class struggle, the Veblenite antithesis is the tension between producing and consuming. The downfall of Charley Anderson, which Edmund Wilson regarded as "the best part" of the story, is exemplary in that respect. Charley is an inventor; he possesses Veblen's positive "instinct for workmanship." He has a flair for production, but no head for consumption, and consumption is the order of the day. Veblen's negative phrase, "conspicuous consumption," realizes itself in the national spree that Dos Passos satirizes. And, what is economically and politically worse, this is rooted in "conspicuous waste"—waste of energy, of resources, and of lives. "It's the waste," Mary French cries out bitterly in the last scene of the trilogy. "The food they waste and the money they waste while our people starve in tarpaper barracks." These conflicting issues are counterpoised in the epilogue, "Vag." Dos Passos, as a life-long traveler, had played the vagabond. Here the valedictory young man, who hikes on the transcontinental highway as the young man in the prologue walked the city streets, could obviously be picked up and booked for vagrancy. The contrast, as he seeks to thumb a ride, is with the airline passengers overhead. There is no longer such a contrast today, when the norm of travel is by air, as there was forty years ago, when it was a luxury of the rich to be skyborne.

The decade of this work was the crucial one for commercial aviation, and one of Dos Passos' plays had been *Airways, Inc.* It is not a coincidence that the tragic fall of Charley Anderson or of "Daughter" should be literally enacted as an airplane crash. "Vag" is still vainly thumbing when the long-drawn-out chronicle draws to a close: "A hundred miles down the road." The road is still open nowadays, and the traffic has greatly increased. As a Harvard student, Dick Savage won a prize for a sonnet sequence from *The Reader's Digest;* but the editors wanted it to terminate on "a note of hope"; and he very readily supplied the amelioration, which may have been the first of his many intellectual compromises. Writing back to Malcolm Cowley, who seems to have wanted something more affirmative from *The 42nd Parallel,* Dos Passos promised "a certain amount of statement of position in the later Camera Eyes"—possibly what came out in regard to Sacco and

Vanzetti, or what would be made more emphatic by his Veblenite adherence. "But as for the note of hope," he concluded in his sincere and straightforward way, "gosh who knows?" No novelist is under obligation to offer reforms or remedies for the state of affairs he undertakes to expose, and Dos Passos would be far less effective in making such an attempt than was his illustrious and wrongheaded predecessor, Tolstoy.

Veblen could have taught him the futility of his hope "to rebuild the past," to recover the "storybook democracy" of Whitman and Jefferson, and consequently have spared him the embarrassment of campaigning for Barry Goldwater. "The American Dream: What Has Happened to It?" This inquiry was raised in a pair of articles by Faulkner, who lectured and planned a book about it. It has been pursued, in one way or another, by many of the other major novelists of our century. The readiest instance may be the concluding page of *The Great Gatsby,* with its flashing realization that "the last and greatest of all human dreams" has receded from the future into the past. If history has truly become a nightmare, better to reveal it than to keep it veiled in outworn fantasy. Speaking to the students of the Choate School, after having received its Alumni Prize, Dos Passos affirmed:

Writing is and I guess it ought to be one of the hazardous professions. . . . The first thing a man—striving to come of age in any period of human history—has to do is to choose for himself what is true and what is not true, what is real and what is not real in the picture of society established for him by his elders. . . . In the search for truth there are no secret formulae that can be handed down from one generation to another. Truth I believe is absolute. Some things are true and some false. You have to find it.

No further explanation was necessary for presenting the panorama as he had found it in *U.S.A.* The achievement was that he had caught so very much of it, thereby enabling Lionel Trilling to say that the whole seemed greater than the sum of its parts. Dos Passos did not need to be—he should not have later become—an ideologue. He was always enough of a moralist to be a genuine satirist. As a reporter, he saw a story in everything, a connecting issue everywhere. As a technician, he developed his own new modes for expressing the complications of modernity.

WILLIAM CARLOS WILLIAMS
AND THE OLD WORLD

My cultural bearings have always been reckoned by points of convergence between America and Europe. William Carlos Williams has embodied a special paradox in this respect, since he was ancestrally and temperamentally rather the Americanized European than the Europeanized American— a hyphenation common enough among citizens but fairly rare among artists. The contrast with Ezra Pound has been striking, in view of their friendship, and Williams is more readily linked with Mark Twain than with Henry James. As if to take note of the distance, we had to correct the spelling of many foreign names in reprinting the novel A Voyage to Pagany (*New York: New Directions, 1970*). *My introduction to that reprint was written at Mr. Laughlin's behest, prepublished under the present title in* The Yale Review (*Summer 1970*), *and included afterward in my* Grounds for Comparison (*Cambridge: Harvard University Press, 1972*).

•

The Atlantic Ocean has tended to act as a magnetic field for American writers, no two of whom have come to quite the same terms with those cultures on the other side. Critics like to polarize their problems into such dichotomies as Highbrow/Lowbrow, Paleface/Redskin, Virgin/Dynamo. But simplification is hazardous because the presence of Europe has so pervaded our background that the stance of every significant writer has been affected by it in some way or other. Whitman's reaction, to be sure, was at odds with Longfellow's response. Yet the strongest testimony has been lodged *a fortiori*, not by professed cosmopolites like Henry Adams or committed expatriates like Henry James but by local colorists like Irving, who celebrated Old Spain and Merry England as fervently as the Hudson River Valley and the Western fur trade, or peripatetic regionalists like Cooper, who vainly sought to turn from *Leatherstocking* to European romances. It was through the grand tour chronicled in *The Innocents Abroad* that Mark Twain emerged as the humorous voice of America. Most of Hemingway's fiction, which the world accepts as the exemplification

of a strenuous Americanism, takes place on foreign soil. This transatlantic impetus reached its fullest intensity with the artistic movement
that surfaced after the First World War. Its impatient manifesto was
a symposium of thirty intellectuals, edited by Harold Stearns and published in 1922 under the heavily ironic title, *Civilization in the United
States*. Its inevitable break-up, under the economic and political pressure in the Nineteen-Thirties, was indicated twelve years afterward by
Malcolm Cowley in his journalistic memoir, *Exile's Return*.

Meanwhile all sorts and conditions of Americans, doughboys and
playboys, gold-diggers and prophetesses, loners and joiners, business-
men and bums as well as bohemian artists, had been making a continental sojourn, or at least a trip. Merely to list a small handful of titles
and dates would be to suggest at how many levels this had become a
part of the national experience: *Three Soldiers* (1921), *The Enormous
Room* (1922), *Mr. and Mrs. Haddock Abroad* (1924), *Gentlemen
Prefer Blondes* (1925), *The Sun Also Rises* (1926), *Dodsworth* (1929),
Eimi (1933), *The Autobiography of Alice B. Toklas* (1933), *Tender Is
the Night* (1934), *Tropic of Cancer* (1934), *Of Time and the River* (1935),
Nightwood (1936). The point of convergence for these various pilgrim-
ages would be what was then the world's capital of the arts. Someone
has told the hero of the book that lies before us, "You know, dear, all
good Americans go to Paris when they die, and we are dead, as far as
they over there are concerned." To which his interior monologue frames
a reply: "Yes, but are we good?" Having been there twice before, he
clearly realizes that its touted frivolity is "America, not France." For the
serious artist, if not for the *flaneur* of Montparnasse, Paris looks beyond
the pleasure principle—here Freud is echoed in the original German.
On the verge of his return, the pilgrim hails France as the "blessed
home of all wanderers." But he is not at heart a wanderer, any more
than William Carlos Williams himself, who managed to live within a
half-mile of his birthplace for nearly all of his eighty years (1883–
1963).

A Voyage to Pagany is the fictional reminiscence of a rare interlude
during that firmly rooted existence, so much of it devoted to the practice of pediatrics and general medicine in the middle-class community
of Rutherford, New Jersey, not far from the dreary industrial town
whose epic he composed in *Paterson*. The paradox of his career was
strengthened by the mixed strain of his parentage. From his mother,
who seems to have exercised the greater influence on him, he inherited

both Spanish and French blood. His English father, who had traveled widely in Latin America, never gave up British citizenship. Young Bill spent his fifteenth year in Switzerland, in the school at the Château de Lancy near Lake Geneva that he mentions here. During the following year in Paris he was privately tutored, since his French turned out to be inadequate for the Lycée Condorcet. As a medical student at the University of Pennsylvania, he contracted his lifelong friendship with Ezra Pound, then pursuing his graduate studies in Romance languages. Theirs was a complementary relationship, sustained on both sides by personal affection and mutual respect, though they would be moving in opposite directions: Pound abroad on his quest for the spirit of romance, Williams homeward to push his own roots deeper into the soil along the Passaic River. It is not hard to read Williams' position between the lines of Pound's letters over the years; even the burlesque Americanese of the expatriate seems to mock the convictions of the nativist. "You'd better come across and broaden your mind (1909)" has its dialectical counter-thrust in "I note your invitation to return to my fatherland (1917)."

If there is a touch of asperity in that last remark, it is because Pound, with "the virus . . . of nearly three bleating centuries" in his veins, was haughtily retorting to an American of the second generation. "And America! What the hell do you a bloomin' foreigner know about the place?" Williams has not even been west of the Maunchunk (N.J.) switchback. This letter was quoted in the polemical prologue to *Kora in Hell,* where the London expatriates are consigned to Williams' private inferno and Pound is singled out as "the best enemy United States verse has." In a subsequent letter Pound elaborated his clinical metaphor: Williams has avoided the endemic blood-poisoning because he had "the advantage of arriving in the milieu with a fresh flood of Europe in [his] veins." For his own part, from the first, he had criticized Pound's "unconstrained vagabondism." His correspondent, recoiling from the early constraints of Idaho and Indiana, was heading for the center, was putting himself in touch—indeed in command—of what he would later call "a live tradition." The real eccentric was the "dago immigrant" ("Finest possible specimen of course," Pound genially added), since he chose to stay behind and play the "old village cut-up." Williams, scientifically trained, approached his experimental objectives directly, and feared that those bookish courses which Pound pursued and prescribed would lead back to academic conventionality. In any case, the exile recognized that the hyphenated descent of his friend made him an authentic spokesman for the realities of *Patria Mia*, such as they were. From Paris, in 1922, he wrote to Rutherford:

. . . I don't really believe you want to leave the U.S. permanently, I think you are suffering from nerve; that you are really afraid to leave Rutherford. I think you ought to take a year off or a six months' vacation in Europe. I think you are afraid to take it, for fear of destroying some illusions which you think necessary to your illusions. I don't think you ought to leave permanently, your job gives you too real a contact, too valuable to give up.

Williams took up Pound's challenge, arranging a sabbatical leave from his practice. He was busy writing in New York during the last six months of 1923. Thence he and his wife embarked for Europe on January 9, 1924; they would disembark from their homecoming voyage on the twentieth of the following June. He sums it all up in his *Autobiography* as a "magnificent year," and its European itinerary would furnish the framework for *A Voyage to Pagany*. When the book appeared, it would be loyally dedicated to Pound, "the first of us all"—a vernacular counterpart for Eliot's dedication of *The Waste Land* to "*il miglior fabbro.*" But, significantly, *A Voyage to Pagany* did not appear for four years; the immediate consequence of the journey was the renewed commitment of *In the American Grain*. D. H. Lawrence had recently brought out his seminal *Studies in Classic American Literature*, stimulating American writers and critics in their perennial search for a usable past. There was no flag-waving or eagle-screaming in Williams' rediscoveries among the explorers, the settlers, the founding fathers, and other predecessors. Mencken could not have been sharper in attacking "the inevitable Coolidge platform." Williams sometimes waxes apocalyptic, as he looks beyond the blandness of American life to "its—horrible temper," beyond its technological achievement to its "gross know-nothingism," beyond the puritanical inhibition to the lawless violence. From his six weeks in Paris he recalls a congenial dialogue with Valery Larbaud. Though the French had been much more humane than the English to the Indians, their colonies had failed because of their Latin sense of history. America's strength is its break with the past, Europe's weakness.

The Great American Novel—a parody of the genre, like the preliminary efforts of so many novelists—was written just before Williams' *Wanderjahr*, and is more intransigently nationalistic: "Europe's enemy is the past. Our enemy is Europe." *In the American Grain,* coming subsequently, illustrates with historical *collage* and critical commentary "the battle to establish a European life in the New World." Hence it may be read as a sequel to *A Voyage to Pagany,* wherein a copy of it retrospectively figures as "a keepsake." Its final emphasis, on grounds of immediacy rather than patriotism, is "Here not there." But the interaction would continue, prompting Williams to his brief sortie in the wake of Pound, his own exploration of "there," *là-bas,* Pagany. The collective name that he chose for Europe, though it had scarcely been repeated since the sixteenth century, was appropriate for his purposes. Pagans had originally been dwellers in rural villages; the early Christians used the term at Rome for those who still practiced idolatry; more neutrally, a *paganus* was a person who did not share the prevailing beliefs. This relative concept could be reversed, as would be demonstrated in 1930–32 by the publication in Boston of the little magazine, *Pagany: A Native Quarterly,* with Williams as a leading contributor and nativism as its literary program. The novel charts a return, via "old Pagany," to primal forces antedating both Europe and America. The central section, "At the Ancient Springs of Purity and Plenty," seeks to revive a sense of power and beauty through communion with "a resurgent paganism, still untouched." Long obscured by Christianity, and by the Renaissance, the pagan gods survive as stone images in the cathedrals.

In the *Autobiography* Williams speaks of *A Voyage to Pagany* as "my first (limping) novel." Since the junket of a husband and wife would hardly make much of a story, he decided to romanticize his material. In *I Wanted to Write a Poem,* based on a series of interviews with him by Edith Head, he describes the genesis of the book more fully. It was composed at Rutherford as usual, albeit in the absence of Mrs. Williams and their two sons, who were then attending his old Swiss school. A laconic diary from 1924 served to nudge his memory and tap his imagination. "The protagonist was, of course, myself; his experiences, in a measure mine." Thus Dr. Evans, a forty-year-old physician from "the New Jersey town of P. where he was born," and born of immigrant stock, wants more than anything else to be a writer. "Loaded up with Americana—his love of America," he believes that Europe is "turning pagan." Since he is traveling alone, the actual Floss Williams—devoted companion, "the rock on which I have built," whose German-Norwegian parentage balanced her husband's admixture of bloods—has dropped out of the overt picture. Nonetheless, "the women figures in the story were frequently my conception of my wife," Williams confessed. And even more intimately: "There are other women, women the American might have desired to go to bed with, sometimes a woman whose face had registered in my mind, a woman out of the crowd." One of his unconformable sonnets may epitomize Floss's role:

> With one woman
> I find all the rest . . .

On the other hand, few writers can have delivered so many babies, or have acquired so special a feeling for the moods and phases of womanhood. Elsewhere, again in the *Autobiography*, he tells us: "Men have given a direction to my life and women have always supplied the energy." In the novel his surrogate has already determined upon a direction, but the women help him to test the alternatives and confirm his resolution with their respective energies—and with his resistance to them. A study of Williams' groping plays, *Many Loves* and *A Dream of Love*, might throw further light on the relation of his marriage to his fantasies.

If Eros does not personally intervene in the narration, which is so susceptible to her sway, it is because she has been deliberately exorcised. The publisher thought that the manuscript was too long, Williams frankly told his interviewer. Accordingly, the author decided to cut out "the best chapter in the book" and to publish it separately as a short story. It is entitled "The Venus," and would have come at the novel's midpoint.* There the goddess is invoked through the painting of Botticelli and the statue from Cyrene; the invocation is heard as a verbal *Leitmotiv;* but our Tannhäuser has definitely left this particular Venusberg behind. The tale, when we take it up, proves to be slight and poignant. It involves a beautiful blonde German girl who is staying at the same *pensione* with Evans in Rome, "the little *fräulein*," "the Cyprian," with whom in the novel he has no chance to speak. In the story there is a conversation between them, little more, while they wander off from an excursion to the antiquities at Frascati. With Teutonic earnestness she raises the question: "What then is it like, America?" How can he explain what he himself, a kind of refugee, has been

* "The Venus" has been added as an appendix to the New Directions edition.

puzzling over? By contrast, the United States "seems less encumbered with its dead." He can show her a flint arrowhead, and she is momentarily attracted to the notion that Americans are almost savage, "not quite civilized." But the ultimate prospect seems "even more lonesome and frightening . . . than in Germany." Daughter of a Prussian general, resigned to taking her vows and becoming a nun, she too has considered and rejected the alternative world to her own.

Williams returned to the theme in one of his finest poems, "The Birth of Venus," which opens with a nostalgic glimpse of the Parade Grounds at Villefranche—the well-remembered vista from his travels that reappears in both the *Autobiography* and *A Voyage to Pagany*. Now it is too late: "we/are not there." The sensory values of love, though reaffirmed, are harrowed by the negations and deprivations of war. Aphrodite, buried or in exile, has played an elusive part in latterday fiction. Exhumed, she takes a stern revenge on a loveless bridal pair in Mérimée's *Vénus d'Ille*. In the guise of the Venus de Medici she fascinated Hawthorne, who evokes her image to symbolize the underground passions of *The Marble Faun*. One might have expected the antipuritan Williams, in a volume contemporaneous with *Lady Chatterley's Lover*, to have advanced the subject somewhat farther. But if Venus is the personification of that chthonic force which his traveler seeks in Pagany, then it must be said that either she eludes him or else he evades her. She has incarnated the artist's goal: "striving to cut between the show and the fact, . . . undeceiving, living—shedding fig leaves." Williams was once persuaded to hold forth publicly on the novel ("a form I have never respected"). Perhaps his disrespect colored his theories. His appeal to Carlyle's philosophy of clothes was more than metaphorical, since novels have so much to do with external appearances; and, of course, it has been their classic function to expose the actualities beneath. For Williams, however, the novel is little more than "a strip-tease"; only the poem can lay bare the nudity of things.

Figures of speech have their limits, and this one would never do to characterize the works of the major novelists. Yet it might help to distinguish between Williams' poetry, where he plays the realist (his word would be "objectivism" or "contact"), and the present novel, which—as he owned—"turned out to be much more romantic than I'd intended." The novels located on his own terrain, *White Mule* and *In the Money*, like most of his stories, would be unequivocally realistic.

In *A Voyage to Pagany* little is made of the novelistic opportunities for characterization, observation of manners, or human relationships. Its burden is reflective and highly subjective, paying less heed to the impressions it gathers than to the impressionist who blends them in with his thoughts—thoughts on art, in the main, and its interconnection with the two hemispheres. "Florence, city of makers," of artists *par excellence*, inspires a meditation on the banks of the Arno, while the river itself, in continuous self-renewal, seems to be the prototype of art. "Reality, romance: it sums up, to make." All novels have combined the two components in varying proportions; the modicum of romance in *A Voyage to Pagany* stands out rather self-consciously because it has been superimposed upon a spontaneous flow of autobiographical reality. Our identification with the problems and preoccupations of Dev (Dr. Evans-Williams) is all but complete. Evans recounts details which Williams remembered specifically from 1924: for instance, the three smiling Japanese tourists at Notre Dame or the joyous walk from Eze to Monaco. The get-together with the *avantgarde* really happened, and the character of Jack Murry was modeled on the Left Bank impresario, Robert McAlmon.

Williams did not aspire to be a Baedeker, and his topographical descriptions are often impressionistic to the point of distortion. When he calls the Santa Croce a cathedral, he is confusing it with the Duomo, and the confusion is triply confounded when he descries within it the tombs of Dante (buried at Ravenna) and of the Medici (adjoining San Lorenzo). Poet though he be, Dev is equally the compatriot of philistines like Sam Dodsworth, Mr. Haddock, and the excursionists of Mark Twain's *Quaker City*. The Forum leaves him cold; he is homesick in Venice; and when he tries to visit Ferney, "old home of the divine philosopher" (Voltaire), the house is closed and the gates are bolted. Nonetheless, like Gershwin's *American in Paris*, he responds with a peculiar zest to whatever comes within his wave-length. His appreciation of a particularly fastidious sequence of French wines is voiced by an indelibly American exclamation: "Wow!" The beer in Switzerland makes him worry about Prohibition at home. It is not surprising that, during his first night in Paris, he dreams of Walt Whitman. Leaves of grass, he discovers on a picnic by the Seine, can be symbols here as well as there. He is immeasurably more concerned with living humanity than with its historical monuments. At Carcassonne his attention wanders from the uninhabited fortress and its medieval legends to the modern settlement at its base, which is not so far removed from New Jersey after all. "People live here! Good God. And they are happy and they sent soldiers to the great war." People, with the consistent exception of Jews encountered on trains, draw out warm sympathies from him wherever he goes.

This cannot be regarded as a travel book, though it was apparently mistaken for such by its limited body of first readers. And no wonder; for its basic pattern is geographical, framed by arrival and departure and by a haunting sense of the oceanic depths beyond. The succession of settings might almost be Dantesque in their triplicity. The focus of the first section is on Dev's affair with Lou Martin, which seems to have motivated the whole adventure. Its principal locale is the Riviera, and the idyll seems to be more closely associated with the place than with the girl. Since he feels no deep chagrin, we need not, when she leaves him to marry her English tennis partner. Thereafter his motivation broadens and becomes more general: he is traveling to enlarge his view. The second section, proceeding from France to Italy, is the most scenic part of the book—although, in the absence of the blonde Venus, it sadly lacks a heroine. Instead we are faced with Dev's esthetic reflections; instead of dialogue, with his monologue, or rather with the interplay between his mind and the masterworks that interrogate it. Sightseeing can but excite "his lust to make," even as antiquity confirms his resolve "to make—new." The third section passes from art to science, insofar as it concerns Dev's professional interests. Now the scene is principally Vienna, where Williams stopped for instruction, though he transposes some memories of a postgraduate year spent in pediatric studies at Leipzig University in 1910. In his admiration of his medical teachers, he can envisage a reconciliation of the sciences and the arts, of the disinterested pursuit of knowledge and the passionate cult of beauty.

Having rambled among the Italian monuments, the protagonist seats himself in the concert hall or the opera house—or, climactically, the Spanish Riding Academy—to continue his artistic education in Austria. Bach's *Saint Matthew Passion* presents him with the highest model, along with the realization that "Art kills time." Here the long-drawn-out message of Proust is condensed into three terse monosyllables, carrying a latent ambiguity: is art merely a pastime or does it confer immortality? A talk among medical colleagues, reflecting back the less permissive sexual attitudes in the States, recalls the exposure of Viennese puritanism that Shakespeare dramatized in *Measure for Measure*. Dev finds a musical mentor, as well as a mistress, in the American bluestocking, Grace Black. While they stroll along the Danube, it is she who voices the sharpest counterstatement against the homeland: its childish athleticism, its materialistic technology, the "political flimflam" of its democracy. Since the lovers are so divided by their cultural allegiances, they have no choice but to part. Heading for France again, Dev joins his sister Bess *en route*. We already know, from an earlier discussion, that she hates America even more than Grace does. Now, as they picnic by the Seine, she too pleads with him to stay in Europe, to quit his job and study it out. "Like Eliot?" he asks, and she answers: "Who is Eliot? Like nobody." Rather than perform his "aesthetic duty to the Stars and Stripes," she would have him settle down with her and learn the secrets of life and art from the French. But he has seen the handwriting on the wall and read his own destiny in it. "Art," he has discovered, "is a country by itself."

Williams declared that the episode of the picnic had been suggested to him by the example of the expatriate brother and sister, the writer Lawrence Vail and the singer Clotilde. Into his fictitious account of the situation he has injected a hint of incest, orchestrated to a theme which re-echoes from a performance of *Die Walküre*, where the Wagnerian siblings join together in the procreation of Siegfried. *"Bruder! Schwester!"* This association would seem to imply that it would be a decadent gesture for Dev to settle down with his "Seine Sister." But the implication is treated symbolically rather than psychologically; Williams' characteristic vein is innocence rather than decadence; Dev and Bess would simply be reverting to their childhood. It was for Thomas Mann to make the most of the same sinister *Leitmotiv* in his "Blood of the Volsungs." Dev's three American women, then, remain in Europe. His most appealing heroine, the German Venus, has escaped from the novel, and the short story about her is a parable in which there can be no meeting between two minds or two worlds. The cycle is revivified by the ending, which is likewise a beginning as with Joyce and Eliot, when Dev catches sight of the Nantucket Lightship. Behind him lie the Seine, the Arno, and the Danube; ahead, once more and forever, the Passaic. It is easy to understand why the author should testify, while admitting freely its imperfections, that "*A Voyage to Pagany* was important to me in my education as a writer." He has told us something about its only previous publication in a modest edition by the Macauley Company of Passaic, N.J., with a jacket designed by his architect brother: " 'The Worm' encircling the world."

Williams regretted the neglect of his book, and hoped to see it reprinted some day. He felt it to be the most lyrical and descriptive of his prose writings, possibly because of its—for him—exotic subject matter. Not that he had been conducting a travelogue or exploiting the picturesqueness of the scenery. The distance he keeps may be gauged by his uncertain handling of foreign names and phrases. This is far less important than the fact that he remains his unaffected self, that he so manifestly wrote to please himself. He was interested not in making an impression but in registering an impact. Though he said that Dr. Evans represented him "as a person—not as a writer," the two are finally inseparable. When he tells us that Evans "was a man who enjoyed writing," he is obviously telling us about Williams. "He wrote because he loved it and he wrote eagerly, to be doing well something which he had a taste for, and for this only did he write." His boyish zest, his wide-eyed openness, and his spontaneous energy made him an especially responsive witness to the American-European encounter. Looking back upon *A Voyage to Pagany*, Williams wondered whether it might conceivably have been influenced by Henry James, who was never one of his favorites. He need not have worried, for we cannot imagine Dev getting into one of those dark entanglements that seduced Roderick Hudson and menaced Christopher Newman. There may be some resemblance to Lambert Strether in the belated curiosity for finding out what one may have missed by living in Woollett rather than Paris. But no Jamesian personage would have made the westward crossing so happily, or found so much that was genuinely poetic in the American scene.

LETTERS OF A WRITER'S WRITER: CONRAD AIKEN

In one of those top-of-the-head questionnaires, the editors of Esquire *had asked a number of people to name both the most overrated and the most underrated American writers of this century. My choice for the former position is currently so much discussed and admired that I see no reason for mentioning him in this context. But Aiken has had such chary recognition, during his lifetime and beyond, that he seemed to me an appropriate nominee in the latter category. When his* Selected Letters *were published shortly thereafter, edited by Joseph Killorin (New Haven: Yale University Press), I was challenged to justify my suggestion by the* Saturday Review *(May 27, 1978). Later I learned from an encounter with the editor of the letters that he was not to blame for the hiatus in material from Aiken's college days: little or nothing of it had survived. Moreover I was pleased to learn that, in response to such criticisms as are voiced here, the publishers had agreed to bring out an additional volume.*

•

Conrad Aiken's position among our writers was an odd one, as he wryly and repeatedly had reason to observe. "In the Pegasus Sweepstakes . . . ," he once put it, "this dubious horse has always been the last in the list of the also-ran." Gradually accepted though rarely acclaimed, and yet always very highly esteemed by his peers, he ultimately won a few of those laurels which compensate for survival if not for achievement. His long and productive development was shy and uneventful, except for—or rather because of—its horrendous beginning. At the age of eleven, he had heard two shots in his parents' bedroom, and rushed in to stumble upon their dead bodies. A transplanted New Englander born in Savannah, Georgia, he completed his "great circle" and made his "eternal return" when he died there at eighty-four in 1973, "back in utero." Depressed in mid-career between the second and the third of his three marriages, he attempted suicide. Happily resurrected, he embarked upon "a posthumous life" which lasted more than forty fruitful years. It is typical of him that, when he left the mental hospital, he went to give aid and comfort to his suicidal fellow poet, John Gould Fletcher.

Voyaging is a continuous *Leitmotiv:* in his first and best novel, *Blue Voyage,* in his nonfiction novel or fictional autobiography, *Ushant,* in his arresting story and play, "Mr. Articularis," and so often in his poetic imagery. Homeless in the parental sense, he oscillated between his ancestral Massachusetts (New Bedford, Cambridge, Cape Cod) and the late Henry James's eyrie on the English Channel, Rye. He was wary of expatriation, and he had little desire or aptitude for mingling, but he felt that abroad he was freer to realize his own potentialities. "England would be so nice if it was inhabited by Americans!" (How an Englishman would have cherished that thought!) In America he preferred Boston to New York as a base of operations, and he steered clear of "the literary crowd," though he had many individual friendships. More and more he thought that poets were to be avoided: "They really stink. Especially in large numbers, when herding." He was consistently independent from the movements with which he was vaguely associated. "Must we share all of Mr. Pound's growing pains with him, page by page?" he asked *Poetry* magazine in 1913. He expressed second thoughts about Imagism to Harriet Monroe, and expounded the merits of rhyme and meter to F. S. Flint.

A forthcoming bibliography will show both the wide range and the sustained continuity of his writing. It did not gain him a living; poetry seldom does that for anyone; but he worked hard to make ends meet with fiction, continual reviewing, potboiling for the W.P.A. in the Roosevelt period, taking apprentice writers as paying guests—even at one point having to sell his first editions. Characteristically, one of his stories best known today, "Silent Snow, Secret Snow," was aimed at *Harper's* for $375 and finally placed in *The Virginia Quarterly* for $75. Ruefully he complained to his editor at Scribner's, Maxwell Perkins; but Aiken, despite the subtle psychology of his lyrical novels, was not a Fitzgerald, a Hemingway, or a Wolfe. During two years spent as poet in residence at the Library of Congress, he was uncomfortable amidst the bureaucracy. Nor could he find a haven for his restlessness in the Academy. His lifelong reluctance to appear in public had led him to drop out of Harvard College shortly before his commencement, rather than compose and read aloud a poem for that occasion. Later on he tutored at his Alma Mater for a single year, and—later still—refused an honorary degree from his former student, subsequently President Nathan Pusey.

The hard-won privacy of his career lent strength to his artistic integrity. Thus he withdrew from a projected journal because, for shrewdly opportunistic reasons, Robert Frost wanted the editorial board to include the entrepreneurial anthologist, Louis Untermeyer. When Random House self-righteously refused to reprint the section from Ezra Pound in Aiken's own anthology (one of his few publications that drew decent royalties), his objections were unappeased by a publisher's note stating that the excisions had been made against his judgment. Given his aloof mode of existence, correspondence took on a special importance for him and his friends. In it he is predominantly warm and genial, often playful if sometimes depressed, salting the discourse with occasionally ribald humor, lively doggerel (including a sardonic parody of *The Waste Land*), and joshing colloquialism (somewhat like Pound's but friendlier in tone). Generally speaking, it might be noted that the style is more spontaneous when he is addressing such correspondents as the publisher Robert Linscott, the bookseller Maurice Firuski, the composer Walter Piston, and the psychologist Henry Murray. With professional men of letters he tends to be more guarded.

This was peculiarly true in his relations with T. S. Eliot, whose lengthening image so overshadowed Aiken's. Their careers had run parallel since their days at Harvard, where Eliot was one year Aiken's senior. Each of them, independently it seems, had totally changed his initial conception of poetry after picking up a copy of Arthur Symons' book on the Symbolist Movement then in the library of the student union. Aiken's earliest poems had been realistic narratives in the Edwardian manner of John Masefield. Aiken himself was first to appreciate the ironic new style of "Prufrock," and instrumental in recommending it to Pound for publication. But his own "Senlin" appeared not very much later than "Prufrock," and earlier than Pound's "Mauberley," while Eliot's late *Quartets*—like some of Wallace Stevens' meditations—have qualities previously cultivated by Aiken in his "verbal symphonies." Though he and Stevens were never intimate—Stevens being another kind of private man—their admiration was mutual. The older poet credited Aiken with having stimulated him to resume his writing a decade after *Harmonium*. Aiken's comment upon that first volume was prescient: "I think him as sure of a permanent place as Eliot, if not surer."

Stevens, in his epoch of recognition, would deplore the limited amount of it that Aiken had received. So would Eliot, who considered him "equally gifted" with himself, and expressed regret at the critics' neglect. Yet, despite their stylistic similarities, Eliot had the flair for catching attention. Aiken was as musical and evocative, but less incisive or quotable. With the ascendancy of Eliot, he felt that their relationship had become increasingly one-sided: there was something in it of Melville's warmth and Hawthorne's coldness. He was deeply offended when Eliot, the "Tsetse" of *Ushant*, responded to a generous fan letter with a crude joke. Moreover, Aiken raised his eyebrows over "the Great Retreat," Eliot's submission to orthodoxies, "with its smell of mummy and exhaustion." He regarded himself as "a cheerful pessimist," taking a biological view of nature and an interest in psychoanalysis—an interest returned by Freud, who was impressed with *Blue Voyage*. Not for nothing was his book of essays called *Scepticisms*. He was not much interested in politics, though he applauded Kennedy and deplored Nixon. Above all he hated war, and was proud to be exempted from the draft on the grounds—doubted by his philistine brother—that poetry was work.

The publication of his letters is welcome indeed, though the present edition can only be taken as a mere sampling. Almost 3,500 were available, according to the editor, a Savannah professor of literature who is preparing a biography. Out of these he has selected 245—less than fifteen percent. The odds become problematic when he tells us that "Of those unpublished at least a thousand are as interesting as those included," inasmuch as the amateurish editing, the minimal commentary, and the inadequate identification of names do not reinforce our confidence in his capacity for selection. From Aiken's critical college years, for example, there is nothing except a letter about a European vacation. On the other hand, it must be said that nearly everything printed here whets our appetite for more. Via the preoccupation with his own psychology, the connections between Aiken's life and work were unusually close; and these letters, along with *Ushant*, reveal that linkage. One of them, in response to questions arising from Jay Martin's doctoral research, explicitly distinguishes the "autobiographical element" from the invention in his fiction. But another admonishes the young scholar to allow more leeway for the processes of imagination and language.

As a younger poet he had criticized the "lack of human warmth" in current poetry, but had likewise called for a "psychic distance" from bare actuality. At the crisis of his mid-career, he already felt *vieux jeu;* his high poetic ambitions were unnerved by feelings of "self-distrust and self-disgust." Had he "somehow missed the way?" Or were his contemporaries trying to be "too contemporary?" As for his juniors, well, he had caustic words for "W. H. Whoreden," whom he personally professed to like and respect, but whose influence he considered "lethal." He himself was more than once the victim of Randall Jarrell's assaults, and he protested against them as displays of "malicious preciosity and highbrow autointoxication." Aiken was—among so many other things—one of the most perceptive critics of his time, and his criticism includes three modest and candid reviews of his own books. He drew comfort—more than he should have needed—from the praise they had been accorded by Marianne Moore and Graham Greene. His very last letter, dictated from his deathbed, was a note to a high school student. The boy had written to express his liking for a poem of Aiken's reprinted in a textbook and skipped over by the teacher.

No, I don't have any great notion about where I stand as a poet. That will be taken care of by those wiser people who come later on the scene than we do. Thus, as in their turn, those opinions too will be revalued over and over. None of us knows in what direction poetry and those other arts will turn—that's part of the cruel fascination of being interested in the arts as you are, and keeping your head about it.

Posterity not only sorts out the major and minor figures; it realigns them as it revolves. Aiken's muted success, he suggested philosophically, might "make a very entertaining study in the dynamics of a reputation—and how unlike Tom Eliot's." Unlike Emily Dickinson's too, since she wrote without thought of readers. Aiken could agonize over or gossip about the literary stockmarket, yet he stuck undistractedly to his self-elected and ill-rewarded vocation. He was so punctilious with regard to such traffic that, when Amy Lowell died (herself the high priestess of coteries), he tried vainly to withdraw his unfavorable review of her *John Keats*. It is touching to get a glimpse of him in the company of that even more reticent writer, E. A. Robinson, trading quips with whores on an English pub-crawl. With Malcolm Lowry, who might have fitted more expectably into a setting of this sort, Aiken's difficult role was that of chosen mentor and authorized guardian, bringing out his disciple's talents while gently but firmly curbing his escapades. Furthermore, it may well be one of the ironies divulged by Eliot's forthcoming *Letters* that, before he met Pound, he had counted most upon Aiken for advice, indeed had looked on him as *"il miglior fabbro."*

A LITERARY ENORMITY:
SARTRE ON FLAUBERT

This review-article—perhaps it could be termed a counter-polemic—made its original appearance in The Journal of the History of Ideas (*October-November 1972*). *It was occasioned by the first two volumes of* L'Idiot de la famille: Gustave Flaubert de 1821 à 1857 (*Paris: Gallimard, 1971; 2,136 pages*). *A third volume, which I have not read but had scarcely expected to avert, did appear in 1972 (665 pages). There has been no translation thus far. Presumably this enterprise would have continued well beyond that point, but for the silence imposed upon the author by the onset of blindness. I hope one may, while retaining the kind of literary reservations here expressed, sincerely regret the recent loss of his courageous voice in formulating timely social problems and dramatizing perdurable moral issues.*

●

It is recollected of Mr. Dick, the amiable but addled friend of David Copperfield, that somehow King Charles's head kept turning up in everything he wrote. Those who have followed Jean-Paul Sartre's career, through its prolific turns and dramatic stands, will have no hesitation in recognizing that his King Charles's head has been Gustave Flaubert. In the critical manifesto *Qu'est-ce que la littérature?*, where Richard Wright was proposed as a role-model for the novelist *engagé*, Flaubert was dismissed as *"un rentier de talent,"* and his detachment was blamed for the repression of the Paris Commune. (Flaubert himself blamed the events of 1870–71 on a general failure to comprehend his *Education sentimentale*.) In spite of such dismissals and occasional sideswipes, Sartre has returned to Flaubert in his current philosophical work, *Critique de la raison dialectique I*, with a long excursus and the promise of an ultimate full-length treatment. Meanwhile he had published an "existential psychoanalysis" of Baudelaire, wherein he reduced the poet to his weaknesses—in the evaluation of Richard Ellmann, who himself has taken such rewarding pains to discriminate the complexities in the life and art of James Joyce. Furthermore, the introductory volume to a collected edition of Jean Genet has given

Sartre the opportunity to make out his inflationary and paradoxical case, *Saint Genet, comédien et martyr*. It is ironic that he should now be referring to the leading Flaubertian scholar of the last generation, René Dumesnil, a physician who has sometimes been quite clinical in his diagnosis of his author, as Flaubert's *hagiographe*. Genet's hagiographer, as a literary critic, has invariably chosen his subject with an eye to grinding some axe of his own. This, then, marks the fulfillment of a lifelong vendetta, and is as dedicated a hatchet-job as can be encountered among the curiosities of literature.

How much can we know about a human being today? That is the problem which Sartre tells us he has set for himself. Against his eclectic backgrounds in existentialism and phenomenology, he proposes to utilize the more concrete approaches of Freud and Marx and, out of this compounded revisionism, to devise a newer and more personal anthropology. To study a case history in such totality, if it happens to be that of a writer, is to establish the precise relations between his life and his work—and thereby to perfect a method of inquiry which, so it is claimed, has broken down since the efforts of Sainte-Beuve. *"Que savons-nous—par exemple—de Gustave Flaubert?"* Of whom else would Sartre be inquiring? That *par exemple* would be disingenuous, were it not so eagerly self-revealing. The choice is justified by the objective statement that, as creator of the modern novel, Flaubert stands *"au carrefour de tous nos problèmes littéraires d'aujourd'hui."* More candidly, Sartre likewise admits that he has long had a score to settle in the present quarter; but, over the years of rereading and reconsideration, his earlier antipathy has been converted to empathy. As a sometime student of German esthetics, he must be well aware that *Einfühlung*—the projection of one's own emotions into one's object of contemplation—offers a highly subjective basis for criticism. If Victor Hugo really was a madman who happened to think he was Victor Hugo, as Jean Cocteau once suggested, then possibly we are dealing here with an obsessive who has convinced himself that he is Flaubert. At all events, now that Flaubert may count Sartre among his friends, he no longer has any need for an enemy. And if he were seeking a *mot juste* for the occasion, he might repeat a favorite adjective, *énorme*, which expresses both grandiosity and outrage when his letters touch on happenings that go beyond all normal bounds.

It is hard to believe that the effectual substance of these two enormous volumes could not have been trenchantly imparted by a few provocative essays in revaluation. Yet Sartre can unself-consciously quote, in a discussion of style (not, of course, his own), Pascal's remark about lacking the time to make his writing shorter. The inordinate number of Sartre's pages hardly gives due measure to the scale he works upon, since they are so very much larger and more crowded than those in the standard Gallimard edition of his other books. The titular dates are also misleadingly broad, for the chronological sequence barely carries Flaubert to within a decade of 1857, the date of his emergence as a writer with *Madame Bovary*. And though a "progressive-regressive method" allows Sartre to anticipate such episodes as the lovers' rendezvous in the carriage, other matters are frequently postponed for consideration in some future volume. However, there is more wordage to this mere beginning than to the whole of Flaubert's publications during his lifetime. Moreover, I suspect, a word-count would show that Leon Edel's five volumes have observed a stricter economy in narrating the seventy-three years of Henry James's biography. Not only in the richness of documentation and in the artistry of organization but in the handling of psychological inference, any comparison with Edel would show up Sartre as an ineptly amateurish biographer. *L'Idiot de la famille* makes use of its bulky proportions not for thoroughness of detail nor for refinement of shading, but in order to thicken a crude and obvious outline with redundancies and repetitions. Sartre is always the impassioned moralist, never the disinterested observer; hence his mode of analysis is not psychology but casuistry; he is less concerned to canvass the facts or to understand the situation than to pass dogmatic and facile judgments on human behavior at large.

His biographical reinterpretations, though they are not strikingly novel, come rather closer to twentieth-century literature than to nineteenth-century social history. To be sure, he has surprised us with a sympathetic account of his own childhood in *Les Mots;* but his domestic principles have more generally accorded with Gide's early watchword, *"Familles, je vous hais!"* Flaubert, on the other hand, is well known to have been a devoted son, and a recent memoir by Lucie Chevalley-Sabatier corroborates the record of his devotion as the bachelor uncle of an orphan niece. The pattern of the hypersensitive son all but crushed by a dominating father has been etched in the consciousness of our time by Kafka. Sartre cites *Die Verwandlung* as if it were evidence, and superimposes the image of Gregor Samsa on Gustave Flaubert. Now, if the Oedipal urge is as universal as Freudianism would have it, then it offers no particular grounds for distinguishing one man's motivation from another's. Writers as different as Sophocles and Seneca, Shakespeare and Dostoevsky, Synge and Camus, Thomas Mann and Robert Penn Warren, all have paid their respects to the theme of parricide. Since Flaubert belatedly did so too in *La Légende de saint Julien l'hospitalier,* Sartre makes much of that traditional tale, calling it Flaubert's swan song but insisting that it would have been exactly the same if it had been written thirty years before. Flaubert's own affectionate tribute to his father, in the posthumous *Souvenirs, notes, pensées intimes,* is conveniently overlooked. Sartre defers the question of Dr. Larivière, one of the few admiring portraits in *Madame Bovary,* which is commonly identified with the elder Flaubert. Yet he goes out of his way to identify the latter with the arch-philistine M. Homais, perhaps forgetting that Homais is put down by a contemptuous remark from Larivière.

Sartre's reductive thesis casts Dr. Flaubert, the distinguished director of the municipal hospital at Rouen, in a part which combines the ignoble traits of the *arriviste,* the professional, the bourgeois, and worst of all the paterfamilias, *"le Géniteur."* He rules his grim household with a kind of "private Stalinism," and satisfies his exigent ambition by bringing his older son up to be his medical successor. Gustave, the younger, was indeed slow to learn his letters; and on this small figment of truth, generally regarded as a paradox, Sartre has constructed a monument of unattested hypotheses, serving to advance his formula: *"un idiot qui devient génie."* The eyebrow-raising title is supposed to define Flaubert's relationship with his family. But how did this far-fetched phrase ever get applied? Sartre can back his own surmise with nothing stronger than a vague subjunctive guess: *"Il faut qu'on ait plus ou moins déclaré à Gustave: tu es l'idiot de la famille."* Ultimately it will be asserted that Shakespeare's (or, rather, Macbeth's) view of life as "a tale / Told by an idiot, full of sound and fury," would be the last word for Flaubert. For Faulkner's Benjy, yes, but for the author of *La Tentation de saint Antoine?* The so-called *hébétude* of Flaubert's schooldays is further molded to Sartre's preconceptions. Parents and teachers are imagined saying, on no authority whatsoever, *"Fais comme ton frère, Gustave!"* The records seem to indicate that this problematic schoolboy won fairly good grades and even prizes. *"C'est formellement vrai,"* concedes Sartre, *"mais con-*

tredit par le témoignage de Gustave lui-même qui se dit, dans les Mémoires . . ." In the name of veracity, what memoirs? Here an appeal has been made from fact to fiction—to a youthful story whose unabridged title, *Mémoires d'un fou,* would give an explicit indication that the narrative spokesman is not Flaubert himself but a heavily romanticized *persona.*

The inferiority complex that Sartre labors to instil in his victim retroactively is belied by the conscious precocity of Flaubert's juvenilia, which will be employed to strain the argument in another direction. A basic conflict is located between two ideologies, his father's scientism and his mother's faith. Actually Madame Flaubert was not much more of a believer than her rationalistic husband, and their son worked his way through a religion of art toward belief in a Spinozistic pantheism. From a childish manifestation of interest in theatricals—and from the sort of testimony that abounds in other childhoods, such as that of Dickens—Sartre infers that Flaubert wanted to be a comedian. Undoubtedly he wanted to write comedies for the stage; unhappily he never relinquished that hope; and that preoccupation fits in well with the antipaternal bias, since Molière was a notable hater of doctors. Through Gustave's humiliating position at home and at school, he was forced into buffoonery; gradually he turned from defense to aggression, from the butt Sganarelle to the mocker Scapin; and somewhere along the way he evolved the monstrous figure of *Le Garçon,* who led him into the comic nihilism of *Bouvard et Pécuchet.* Only when his parents frustrated his histrionic vocation, it is argued, did he turn to literature as a *pis aller.* The responsible profession they held out to him was the law, at which he proceeded to dawdle and fail. The roadside seizure that overtook him soon afterward, the crisis of his career, has been alternately diagnosed as epileptic or hysterical. Treating it as a psychosomatic gesture, which made possible his semiretirement, Sartre is not greatly at variance with the accepted trend of interpretation. More mystically, he conceives this fall as a symbolic death, and credits Flaubert with having successfully willed a final release through his father's impending death.

Sartre likes to theorize about methodology, but in practice everything yields to sheer verbal barrage. Lacking direct access to his subject's infancy, it is admitted, *"le biographe bâtit sur le sable,"* and his materials can be obfuscating as well as insubstantial: *"il construit sur la brume avec du brouillard."* The *Correspondance,* which so richly illuminates Flaubert's maturity, is sporadic during his adolescence. No matter; for the adolescent was wildly engaged in writing stories; and it is to the *Oeuvres de jeunesse* that Sartre has turned for autobiographical documents. If these were macabre, melodramatic, and exotic in tone, if they dwelt on madness, suicide, and crimes of passion, they did no more than reflect the romantic conventions of their day. All over France bright schoolboys were indulging in similar exercises, as Louis Maigron once demonstrated in *Le Romantisme et les moeurs*. More recently, in *Les Débuts littéraires de Gustave Flaubert, 1831–1845*, Jean Bruneau succeeded in tracing those derivative tales to their conventional sources. But, though his authoritative study was available to Sartre, he discounts it whenever he finds a theme that can be connected with what he is looking for in the personality of Flaubert: the patricide of *L'Anneau du prieur*, the fratricide of *La Peste à Florence*, the extermination of a whole family in *Passion et vertu*. Flaubert *père* must be the moribund protagonist of *Les Funerailles du docteur Mathurin*, in spite of the proved French influence of the Anglo-Irish Gothic novelist Maturin. Distrusting the sincerity of Flaubert in the first person, Sartre hears his authentic voice from the Faustian Smarh and a motley succession of heroes and heroines. At one point we are characteristically told to abandon the correspondence, since it constitutes *"un discours aux autres,"* and to reread the early novel *Novembre*, because it is *"le discours que s'adresse à lui-même."*

This might be summed up as *vie romancée* with a vengeance (and Sartre applies the same *reductio ad hominem*, in a lengthy digression, to the admittedly talentless compositions of Flaubert's short-lived friend, Alfred Le Poittevin). A typical description presents Dr. Flaubert exasperated by his vain endeavors to teach Gustave the alphabet. Sartre anticipates the reader's curiosity: *"On demandera comment je sais tout cela. En bien, j'ai lu Flaubert . . ."* What he has read in *Un Parfum à sentir*, another of those *contes noirs*, is a passage where an acrobat teaches his son a stern lesson in walking a tightrope. Using a writer's work to interpret his life becomes a particularly circular procedure, when one begins by reading into the work a prior speculation as to the life. Now and then Sartre is willing to label his view a conjecture, as when he suggests that, though Louis Bouilhet was Flaubert's closest companion in middle years, they were not on friendly terms at school. That suggestion is controverted by the protest that Bouilhet signed when Flaubert was about to be expelled, as well as by the retrospective preface that Flaubert contributed to Bouilhet's *Dernières Chansons*. All too often the critic, in the absence of adequate testimony, reads minds and invents quotations freely. Phrases like *il va de soi* . . . , or less confidently *qui sait si* . . . , or frankly *j'imagine* . . . strive to validate the hypothetical. Sentences may run to more than 250 words, paragraphs to as many as five pages. As if to sharpen the antithesis between himself and the master stylist he is confronting, Sartre pushes language to a rebarbative extreme. His torrential rhetoric is slowed down by his hypertrophied vocabulary. The opacity of his Latinate neologisms seems to outdo the jargon he has gleaned from German metaphysics. To echo a habitual example: *"la totalisation est intériorisée."*

Since there is so much talk about "totalizing," since the professed intent is to marshal all the pertinent information, it should be pointed out that Sartre makes very limited use of Flaubertian scholarship. Predictably he takes no notice of the significant studies in other languages than French, notably the well-documented biography by the American B. F. Bart. English being one of Sartre's blind spots, he refers to Defoe as "Foe" and claims to have learned from Marx that Milton *"produisait ses poèmes comme un oiseau produit son chant."* Knowing Milton at first hand, as Sartre clearly does not, Marx would never have characterized the poet so inappropriately. What he said, in discussing motives for production, financial or otherwise, was that Milton produced his poems as a silkworm produces silk. A footnote mentions "Sterkie"—evidently the late Enid Starkie, whose biography has been translated into French—and takes her to task for interpreting a newly discovered letter from Flaubert to Bouilhet as a testimonial to a homosexual relation. Skepticism would seem to be warranted here; and the evaluation of Flaubert's sexuality seems plausible enough, emphasizing as it does passivity, somewhat androgynous sensibilities, and an attraction to maternal types. But these implications of temperamental weakness, at least as apprehended from a strongly masculine point of view, are exploited to support the notion that Flaubert was incapable of will power and that literature was for him "a passive activity." In a lugubrious jingle, *névrose* is equated with *nécrose;* arrested development is seen as the precondition for everything else; and the consummation of art is a form of living death. In other words, the political activist has been spelling out an elaborate rationalization of the positions he has been taking against the esthetic recluse all along.

In consequence, we learn much less about Flaubert than we do about Sartre. When the latter accuses the former of not being sufficiently aggressive in his reading, the accusation throws a ray of light back against itself. Sartre's attempt to read over Flaubert's shoulder as it were, to go over his homework with a blue pencil and clarify his slightly confused impressions of *King Lear,* ends by heavy-handedly confounding the confusion. Flaubert, the clown *manqué,* possessed neither wit nor a sense of irony, according to Sartre, whose conception of laughter is based on derision, stressing hostility at the expense of play. His tendency to be literal about *façons de parler,* to take the black humor of the letters more seriously than may have been intended, is a continual source of misunderstanding. But comedy, for him, is basically unreal: *"rien n'est réel qui ne soit sérieux, rien n'est sérieux que ne soit réel."* And who, if not an existentialist, has the right to define reality in his own terms? Ever since his earliest philosophical treatise, *L'Imaginaire,* Sartre has held the imagination in almost Pascalian suspicion. The fundamental charge against Flaubert is that, escaping from reality into fantasy, he *"réalise la déréalisation du réel."* What does this word-play mean, if not that he succumbed to that very romanticism from which—in his own intention and in the world's estimation heretofore—he escaped with some success? *Madame Bovary* is yet to be surpassed in its exposure of romantic vagaries, as is *Bouvard et Pécuchet* in its satire upon the bourgeois mentality. And it is curious that, drawing so uncritically on Flaubert's juvenile phantasmagoria, Sartre pays so little attention to those mature works of realistic fiction which are known to have tapped a vein of intimate reminiscence, especially *Un Coeur simple* and the second *Education sentimentale.*

Sartre does acknowledge, though he does not begin to explain, that there has been, or might be, such an event as a "Flaubertian revolution." This is grounded in a critical attitude toward the language itself, and it can be formulated as *"le principe de la non-communicabilité du vécu."* It can make itself felt by exposing the inadequacy of attempts to communicate the stuff of experience, even as a way of life was exposed when romance was tested by Don Quixote empirically. Elsewhere I have ventured to term that process "the Quixotic principle"; and, since each generation must liberate itself from the presuppositions it has inherited, Flaubert was no less revolutionary than his forerunner Cervantes, with whose outlook he warmly sympathized. Just as the Spaniard had vainly practiced most of the artificial forms in vogue at the time, so the Frenchman had scrawled the extravagant fictions of his nonage; and *Don Quixote* was an exorcism for the one, as was *Madame Bovary* for the other. In both instances, the novelist developed by recoiling from his apprentice-work—which, though it is worth reconsidering as a primary stage of development, holds no key to his enlarged apprehension. All that can be found out should be welcome, when it elucidates the creation of masterworks. So, when Taine was writing *De l'intelligence,* he interrogated Flaubert as to the imaginative impetus that had prompted *Madame Bovary.* Theodor Reik, pioneering sixty years ago, devoted a psychoanalytic monograph to *Flaubert und seine "Versuchung des heiligen Antonius": Ein Beitrag zur Künstlerpsychologie.* Flaubert was far from being a man of action like Luther or Gandhi, the crises of whose careers have been recounted so dramatically by Erik Erikson. Insofar as we judge by a Flaubertian esthetic, we accept the impersonal and self-effacing role to which the artist assigned himself.

Yet, insofar as we have been taken into his confidence through his letters, and into his workshop through his manuscripts, he has revealed to us an object-lesson which we are bound to study for better or worse. For better, for integrity and perfectionism, his admirers have viewed him as a secular saint committed to an artistic martyrdom, a fastidious upholder of jeopardized values, a latterday mandarin in a world of encroaching semiliteracy. Now, after having canonized the martyr Genet, the Sartrian dialectic goes on to assume the worst of Flaubert, viewing him as the composite product of those ignobilities against which he exhausted all his gifts and energies in protesting. As a *tour de force* of devil's advocacy, *L'Idiot de la famille* is a not illogical successor to Flaubert's *Tentation de saint Antoine* and Sartre's *Diable et le bon Dieu.* Unremittingly, like the devil himself, it nags and sneers, it debases and trivializes whatever it touches. One is truly at a loss to imagine whom it will convince, since the reader who knows what it takes for granted is likely to know better, or when it will end, if ever—*Les Chemins de la liberté* never did. Justice would collaborate with mercy if the monument were halted at this substructural phase. But, though it closely depends on minor writings of Flaubert still untranslated into English, a complete translation of the book itself has already been announced, bravely disregarding the Anglo-American fate of *L'Etre et le néant,* which has carried more weight to remainder counters than to departments of philosophy. It would be gratuitous, under the circumstances, to deplore the characteristic absence of an index. If *Madame Bovary* is an *anti-roman* (and Sorel used the term three centuries before Sartre), then Sartre himself is an *anti-romancier* and his critique of Flaubert is a furious and infuriating assault on nothing less than literature itself.

34 RUE LHOMOND:
FRANCIS PONGE

This is a testimonial not only to the gifts of a highly original poet, whom I should have admired at a distance had we not been brought closer, but also to the cultural mobility of our time, which has so extended the range and the serendipity of literary friendship. When the biennial award of the Books Abroad/Neustadt International Prize for Literature *to Francis Ponge was celebrated by* Books Abroad (Autumn 1974), *the editor and animator of the celebration, Ivar Ivask, suggested that I contribute this informal note of personal reminiscence.*

•

Can it really have been all of twenty-one years since we became acquainted? Yes, in sober fact, plus a few months more. As it happened, I was a professor on exchange from Harvard to the Sorbonne, looking for quarters in Paris at a time when they were scarce. The apartment that turned up was rather crowded for the three of us: my wife, our eleven-year-old daughter, and myself. It constituted most of the cement-floored *rez-de-chaussée* of a small and shored-up building which dated from the fifteenth century, and indeed had been condemned to be torn down almost forty years before. It faced toward a pleasant courtyard and away from the street, which was aptly named— as I was to realize—for an eighteenth-century grammarian, the Abbé Lhomond. One direction led there from official Paris: the *grandes écoles,* the Pantheon, the University. The other dipped down into the winding market of the Rue Mouffetard, and into the very oldest part of the city, with its Roman arena and other ruins. Across our corner ran the Rue du Pot-de-Fer, where the language heard was Arabic. Near the head of the street was the Ecole Normale, and at that conjunction two *clochards* slept regularly over a Métro grating. Our distinguished neighbor, when we got to know him, proved to be a proud and knowledgeable guide to his *quartier*. Here if anywhere was the ancient Lutetia, he liked to point out, as well as the medieval Latin Quarter that harbored François Villon. Jean Valjean had once escaped

145

from Inspector Javert by climbing over the convent wall across the street, and a stone's throw away was the *pension* where Eugène de Rastignac had met Père Goriot.

We were determined to put up with the constriction because we were attracted by the location, and because we did not have much choice. But we had no conception in advance of the luminously silver lining that lay behind our little cloud, until at the booth of the *concierge* we glimpsed the name of our fellow tenant and at certain times the exquisite politeness of his person. The name was not, of course, unknown to me. Francis Ponge's reputation had crystallized during the Second World War, with *Le Parti pris des choses.* As between French and Anglo-American poetry, there has been a fruitful cycle of interaction: i.e., Poe-Baudelaire-Laforgue-Eliot. Ponge, although completely original, struck a note which was evoked in English a generation earlier by Pound, by T. E. Hulme, by the Imagists, and by the red wheelbarrow of William Carlos Williams—generally speaking, by a rededication to visual perceptiveness and verbal exactitude. My own long correspondence with Marianne Moore over her translation of La Fontaine had greatly sharpened my appreciation of this modern poet who has been called *"le La Fontaine des choses."* Neglected in his youth, he was being hailed in his middle years as a fellow existentialist by Sartre and Camus. Still later years have shown him to be a precursor of the *nouveau roman* on the one hand and of structuralist criticism on the other. As a student of realism, which finds a semantic parallel in *chosisme,* I had been acutely impressed by his example. The exact delineation of particularities—the quest for what Joyce, in his scholastic jargon, termed *quiddity*—had found no more rigorous proponent.

And this was the man that, as we so happily discovered, was now living just above us, on the *piano nobile* of our decaying edifice—in a flat inherited not too long before, with artistic appurtenances left over, from the previous occupant, Jean Dubuffet. We had mutual friends in two brilliant young men who had recently studied with me at Harvard, and were just then setting out on their careers as French writers, the poet André Du Bouchet and the art critic Pierre Schneider. We must have been introduced by the one or the other, or possibly both. In any case, the Ponges were the kindest and friendliest of neighbors. They comprised, like ourselves, a closely knit circle of three. Odette was the gracious and intelligent wife, who coped with everything for her two charges. Armande was the charming *lycéenne*, who worked hard at her English, and amiably consented to become the perfect baby-sitter and the adored companion of our little girl. (Does she still have the battered *Concise Oxford Dictionary* we left with her as a memento of that year?) Francis was not publishing very much, except for an occasional and felicitous venture into art criticism, and he was supporting his family by teaching at the Alliance Française. (How he ever could have sold insurance, in his prior job, is beyond surmise.) German was his foreign language, not English; "My Creative Method" was a title which he had accepted—unfortunately, I think—from a commentary by Betty Miller. We conversed in French; but I shall not try to render his conversation verbatim because, after the interval of years, I could not recapture the precision, the elegance, or the succinctness of his phrasing.

The everlasting relation of words to things, than which life could scarcely hold a more critical relationship, was for him both a perpetual challenge and a persistent criterion. And if he saw the word as an object, he envisioned *"l'objet comme idée."* His talk—like so much of his writing, wherein he talks about writing—took the French language as its habitual point of departure and of return. Littré was his breviary; he was adept at glossing the archaic twists of Villon; his gift for explication was to unfold itself monumentally in *Pour Malherbe*. It was characteristic of him to note that *oiseau* contains each one of the five vowels, as well as to speculate on alternatives for its single consonant. But all such speculations ended by bringing home the linguistic elusiveness and the inherent reality of the bird itself—or whatever theme he was contemplating, animate or inanimate, grand or minuscule. *Le Savon* and *La Pomme de terre* had virtually changed into crystal balls in his firm hands and under his penetrating eyes. It was good to be dwelling in quotidian proximity with one who could confer such depth and dignity on the humble and solid things of every day. Given the intensity of his gaze, it could become a short leap from the familiar to the cosmic, not to say the apocalyptic: *Le Soleil placé en abîme*. Observing the behavior of a fly, he discerned an analogue in the figure of Coriolanus, during a year when the Comédie Française was interpreting Shakespeare's play as a portent of authoritarianism. (Could that fly be also interpreted as a portent of Robbe-Grillet's centipede?) With what interest Monsieur Ponge would savor the Parisian locutions of our common *femme de ménage*, Madame Tissot!

Usually we encountered in the hallway, where he would often stop for a cordial interchange. Occasionally, after our respective family dinners, we would get together upstairs or downstairs for a demitasse and a liqueur. One of those occasions has lingered in my memory with a special glow. That afternoon I had attended the funeral of Paul Eluard, where the flamboyant Louis Aragon and other Communist orators had tried to turn the crowd of mourners at Père-Lachaise into something like a political manifestation. Ponge, who had been a close friend of Eluard's for many years and was godfather to his daughter, had seen little or nothing of his fellow poet since he himself had resigned from the Communist Party. Having missed the ceremony on principle, he was nonetheless sympathetic and eager to hear about it in some detail, and was ruefully meditative in his comments. Then, upon our questioning, he launched into a candid, eloquent, and excruciating account of his own experiences as a party member. After he had spoken at some length, my wife, whose Russian revolutionary background made her a particularly attentive listener, voiced two questions which he had aroused in her mind. If the discipline was as shackling as he had attested, why had he joined the party in the first place? And how, if he had been so intricately involved, had he ever managed to get out? His reply was a clear-eyed self-appraisal and likewise a reverberating confession: "There is one thing you must understand about me. I was born and bred a Protestant. Hence what is difficult for me is what I must undertake." His difficulties were not those of Gide or Rousseau. But it is easy to understand what he means when he says that poetry, for him, is *"un besoin, un engagement, une colère, une affaire d'amour-propre et voilà tout."*

At the end of the term we took our leave from the address that we had shared with the Ponges, rather precipitately because of the housing pressures. And, although we exchanged publications and New Year greetings, we did not see them during the next twelve years. But then, in 1965, our old neighbors made their first visit to the United States. Ponge was on a heavy schedule of public readings at colleges and other institutions. However, they were able to save a weekend for reunion and relaxation in what he would describe as *"ce bel automne de la Nouvelle Angleterre."* Though the fringe around his head was no longer so dark, his eyes were as sharp as ever and his voice was as clarifying. It was an enormous pleasure to witness his spontaneous reactions, at the age of sixty-six, to our American vistas. Fall is the

best season in New England; the leaves were outdoing themselves in
their annual spectacle. We took them on our standard tour for European friends—Concord, Lexington, and Walden Pond. We tested them
on clam chowder, which they enjoyed. What seemed to please him
best was the North End of Boston; its Italian markets and eighteenth-
century houses appealed to sensibilities deeply rooted in the Midi.
Though he has returned to this country since, we have not seen him
again, and I shall be at Oxford when he comes back this spring to
receive the international prize he has so richly deserved. Yet I continue
to cherish vivid and frequent recollections of those privileged months
we spent on the Rue Lhomond. It was the closest approximation that
I can imagine, as a stranger who came along two generations afterward, to having been a guest of Mallarmé's at his Tuesdays on the
Rue de Rome.

RECOLLECTING
W. H. AUDEN

In 1975, the year after Auden's death, The Harvard Advocate *devoted a special issue to the memory of the poet and his work. I had been invited to contribute this brief recollection, which was there entitled "Auden at Harvard." Later on his literary executor, Edward Mendelson, told me that I need not have worried about keeping—or even quoting from—the cited correspondence, since it does not deal with personal matters. Nevertheless, I have adhered to my original compromise between the spirit and the letter of Auden's request. I might also note that the recent unauthorized biography,* W. H. Auden: The Life of a Poet *by Charles Osborne (New York: Harcourt Brace Jovanovich, 1979), makes unacknowledged use of my article.*

•

Now that he has taken his place in the tradition of English poetry—a tradition he so knowledgeably mastered and so ingeniously deployed—I find myself recalling his earliest impact. "Bliss was it in that dawn to be alive, / But to be young was very Heaven." Well, if even the good gray generation of Wordsworth had pulsated through an iconoclastic youth, how much more exciting it was for my college contemporaries to hear fresh voices being raised from the land of our literary textbooks! The Spanish Civil War was soon to become their French Revolution, and the following decades were to register a more conventional pattern of conversions and tergiversations. But the ideological queries that ushered in the Nineteen-Thirties were strengthened, in our young imaginations, by such revolutionary fanfares in the arts. It was my teacher best attuned to those times, F. O. Matthiessen, who lent me his copy of *New Signatures*, together with British periodicals which were beginning to publish the new school, recently graduated from Oxford or Cambridge. Cecil Day Lewis, who was to top a rather tame career by becoming Poet Laureate, issued their challenging manifesto, *A Hope for Poetry*. Naturally the talents were uneven, though Louis MacNeice and Stephen Spender already stood out

150

among them. But Wystan Auden was already the master he never ceased to be, both in the resourcefulness of his technique and the individuality of his outlook.

My own introduction to his work continued under the happiest auspices. During my senior year at Harvard, T. S. Eliot was living at Eliot House (where else?) as the Charles Eliot Norton Professor of Poetry, and to literary-minded undergraduates he was very generous with his time and his conversation. With that same generosity, on a much higher plane of perception, he had recently become the mentor and publisher of Auden and the other new signatures. Their affinities with him were obvious—and not least in that they seemed to be taking over where he would be leaving off. If it could be said that he had brought English poetry into the twentieth century, it might now be added that they were eager to adapt his diurnal idiom and formal elaboration to attitudes and events that went beyond his traditionalistic stand. Faber and Faber, his house, was then publishing *Paid on Both Sides* and *The Orators*, with their pyrotechnical trajectories from schoolroom to aerodrome and from Old English metrics to Hyde Park forensics. Eliot was warm in his commendation and recommendation of both volumes, while his predictions for Auden's future virtually constituted a laying on of hands. Yet he hinted at one slight caveat against the hazards of facility. In retrospect this judgment seems particularly farsighted, since it would take Auden many years to move from the succinct austerity of his original output to the almost Swinburnian flow of his later occasional writing.

Unlike Eliot, for whom expatriation had meant assimilation, Auden remained a British cosmopolite during the latter half of his life, when his principal base of operations was New York. To be sure, he took out naturalization papers; he took a sympathetic and uncondescending interest in our language and folkways; he made numerous friends among American writers; and he did much to establish the circuit that has provided our campuses with periodic visits from poets reading their works. It was a round which later killed Dylan Thomas, but Auden steered his course with grace and wit. Soon after his arrival in 1939, he must have given the first of his Morris Gray readings at Harvard. He was the embodiment of what we looked up to and wanted to hear from: lean-faced and sandy-haired, not much older than the graduate students in his audience, clipped and sardonic in his casual elocution, brittle yet spontaneous in his interwoven comments, which had not yet become a magician's patter. His host and ours at the reception afterward was Theodore Spencer, beloved teacher of Shakespeare and modern literature, an accomplished poet in his own right. At a period when social intercourse between the academic and the literary worlds was more standoffish than it has since become, Spencer had a special flair for bringing them together. To make Auden's personal acquaintance under these hospitable auspices turned out to be a good omen for later encounters.

On one of these he was our overnight guest; and though we found him most congenial, I doubt if the official occasion for which he came could have been so described. He had been invited to deliver the Phi Beta Kappa Poem for 1946. It is true that he arrived at our home wearing sneakers and conspicuously shabby clothes, and that the small kitbag he carried with him promised nothing in the way of more formal finery. But, as it turned out, he had taken the pains to produce a *pièce d'occasion* whose epigrammatic elegance rose far above the standard expectations for these ceremonial routines. Entitled "Under Which Lyre: A Reactionary Tract for the Times," it could be subsequently read and properly savored in one of his verse collections, *Nones*. With good-humored and evenhanded dialectic, it balanced the kind of educational arguments that have since been labored so heavily in the Leavis-Snow polemics over the Two Cultures. The setting for which he had fondly and mistakenly framed it ought to have been an intimate evening meeting, where it might well have formed the appropriate climax to a sequence of after-dinner speeches and frequent toasts. Instead, the epigrams bypassed the superannuated alumni and thudded against the hollow rafters of Sanders Theatre during the cold sobriety of ten o'clock in the morning—an hour which Auden regularly eschewed. The statues flanking the platform looked the other way.

Our spectators had more reason to be bewildered when Auden lectured to them in 1947–48. This marked the long-awaited culmination of a series commemorating the quadricentennial of the birth of Cervantes, and many of the previous speakers were present—some of them well-known authorities—to hear the general summing-up. Auden's preparation had included a certain amount of browsing among Martinis, and he did not put his hearers at their ease when he began by apologizing for his new set of dentures. Nor did he disarm the professional Cervantistas by remarking that no one could really claim to have read *Don Quixote* in its entirety. It was no worse than a scholastic leg-pull, innocent if brash; but it led us on into a double loss; for, when he was nominated as professor of poetry not long afterward, it was combined with narrower personal objections to dissuade the Administration from offering him the appointment. Years later, when I had something to do with these matters, we were able to reopen the question and to make him a serious invitation. Auden then replied, with characteristic openness, that he would have enjoyed a year at Harvard—where he would assuredly have been a most engaging and welcome visitor. But, as he scanned his current plans and projects, he had in mind no undertaking that could be expounded in half a dozen weekly lectures or ultimately synthesized into a book of critical prose.

It is a pity we missed him at the right moment. Elsewhere he enunciated his thematic study, *The Enchafèd Flood;* he propounded a commentary on Shakespeare's sonnets for the New School of Social Research; he spent a fruitful year as visiting professor at Swarthmore College; and he inaugurated the T. S. Eliot Lectures at the University of Kent. The National Institute of Arts and Letters is one of those professional societies which exist primarily for mutual admiration, but it carries one responsibility which he undertook with the utmost conscientiousness: the discernment and encouragement of younger writers and artists. At a private dinner after one such conference on awards, the discussion turned about and brought up a point which led to our single argument. All of those present had been shocked by the recent suicide of F. O. Matthiessen, an act which Auden declared he could never forgive. I was surprised that such a moral stance could be taken by a friend professing Christian principles. Since I had known Matthiessen much better, I tried to explain that his political protest had been compounded by the death of his personal companion and his increasing desperation over his sexual life. Wystan understood that situation better than I did, in most respects; his response was bluffly British and somewhat Boy-Scoutish; he thought the whole thing might have been averted if he and Matty had somehow got together for a heart-to-heart talk. He had come to cheerful terms with the problem that Matthiessen could only meet as a tragedy.

Auden happened to be again in our Cambridge when Isaiah Berlin first arrived, and I remembered sitting on packing cases under a dangling lightbulb in an unfurnished room at Lowell House, while the two of them—with their uniquely chatty authority—reanimated the Oxford of the Twenties. It seems fitting that Auden should have rounded out his expatriate cycle by returning thitherward, first as professor of poetry and finally as honorary fellow of his old college. It is saddening that he seems to have felt something like an Oxonian Rip Van Winkle, and that—having braved the onslaughts of Manhattan for nearly thirty years—he should have been mugged and robbed in the very purlieus of Christchurch. Shortly before his last departure for England, he had given his finest performance at Harvard. Having reversed the Wildean expansion of middle years, his face had now become a deeply wrinkled mask. He had given up the conversational patter, and simply interspersed the poems with moments of silence, conceivably meditation. Students were then at the height of their dissatisfaction with elders; yet here was one who presented himself unabashedly as "an old party," and whose every word they attended with respect and rapport. The only other poets who have gained such plaudits at Sanders were Eliot and Frost. But they had always been father figures for most of us, whereas Auden had passed from youthful rebel to venerated sage within an accelerated and turbulent generation.

Once I reviewed a book of his poems, respectfully though not ravingly, and he was gracious enough to send me a postcard of thanks. To my cavil—that certain lines had sounded oversimplified—his answer was lucidly practical. He had been writing for music in this case, and had discovered that the lyricist was lucky if he could emphasize one word in a single line. We had further opportunities to discuss the question, and I realized how much thinking and reading and listening he had spent upon it. It was his conclusion that Ben Jonson and Thomas Moore had fitted words to sounds most effectively in English, and many of his own experiments may profitably be scanned for such effects. In a less technical vein, I retain a letter which reads like an apologia for his increasing conservatism. Though I have no copy of what I had written to him, I must have echoed the common charge that he had been abandoning his earlier sociocritical stance. He begins by expressing skepticism toward all literary ideologies—a view which then was prompting him to revisions and excisions, and which would leave him more of a virtuoso than an iconoclast. He was careful to keep his religion in a separate category, deprecating the pseudo-mysticism of Aldous Huxley. For Fascism and other modes of authoritarianism his contempt remained intransigent, because he could not see such absolutes imposed upon the fallibilities of man's Augustinian condition.

In paraphrasing from his correspondence rather than quoting it directly, I am aware of having awkwardly compromised. I am not anxious to disregard his executors, who have transmitted the wish that his letters and papers be destroyed. Literature, on the other hand, would be infinitely poorer—would have had to do without the *Aeneid*, the *Canterbury Tales*, the novels of Kafka—if such deathbed wishes had been faithfully executed. In the present instance we are still allowed the *oeuvre*, though the author seems inclined to take refuge behind it. Yet it speaks to us so personally, having been fashioned and refashioned before our eyes, having responded to our dilemmas with such original insights, that we scarcely can be asked to look upon it as an anonymous artifact. Moreover, we have witnessed some discouraging examples, lately that of T. S. Eliot, where such injunctions have merely opened the way for biographical potboilers by ill-qualified hacks. As for the intimate character of Auden's personal experience, he has maintained a model of candor and integrity which should not be undiscussible today. His keen concern for other writers' lives was brilliantly manifest in his *New Yorker* review of Chekhov's letters just a short while before his death. "Private faces in public places"—how well we have been learning that lesson!—"Are wiser and nicer / Than public faces in private places." The privilege of having known Auden is one which I shall not forget, and which my younger friends will not reproach me for attempting to share with them.

DELMORE SCHWARTZ'S GIFT

Some years after Delmore Schwartz's death in 1966, The Harvard Advocate undertook to memorialize him. Again the editors invited me to explore my memories for the occasion, and I tried to do so in this paper. But they seem to have met with delays and obstacles in gathering material for a full symposium. After two years, during which the originators had graduated, another editorial board consequently gave up the notion. Meanwhile James Atlas, whom I had known as a student, had undertaken what was to prove a serious, illuminating, and well-balanced biography, Delmore Schwartz: The Life of an American Poet *(New York: Farrar, Straus & Giroux, 1977). I was happy to let him see my manuscript, and he made incidental use of it with due acknowledgment. The text itself was published belatedly in a new magazine,* Canto *(Spring 1978).*

•

Irony can be overdone, as Delmore Schwartz might have said, had he realized that his personality might emerge as the posthumous model for a prize-winning best-seller. He is physically recognizable from the opening page of the recent *roman à clef* by Saul Bellow, *Humboldt's Gift*, though he might have lived a happier man if he had known that someone would some day be calling him "handsome"—the first of Mr. Bellow's string of introductory adjectives. His unhappiness about so many things began with himself, his name, his appearance, his uneasiness over what his teacher A. N. Whitehead called "the withness of the body"—a feeling voiced in one of his most memorable poems, "The Heavy Bear." Mr. Bellow has caught his features very clearly: the scar across his forehead, the Asiatic cheekbones, the fair and wavy hair, the teeth discolored and irregular, the eyes large and wide-set. These, perpetually animated by his talk, added up to a *laideur sympathique* for most of us who knew him. For me his face resembled a mottled mask by Jacob Epstein. As for his given name, he hated its irrelevance; and indeed it sounded rather more like a resort hotel than a Jewish poet. He once expressed an unexpected affinity with an otherwise uninteresting fellow sufferer, a Harvard dean named Delmar Leighton. The trauma came to be symbolized in his play about a cir-

156

cumcision, *Shenandoah,* and Shenandoah Fish became a recurrent spokesman in his stories.

If "Shenandoah" was improbable, "Von Humboldt" is even more so. The Indian place name makes for a certain amount of incongruous sense, in view of Delmore Schwartz's concern with the adaptation of immigrants to the New World, whereas Mr. Bellow has baptized his co-incidental protagonist "after a statue in Central Park." The German polymath contributes no meaningful overtones, and the aristocratic particle dangles quite ineffectually. The novel itself is exceptionally rambling and loquacious, even for its author, even if the exaggeration be credited to his powers of imagination. Its credible point of departure was the shock so widely felt when newspapers announced that Delmore Schwartz had suddenly, during middle years, "dropped dead in a dismal hotel off Times Square." Much of this twice-told tale has been concocted out of literary small talk and academic gossip, such as the malicious caricature of the late R. P. Blackmur. But the novelist reserves his sharpest treatment for his own first-person surrogate, the symbiotic friend and fellow writer whose worldly success is counter-pointed by Humboldt's falling-off. The latter is romanticized into a tragic clown, another one of our most gifted writers who failed to meet his second act, a heroic failure whose human weaknesses some-how compensate for his artistic imperfections—in the train of Scott Fitzgerald, James Agee, and how many others? After all, the facts fit well enough with the picaresque role in which Mr. Bellow has cast him.

Except for the physical likeness and the sudden obituary, and pos-sibly some twists of conversation, I cannot say I really knew that way-ward hero. The figure who held forth at the White Horse Tavern, who followed the primrose path of Dylan Thomas, who cruised so jauntily through Princeton and Greenwich Village, who moved in and out of mental institutions, had—by his own volition—relinquished our friend-ship not long after it was consolidated. During the late Thirties, when he spent two years at Harvard as a graduate student in philosophy, I cannot remember just how we had become vaguely acquainted; but I have a vivid remembrance of first hearing about him from two pro-fessors who were our close mutual friends. Both of them were bache-lors, large-minded and keenly sensitive men, who gave a great deal of their time and interest to students. One was David Prall, whose course in esthetics must have been more congenial to Delmore than the trend toward mathematical logic in his department, and whose head tutor's suite in Leverett House was a hospitable center for promising younger talents. The other was F. O. Matthiessen, then in the ascendant phase of his tragically abbreviated career as an interpreter of modern poetry and of American literature. True to his discerning intuitions, Matty singled Delmore out and welcomed him. He would write a review of *Genesis* that helped to establish its author's reputation, and devote several pages to his poems in his own last publication, *The Oxford Book of American Verse.*

Actually it was another friend, closer to our ages and directly involved with our respective early publications, who brought us into the most literal propinquity. This was James Laughlin IV, who had founded the *avant-garde* publishing firm, New Directions, shortly before his recent graduation from Harvard. Delmore was among the earliest of the numerous literary discoveries that J. featured on his list and in his annual. "In Dreams Begin Responsibilities," the story with which Delmore made his initial impact, and possibly the finest thing he ever wrote, was published in *New Directions for 1937* as well as in the *Partisan Review,* and became the centerpiece of his first and most striking collection of prose and verse. Since Delmore ultimately turned against J., as he did against everyone sooner or later, and all the more rancorously because he had been so warmly befriended, it is important to realize how much the recognition and the support of New Directions had meant to him at the time when he needed them most. It was at J.'s well-meaning suggestion, in the hope of helping Delmore to pay off an advance, that his translation of Rimbaud's *A Season in Hell*—intended as no more than a private exercise—was put into print. Delmore was aware of the chance he was taking, for his French was weak, as reviewers were quick to point out. Thereupon J. handsomely withdrew it at no cost to Delmore, later substituting another version by the sharpest and most expert of his critics, Louise Varèse.

Twice it has been my fortune, and I count it a lucky recurrence, to be dwelling where a poet was my nearest neighbor. The other occasion came twenty years afterward, when Francis Ponge occupied the apartment above our *rez-de-chaussée* in Paris; but that is another memory. For several years my wife and I made our home at 909 Memorial Drive, in a little row of four yellow wooden houses owned by the University, facing the Charles River on the present site of Peabody Terrace, the apartments for graduate students. Each of these Mansards held six small rooms, and our hall bedroom was set aside for the child

we were expecting. For the first two years, 1940–42, we had Delmore
and Gertrude Schwartz as our next-door neighbors at 908. Those prem-
ises were rented by New Directions, which had its local office downstairs. In charge was Albert Erskine, who resided elsewhere (previously the business manager of *The Southern Review* and currently a
vice-president of Random House). Gertrude worked full-time as his
assistant, and the Schwartzes had their quarters upstairs and made
use of the kitchen. Not long after our small daughter arrived, Delmore—who, childless himself, had a humorous fondness for children—
celebrated her by composing a blues (to the tune of "Frankie and
Johnnie"). My wife had fallen into the quaint habit, adding a Russian
suffix to an English adjective, of addressing her as "Goodka" when she
behaved well and as "Badka" when she was mischievous. This, appealing to Delmore's latent Manichaeanism, inspired a series of varia-
tions on the following theme:

> Goodka and Badka were sisters,
>   The daughters of Mrs. Levin.
> Goodka she was a good little girl,
>   But Badka was bad as sin.

If there was a refrain, I have forgotten it. But the significant stanza
was the wry one that pointed back to himself:

> Next door there lived a poet.
>   His name was Mr. Black.
> He sent his verse to the editors,
>   And the editors sent it back.

Our recollections of Delmore and Gertrude from those two years
follow a pattern of lively intimacy for the first year, receding into a
studied coolness for the second. Occasionally we had dinner and more
frequently drinks together, though none of us drank anything strong
or voluminous. I have heard aggressive and alcoholic details about
Delmore's subsequent lifestyle, and Bellow makes a roaring boy of
Von Humboldt Fleisher; but in those days I must testify that he was
gentle and temperate, albeit prone to sadness and sometimes bitter-
ness. After our dinners at 908 and 909, he and I often chatted for an
hour on the front steps we shared. My wife spoke of this dialogue as
"talking pessimistic," and it was unquestionably Delmore who set the
tone. Though I am far from immune to melancholia, I found that these
exchanges usually ended—on a relativistic basis—by cheering me up.

Delmore in his turn was called upon to cheer up John Berryman, during the brief period when he was teaching with us. At one particular moment, John had to be dissuaded from throwing himself into the Charles. Since he proposed to do this from the Weeks Bridge, a very low footbridge over a mild and miniature river, it is not clear how serious the consequence might have been. But I have seen the high bridge from which he finally jumped to his death in the Mississippi River three decades later. And it is now evident that a whole generation of poets, with Delmore conspicuous among them, experienced and reacted to that vertiginous impulse.

Invariably, he was an avid and interesting conversationalist. Our actual conversations have receded too far into the distance for me to recall them with any particularity; but I retain a warm impression of having enjoyed them, having struck a balance between agreement and argument with him, and having had to temper my acceptance of his opinions and anecdotes with occasional pinches of salt. Though he ranged from personalities to critical theories, his concerns were predominantly literary. I do not recollect that he ever talked much about his teaching or pupils; it was mostly about himself and his work. I myself was implicated in an effort to introduce the Teachers' Union at Harvard, and sympathized with various left-wing causes of the decade. So did most of our acquaintances, including Delmore, who had a theoretical sympathy for the more or less Trotskyite ideology then espoused by the *Partisan Review*. Yet he maintained an aloofness from political activities. All of us were beginning to live in the shadows of the Second World War, many of us expecting to be called up in a month or two, and consequently clinging to the arts as devotedly as we could, while turning aside from previous ideological disillusionments. This conflict may have been neutralized for Delmore, to some extent, by the deeply subjective nature of his approach to any subject. Nearly all of his writing was directed at, and delimited by, two of his most personal involvements: his family background and the New York intelligentsia.

To this day my wife and I continue to wonder why, toward the middle of our second contiguous year, he decided to cut us. The act—or non-act—of cutting would seem to be a childish gesture, if not a denial of reality, especially when not supported by reasons. Yet something comparable would apparently happen to every one of his friends in an accelerating succession, and some light may be cast upon that proclivity by his haunting poetic expression of paranoia, "Do the Others Speak of Me Mockingly, Maliciously?" We others never did anything to justify such suspicions, insofar as I can report. Life is simpler than that, as Einstein said of Kafka. We could never have done otherwise than to mingle our respect and regard with our perplexities. Nor can I believe that Delmore resented my lack of enthusiasm for a story he showed me, "An Argument in 1934," since he had expressed some doubts about it himself and never saw fit to reprint it between hard covers. His self-absorption, one must fairly acknowledge, did not preclude the candid habit of self-criticism. In retrospect, it is now clearer to me how obtuse we were in not realizing that at this time his first marriage was coming apart. Increasingly his daily *confidante* was another row-house neighbor, a painter whose husband had gone abroad and would be lost in the war. Moreover, during the next year or so, Delmore fell in love with one of my brightest doctoral candidates, and found himself the rival of a venturesome senior colleague, who has also passed beyond the limits of reckoning.

What his Harvard experience may have signified to Delmore I have some difficulty in guessing. One explicit allusion that comes to mind is his sonnet beginning "The Ghosts of James and Peirce in Harvard Yard." One of its sound effects was based upon the adjective "Episcopalian," reverberating onomatopoetically like a peal of chapel bells. This reveals a curious unawareness of the situation at hand, or of history, inasmuch as Harvard—originally Congregationalist, then Unitarian, then Protestant/nonsectarian—never had any Anglican connections. Manifestly Delmore never ceased to regard it, from the vantage point of a different parochialism, as enemy territory. He scented anti-semitism everywhere. Now, having grown up in the Middle West, I was accustomed both to living in a Gentile community and to taking an outsider's position. Coming to Harvard, where "indifference" was a liberating watchword and *laissez-faire* was a social principle, I encountered little in the way of ethnic prejudice. Delmore, on the other hand, had been born in Brooklyn, brought up on Washington Heights, and mainly educated at New York University. Before he came to Cambridge he had seldom moved outside of Jewish circles. Hence his diffidence conspired with his suspicion to intensify feelings of mistrust toward his new environment. Yet we cannot disregard his trenchant epigram: "Even paranoiacs have enemies." And it is undeniably true that a strong professional bias then operated to discourage Jews from university careers in departments of philosophy and of English literature.

Delmore, from whatever motivation, dropped out of his philosophical studies shortly before the close of his second year, and left the Harvard Graduate School without taking a degree (having won a prize for an essay on poetics). The next two years witnessed his emergence as a recognized writer, and it was in that capacity that he returned in 1940 with a teaching appointment in English. This was one of the newly established Briggs-Copeland Instructorships, posts especially designated for talented young writers. Each of them was assigned a section of the course in freshman composition, whose quality was thereby much improved. Beyond that, they could offer their own courses in more advanced writing, and their schedules were expected to include free intervals for continued writing of their own. It was a hopefully comprehensive program; a full schedule hardly left the time for all three commitments to be pursued with the same degree of attention. One of the drawbacks to that benign impulsion which has been installing writer-teachers on the campus is that usually they must cultivate one concern at the expense of the other. But it has been an unmitigated enrichment for us academics to welcome such colleagues as Delmore, John Berryman, Wallace Stegner, Mark Schorer, Howard Baker, Richard Wilbur, and Kurt Vonnegut—to mention but a few. The regrettable part of the arrangement, for Harvard, was that none of them proceeded up the ladder to local tenure. Although Delmore was promoted to an assistant professorship, he resigned before its termination.

He was to have almost twenty years for further writing, yet they were appreciably less prolific or successful than his Briggs-Copeland period. Moving freely and effectively from verse to prose and from fiction to criticism, he was never sure what his particular genre should have been, as he had confided to me in our front-step talks. His own label, "Poems of Experimentation and Imitation," was just. In spite of their intensity, they never outdistanced some of their literary influences (Eliot, Yeats), while his will to experiment was sometimes impaired by an uncertain touch. It was unfair of Rolfe Humphries to term them "entirely earless," but they appealed more directly to the intellect than to the senses. Since he was less constrained by technique in his stories, his originality came out more fully there. He was like Poe in this respect, as in others. That is to say, he functioned primarily through an incandescent imagination, which could impose its uniqueness upon everything that came its way. His fiction, sharp, dry, nervous, understated, didactic, tended to merge with his criticism, which abounded in suggestive insights. Here again the great exemplar was Eliot, and the stumbling block turned out to be Yeats; for Delmore had uncritically accepted an inaccurate text of "Among School Children," and worked out an ingenious interpretation derived from a misprint. In all of these expressions, he stayed true to his idiosyncratic self. It is worth noting that he did not choose to exploit the themes of madness or Jewishness, as his successors would find it so easy to do.

What he has unforgettably expressed is what he agonized over in his life and death: estrangement, alienation, disaffection, *anomie*, Melville's "desolation of solitude," Proust's *"chaque personne est bien seule."* He reversed the happy ending of the immigrant legend; instead of joining a transatlantic utopia, the eternal wanderers got lost in a deeper and darker wilderness (see "America! America!"). If he took a stance, it was the opposite of Whitman's; for he wanted compulsively, not to embrace, but to reject everybody. These attitudes could not have been projected with such fervor, if they had not been formulated by a subtle intelligence, well versed in civilized amenities and eminently fitted for intercommunication and reciprocal affection. A propensity for willful misunderstanding turned this paradox into a vicious circle. Let me exemplify with two trivial stories: one his, the other mine. Taken together, they may help to explain why we ceased to communicate, why we may never have communicated, and how he attempted to pass on that noncommunication to his readers. His novella, "The World Is a Wedding," essentially comprises a sequence of reported conversations. The title makes an ironic comment broadly on life itself, but more specifically upon the single feminine character, for whom the world is a funeral, since no one has sought her hand in marriage. She is surrounded by a chorus of sophisticated younger New Yorkers, who have graduated into the Depression, and whose native cynicism is heightened by unemployment or jobs unworthy of their aspirations.

Most of the narration conveys a stylized yet realistic account of their dialogues. The incidental subject of conversation, for half a page, happens to be "a youthful teacher and critic, Mortimer London, who was reputed to be brilliant." It transpires that he was once given a letter of introduction to James Joyce from T. S. Eliot, "in which a great author commends him to a great author," and that—as a kind of existential gesture—he preferred to keep it rather than present it. This is understandably considered "insane" by the story's spokesmen, and the fact that he has divulged it illustrates their belief that "everyone himself tells the worst stories about himself." Well, I must confess that I had happened into that situation, and had talked about it with Delmore. The circumstances were, of course, much simpler. Eliot had been a visiting professor during my senior year at Harvard. He had been very kind to me then and in the following year, when I divided a traveling fellowship between London and Paris. I had been embarrassed by the letter of introduction, since I could not think that such an encounter would be anything more than an importunity. Yet I felt obliged to forward it, together with a covering note which suggested that no answer was necessarily expected. To my great relief, Joyce never answered. I was later told that he would have, one way or another, if only out of courtesy to Eliot, had it not arrived during a crisis precipitated by his daughter's breakdown. Five years afterward, when we had something to talk about (namely *Finnegans Wake*), he voluntarily sent a postcard.

I must therefore recognize myself in the walk-on part that Delmore created, even as he could have identified himself with the profile of the rather more genial personage invented by Saul Bellow. But I am sincerely perplexed by the motive attributed to me, and more so by the non-action to which it seems to have led, apparently some sort of grand refusal—in view of the trepidation and the misgiving with which, so far as I could, I managed to act. How would Delmore, in my place, have acted? What is revealing, for him if not for me, is that the protagonist of the anecdote dramatically refuses an opportunity to communicate at the highest level, engaging in a game of moral one-upmanship which—he seems to imagine—will elevate him to a plane as high as that of his potential interlocutors. I have long since given up this minor enigma, which must have much less meaning for other readers than it had for me. If I ever sought to devise a tale that would bring me credit or discredit, I should hope it would have more point. Mr. Bellow's novel scores a good many points, some of which are the licensed improvements that fiction can so easily score over truth. But I cannot believe very strongly in Humboldt's gift, if it consisted merely in the sophomoric scenario bequeathed to, and described by, the feckless narrator. Delmore's legacy was by no means a practical joke. Delmore's peculiar gift was his *Angst,* his unreassuring certainty that discomfort is a basic component of our psychological condition, his accusation leveled against all who are complacent enough to feel at home in the universe he rejected.

RANDALL JARRELL'S *FAUST*

It was probably no service to Randall Jarrell, who had distinguished himself as a poet, a critic, and a writer of satirical fiction, to bring out posthumously his translation of Goethe's Faust: Part One *(New York: Farrar, Straus & Giroux). Yet, insofar as it can take us into the translator's workshop, it can tell us something about poetic and dramatic style, about the* Sprachgefühl *of German and English, and about the archetypal modernist who composed the philosophical drama. My review-article in* The New York Review of Books *under the title of "Faust: Still Striving and Straying" (November 25, 1976) also took cognizance of the new version of the entire work by Walter Arndt, appearing concurrently in a more academic format (New York: W. W. Norton and Company). I thought I saw some merit in that version, but evidently not enough for Professor Arndt, who engaged me in a further round of discussion (*The New York Review of Books, *February 3, 1977).*

●

Forever striving and forever straying, the role of Faust has been adopted as a historic model for Western man. As an individual bent upon self-realization, and caught up in a devil's bargain with technological forces, he was ideally cut out to be Spengler's prototype of the modern mind. His black magic has been detected most recently, according to a poem by Karl Shapiro, in a mushroom cloud arising from Los Alamos. His persisting legend, which began in a Reformation chapbook and inspired a powerful tragedy of the Renaissance, has extended to the musical fiction of Thomas Mann and the cerebral dialogue of Paul Valéry. Other legends, notably those of Prometheus and Don Juan, have dealt with forbidden knowledge and facile seduction. But it was Faust who, upon its reaction from the Enlightenment, became the culture hero of Romanticism. And Goethe's was the masterwork among the many dramas that reanimated this theme for the *Sturm und Drang.*

But Goethe cannot be ticketed as a mere Romanticist. True, the First Part of his *Faust* may be regarded as his major contribution to the movement. Yet, as a product of intermittent endeavors over some thirty years, it was already overlapped by his Weimar Classicism, which would culminate in the Second Part. The latter, almost twice as long as the former, was written more or less consecutively during the last few years of his long and supremely creative life. Without its cosmic resolution the drama is incomplete. Goethe himself managed, nonetheless, to live with that suspense for sixty years. If the final work is an organic whole, it reflects the changing stages of its author's development. The earliest passage that he composed was the most poignant and untraditional, the domestic episode of Gretchen. Readers—and playgoers even more—have appreciably preferred her "little world" to the imperial allegory and the classical phantasmagoria of the sequel.

These two new translations on my desk—surrounded there by a Faustian gathering of other translations, texts, commentaries, and dictionaries—have been preceded by about fifty versions of Part I and a dozen of Part II. The disproportion accords with a ratio which can also be noted in English versions of Dante's *Inferno* and *Paradiso*. Do translators get tired after the first round, or is damnation more interesting than salvation? That they are perennially drawn to the attempt indicates not only that *Faust* is there, like Mount Everest, but that earlier efforts to ascend it from abroad have not altogether proved satisfactory. Randall Jarrell appears to have felt this challenge deeply and responded to it during the last phase of his career, which all too prematurely ended eleven years ago. Fragments of his translation have been read aloud and published in periodicals. Now, with a short but important gap filled in by Robert Lowell, it stands complete, so far as it goes.

In a candid and devoted afterword, Mary von Schrader Jarrell explains her late husband's motivation: "Poets know that when you can't write your own poetry you translate someone else's." Temporarily blocked as a poet by his successful excursions into prose, Jarrell translated Goethe to prime the pump. A strong sense of psychic identification seems to have determined his choice of subject. Such affinities are not necessarily bilateral. It may well be that Jarrell had more in common with the *persona* of Faust—the romantic Faust of Part I—than with the personality of his creator. After all, both were "intellectuals and professors," as Mrs. Jarrell points out. Moreover, both could be stylistically characterized in terms of sincerity, curiosity, and irony, along with tension, restlessness, and sentimentality. Jarrell counted on his own lyricism and flair for monologue to serve the undertaking. His talent as a satirical phrasemaker, likewise, might have helped with Mephistopheles.

Mrs. Jarrell's references to Goethe are somewhat blurry, and she tends to minimize the linguistic problem. Never a German scholar or even speaker, Jarrell obviously worked hard as a conscientious student of his text. Yet a slightly garbled quotation from Schubert's *Winterreise* (lyrics by Wilhelm Müller) hardly attests connoisseurship in German poetry. Due allowance must be made, of course, for the possibility of revisions and afterthoughts that was unhappily closed to this translator. Given the license that all translators should be allowed, he is reasonably accurate. Very seldom does he cross the thin line between a circumlocution and a mistake. I would merely interpose a few marginal queries here and there. "Have you gone mad?" is a rather stepped-up reading of "What is the matter with your head (*Wo steht dein Kopf*)?" And—to cite another monosyllabic example— "I am afraid of you" is not quite the same thing as "You make me shudder (*Mir graut's von dir*)"—the heroine's last words.

Gretchen indeed gets treated cavalierly. She is "impudent" rather than "pert (*schnippisch*)"; her hand is "disgusting" and "raw," not "filthy (*garstig*)" and "rough (*rauh*)." Since rhyme is very casually observed, the need for bringing in extraneous items should have been reduced. Why, then, is the same un-Goethean metaphor superimposed upon abstract expressions twice in the opening lines of the "Prologue in Heaven": "thunderous footsteps" for "thunderous movement (*Donnergang*)" and "tranquil footsteps" for "gentle conduct (*sanfte Wandel*)"? What we have here is more acceptable as a personal trot than as a poetic equivalent. The claim of speaking plain English is generally made good, though archaism occasionally creeps in (e.g., "many a . . ."). More often the speech veers toward a vernacular extreme. Only an American undergraduate would be asked, "What have you elected for your major (*Was wählt Ihr fur eine Fakultät*)?" And when Valentin uses the expressive term *Schwadronieren* for soldiers' empty boasts, it is grossly cheapened by the reduction to "crap."

Robert Frost spoke too harshly when he declared that poetry is what gets lost in translation. Yet something has got to give, some variable is bound to be disregarded, in a process where a sequence of meanings has to be extracted from its sound-pattern and rematched with a wholly different set of sounds. And when the two languages involved are German and English, George Steiner's question becomes highly pertinent: "Why are German versions of Shakespeare consistently so much better than English versions of Goethe?" Some basis for the answer, to be sure, is that Shakespeare wrote mainly in blank verse while Goethe widely varied his rhyme-schemes, and that English happens to be much less fecund and flexible in rhyming than German. Among the many meters of *Faust,* the characteristic measure is *Knittelvers,* which Goethe developed from the carnival plays of Hans Sachs—loosely iambic tetrameters, somewhat irregularly rhymed with alternating masculine and feminine endings. The quatrain that states Faust's wager with Mephisto offers a memorable instance:

> Werd' ich zum Augenblicke sagen:
> Verweile doch! du bist so schön!
> dann magst du mich in Fesseln schlagen,
> dann will ich gern zugrunde gehn.

The most popular of the older translations, that of Bayard Taylor, keeping to the conventions of nineteenth-century diction, does not stray far from the text, though it achieves its rhymes by a little embroidery along the edges:[1]

> When thus I hail the Moment flying:
> "Ah, linger still! thou art so fair!"
> —then bind me in thy bonds undying,
> my final ruin then declare.

Jarrell's version, condensed to three taut lines, is plain enough but not very memorable (every minute has sixty seconds, and waiting is not quite the same thing as staying):

> If ever I say to any minute:
> "But wait, wait! You are so fair!"
> Throw me in chains, then; then I'll gladly perish.

The other new translator, Walter Arndt, preserves the meaning while almost catching the original meter:

> If the swift moment I entreat:
> Tarry a while! you are so fair!
> Then forge the shackles to my feet,
> Then will I gladly perish there!

It is worth turning back a little, at this conjunction, to the thoughtfully crafted translation of Louis MacNeice, which perhaps comes closest to Goethe here and elsewhere.[2] Though it skips over the alternate rhyme, it catches the double beat of the feminine cadence. It even dares to address the personified instant with the second-person singular pronoun (the metaphorical connotation of *Augenblick* is an irretrievable loss, which three of these four renderings try to offset by introducing an adjective):

> If ever I say to the passing moment,
> "Linger a while! Thou art so fair!"
> Then you may cast me into fetters,
> I will gladly perish then and there.

Typically, there are no runovers in these quotations; Goethe was sparing in his use of enjambment. His syntactic unit was the single line, which often takes on a sententious or proverbial inflection. Consider the Lord's pronouncement which later becomes the key to the tragedy: *"Es irrt der Mensch, solang' er strebt."* This is rendered fairly closely, though not very gracefully, by Professor Arndt: "Man ever errs the while he strives." Jarrell's alexandrine formulation sounds more colloquial, but it sounds too much like Robert W. Service: "A man must make mistakes, as long as he keeps trying." The tone of incantation, so essential to the play, is harder to attain without regular rhymes and repeated phonemes. There are times when Jarrell goes out of his way to avoid a rhyme. Once, for a wonder, two German-English cognates suggest a perfect—if inelegant—one, in the scene "At the Well" (*stinkt/drinkt*). Mr. Arndt is literal and apt:

> It stinks!
> She's feeding two now, when she eats and drinks.

It should be added that he echoes MacNeice, as MacNeice echoes Taylor. Translation is, in some respects, a cumulative enterprise; and those who wish to improve upon the weaknesses of their predecessors are justified in building upon the strengths. Jarrell, by deliberately inverting, breaks away from that consensus:

> It stinks!
> Now when she eats and drinks she's feeding two.

Most of Jarrell's lines move toward a kind of free blank verse, which in English drama is haunted uncomfortably by the ghost of Shakespeare. The avoidance of rhyme is particularly noticeable in the Garden Scene, where it lent a note of mock-symmetry to the pairing off of the lovers. Without it some of the epigrams seem less than epigrammatic, and it comes and goes erratically in the songs. Arndt's version of Gretchen's ballad, "The King of Thule," can be sung to the existing music—unlike Jarrell's. Arndt's treatment of her lament at the spinning wheel runs nearly word for word, and (except for changing a future to a present tense in the third line, and dropping out the first-person pronoun) it is exactly the counterpart of MacNeice's:

> My peace is gone,
> My heart is sore;
> Can find it never
> And never more.

Here, where again the German could ease the rhymer's dilemma (*schwer/nimmermehr*), Robert Lowell—filling in for Jarrell—turns away capriciously from the obvious solution (can he have been acting on the conceivable assumption that Poe's raven has used up "nevermore"?):

> My peace is gone,
> My heart is sore,
> I never find it,
> I never find it.

It does not follow, therefore, that the translator's freedom from the constraints of rhyme invariably brings him closer to the linear purport of the author's language. Barker Fairley, the dean of living Goethe scholars, has given us a Faust in English prose which seeks to convey the ideas as idiomatically as possible by transposing quite freely.[3] Metrically faithful, Arndt has produced a *tour de force*, without deviating farther from Goethe's substance than Jarrell. He has girded himself for this achievement by his rhyming version of Pushkin's *Evgeni Onegin*, which drew down upon him the Olympian wrath of his literalistic rival, Vladimir Nabokov. As with Nabokov, English is not the first of his various languages—a fact which betrays itself in both writers only through self-conscious virtuosity. Arndt makes a spirited defense of rhyme, which is convincing so far as Goethe's esthetic effects are concerned, but leaves Arndt sweating with the other translators when it comes to Englishing those effects.

Thus he goes through too much trouble in calling Faust the Lord's "serf"—rather than "servant (*Knecht*)"—simply to gain a dissonant jingle with "worth" and "earth." On the other hand, with his "Prelude in the Theater" (would it not, more precisely, be "on the Stage"?),

Lustige Person is presented literally as "Merry Person," which does not carry its theatrical overtones, whereas the spontaneous idiom would have been "Clown" or "Comedian." "Paradisiac lucence" for *Paradieseshelle* cannot be technically faulted, though it would sound appropriate only on the lips of an archangel. There are passages where one is reminded of Ben Jonson's remark about *The Fairie Queene:* "Spenser writ no language." Spenser fabricated a marvelous style, but it was eclectic and artificial. Like him, Arndt devises coinages to suit his needs ("perpent," "hexendom"), and rises to the many occasions for wordplay. Nimble and ingenious consistently, if sometimes stilted or circumlocutory, he is at his best with patter, comic scenes, and grotesquerie.

To his verse-text of the total work, Cyrus Hamlin has added lucid and informative footnotes, a succinct commentary, a substantial amount of historical background, and a selection of criticism, both contemporaneous and modern. The reader in a position to take full advantage of that compendious apparatus ought really to have some firsthand acquaintance with German literature. Conversely, it is fair to say that students in the field will find this a useful volume. A comparison with Jarrell's book, wholly apart from stylistics, raises two general questions. No notes are provided with the latter. Hence a good many intelligent readers will find the drama unintelligible at many points. The puns (on *Faust* and "fist" at one point), the Latin (not always correctly transcribed), the allusions to forgotten literary antagonists, the jargon of alchemy, virtually the whole of the topical Walpurgis Night's Dream—why include them if they go unexplained? Do not the three introductory sections have less to do with Part I than with Part II?

This leads directly to my second question, which has been firmly answered by Henry Hatfield in his excellent critical introduction to Goethe: "One cannot understand *Faust I* without reading the second part."[4] Faust need scarcely have invoked the cosmos in order to seduce a naïve girl. His ultimate significance is framed by his adventures in "the great world," and especially by the outcome of his compact. Part I by itself may be considered more fragmentary than an arrangement of both parts which leaves out some opaque or digressive episodes. The MacNeice translation covers about 8,000 of the play's 12,000-odd lines, and the abridgments are clearly signalized. Since it was commissioned by the B. B. C. for the Goethe centennial in 1949, it has stood the test of effectual performance. Though Mac-

Neice did not know a great deal of German, he had line-by-line advice from Ernest Stahl, a perceptive critic of German poetry. The quality and readability of MacNeice's verse is self-evident. To take one sampling:

> I am not like the gods—that I too deeply feel—
> No, I am like the worm that burrows through the dust
> Which, as it keeps itself alive in the dust,
> Is annulled and buried by some casual heel.

There is no smell of the thesaurus here, nor is there much variance from the exact sense and the word-order of Goethe:

> Den Göttern gleich' ich nicht! zu tief ist es gefühlt.
> Dem Wurme gleich' ich, der den Staub durchwühlt;
> den, wie er sich im Staube nährend lebt,
> des Wandrers Tritt vernichtet und begräbt.

Arndt, in his turn, adheres awkwardly to the German in his first line, compounding the inversion and retaining the weak passive, then divagates in the second and third, and recovers effectively in the fourth:

> Not like the gods am I—profoundly it is rued!
> I'm of the earthworm's dust-engendered brood,
> Which, blindly burrowing, by dust is fed,
> And crushed and buried by the wanderer's tread.

Jarrell, except for a second line that parallels MacNeice (plus half of the first), stays farther from his source than the others, yet has assumed no personal control of his material:

> I am not like the gods! I know it too well;
> I am like the worm that burrows in the dust,
> Feeds on the dust—and the foot of the traveler
> Crushes and buries it, there in the dust.

Goethe, who enthusiastically welcomed the French version of *Faust* by Gérard de Nerval, would no doubt have made some mellow comment to his confidant Eckermann, could he have foreseen the perpetual strivings of his English translators. An experienced translator himself, he dramatized the predicament when his hero gropingly rephrased the exordium of Saint John. His belief in poetic universals was shared by the great succession of English poet-translators: Chaucer, Spenser, Dryden, Pope, Coleridge, Shelley, Yeats, Pound. It is gratifying that recent American poets have been involving themselves

in this responsibility—many for more positive reasons than that of un-
blocking their voices. Mrs. Jarrell refers to three of her husband's contemporaries who have been similarly engaged: Robert Lowell, Richard Wilbur, and Robert Fitzgerald. But Racine was not as happily
matched with Lowell as Molière was with Wilbur, while few among
them have dedicated themselves to the task as arduously as Fitzgerald
has to the Greek tongue and the Homeric world.

Jarrell, who subjected himself in his earlier writing to a stricter
technical discipline, proved an admirable translator of Rilke on at
least one occasion, "The Olive Garden." Probably this belated publication of his *Faust* manuscript can best be justified by the thematic interest it may hold for readers of his own allusive poetry. Goethe figures confronting Napoleon in "An English Garden in Austria"; Faust's
wager is turned upside down in "A Conversation with the Devil."
Lamenting that "I don't know enough German," in "*Deutsch durch
Freud*," Jarrell invokes Goethe as "my own favorite daemon," and
characterizes his phrasing as "very idiomatic, very noble; very like a
sibyl." He is fascinated throughout with that theme of flight which
animates the soaring quest of Faust, and which is condemned but un-
checked when it encounters the operatic fall of Euphorion. Above all,
there remain a certain mood and a certain focus that Goethe's poetico-
philosophical drama must have mirrored and reinforced for Jarrell.

The mood is that of the modern intellectual weary and suspicious
of intellectualism, impatient with the limits of the dryasdust academy
and eager to face the immediacies of sensory experience: the mood of
Faust leaving his Gothic study to mingle with the Easter crowd, join
the drinkers at Auerbach's tavern, and regain his youth in Gretchen's
arms. When Jarrell wrote,

> The blacked-out tree
> Of the boy's life is gray
> On the tangled quilt,

he undoubtedly was recalling Mephisto's counsel to the Student (after
a dialogue which has illustrated and parodied Faust's inaugural soliloquy on the hollowness of book-learning):

> All theory, my friend, is gray—
> The golden tree of life is green.

Goethe's running contrast between the Word and the Act, which is
rather similar to Bergson's dichotomy between mental abstraction and

natural flux, oscillates through Jarrell's poems continually. Yet almost as many of them are situated in tranquil libraries as upon fighting planes. "The Woman at the Washington Zoo," herself trapped and caged, cries, "change me, change me!" In "Gleaning" there is a girl inside the old woman who gasps out, "More, more!" It will be noticed that both of these Faustian heartcries are uttered by women.

For the recurrent focus is centered on "Woman," the title and subject matter of a longish, explicit, and sensitive meditation. There is an observation in that poem,

> Man's share of grace, of all that can make bearable,
> Lovable almost, the apparition, Man,
> Has fallen to you,

which parallels the resolving lines of the untranslated Second Part, where it is promised that undescribable ends will be ultimately accomplished for both sexes through the upward progression of eternal womanhood:

> Das Unbeschreibliche,
> Hier ist's getan;
> Das Ewig-Weibliche
> Zieht uns hinan.

One of Jarrell's high notes, not unrelated to his innate masculinity, is a feminine pathos which extends from the Marschallin in *Der Rosenkavalier* to the little black child, Lady Bates. This may help to explain why he was more interested in Part I than in the further adventures of Faust, and why—in spite of some verbal obstructions—he seems to have empathized most fully with Gretchen. It is not surprising to be told by Mrs. Jarrell that his favorite episode was the Dungeon Scene. Dramatically it constitutes the climax of the whole play, and one of the greatest scenes in the world's repertory, even outdistancing in some respects its Shakespearean prototype, the two mad scenes of Ophelia. The poignance of Goethe's half-crazed heroine compulsively re-enacting the deaths of her child and her mother, and gradually recognizing and finally spurning Faust to confront by herself the prospect of execution and the promise of redemption, needed no more than a simple and supple presentation to bring out the emotions that responded to it at Jarrell's public readings.

N O T E S

1 Bayard Taylor, *Goethe's Faust: The Prologues and Part One,* rev. and ed., Stuart Atkins (New York: Collier Books, 1963). Bilingual edition. A companion volume comprises Professor Atkins' presentation of Taylor's *Part Two,* but does not include the German text.
2 *Goethe's Faust: Parts One and Two,* an abridged version translated by Louis MacNeice (New York: Oxford University Press, 1961). (London: Faber and Faber, 1951.)
3 *Goethe's Faust.* Translated by Barker Fairley; illustrated by Randy Jones (Toronto: University of Toronto Press, 1970).
4 Henry Hatfield, *Goethe: A Critical Introduction* (Cambridge, Mass.: Harvard University Press, 1964; paperback edition, New York: New Directions, 1963).

IN MEMORIAM:
I. A. RICHARDS (1893–1979)

Being called upon to write an obituary for a friend, as I was on this occasion by The New York Review of Books *(December 6, 1979), is always a sad burden, to be sure. But the sadness of loss is somewhat lightened by the parting view of a life so fully rounded and widely appreciated. I had first met I. A. Richards when I stopped by his door at Magdalene College in 1933, presented a letter of introduction from F. O. Matthiessen, and was warmly welcomed to tea and conversation. Six years later we both joined the Harvard Faculty: he in a senior post at the Graduate School of Education, I on a junior appointment in the Department of English. We were soon working together through the developing program in General Education, and for a number of years resided around the corner from one another. Until his eighties, he and his wife did not resume their English residence, and after that they paid an annual visit to friends in New England. It is a satisfaction to remember that, during the autumn before his death, my wife and I persuaded this pair of mountain-climbers to come down (in both senses) and spend a few days with us at Cape Cod, where they vigorously trudged the dunes. Since there were friendly disagreements as well as common interests, I might add that I have suggested a more critical view of Richards' methods in* Why Literary Criticism Is Not an Exact Science *(Cambridge: Heffers, 1968), reprinted in my* Grounds for Comparison *(Cambridge, Mass.: Harvard University Press, 1972).*

●

When Ivor Richards was stricken with a terminal illness last spring, he was fulfilling a long, far-ranging, and exceptionally active career as a citizen of the world. During his eighty-seventh year he had been revisiting China, for him the beloved scene of educational ventures and recurrent interchanges many years before. Despite his failing strength, his lectures had been meeting with a triumphal reception. For five weeks he was treated with the utmost resources of Chinese medicine, and finally flown by the government with a medical escort back to Cambridge University, where he died in the bosom of *alma mater* on Friday, September 7. As a young student at Clifton and

Cambridge he had been forced to drop out periodically by the hazard of tuberculosis, and in subsequently rebuilding his health had turned himself into an indefatigable mountaineer. It was on a mountain top that he met Dorothea Pilley, the accomplished alpinist who became his wife. Inseparable traveling companions, they spent most of their vacations in the Alps or in quest and conquest of more distant peaks. Even during their later years in New England, after Mrs. Richards had been seriously injured by a motor accident, they still went backpacking over the academic weekends.

Richards was a person who looked at life, existentially as well as literally, from the heights in panoramic exaltation. If he had professed an abiding religion, it would have been a kind of Wordsworthian pantheism. He signalized *The Waste Land*, when it appeared, as effecting a severance between poetry and belief—a view which T. S. Eliot could hardly accept, though their dialectical friendship was warm and long-standing. Richards viewed himself as a man "without Beliefs," significantly capitalizing the noun; he was rather a man of attitudes, which were bound to change along with his protean development. Facing the problem of values under the early influence of G. E. Moore's ethics, William James's psychology, and C. S. Sherrington's physiology, he proposed to resolve it on an empirical plane. It was not for nothing that he had taken his undergraduate honors in what was known as Moral Sciences, or that his first published article was addressed to the mediating theme of "Art and Science." To the English Faculty, when it was established at Cambridge after the First World War, he brought a fresh approach which was philosophic and analytic, rather than conventionally oriented toward the philological and historical backgrounds of literature.

Literary studies at the time, both in England and in the United States, tended to be either antiquarian or impressionistic, and consequently at internal odds. Theory, redefinition of terms, and conceptualization of problems were matters of little concern within the academy, despite the occasional efforts of such freelances as Kenneth Burke or Herbert Read. The Marxist and the Freudian ideologies, for better and for worse, would be finding their respective critical applications. Linguistics, though seminally related to literature in the thinking of various continental schools, mainly went in its own specialized directions until the comparatively recent campaign for a rapprochement under the flashy banners of an imported Structuralism. Here the great exception has been Richards, who—more than half a century ago—was concerned with the sort of questions that have been cropping up in the latest issues of *Tel Quel.* The starting point was his collaboration with that nimble-minded impresario of ideas, C. K. Ogden, notably in *The Meaning of Meaning* (1923). There, in what would serve as a prolegomenon, Richards helped to survey the ground and lay the foundations, if not for a "science of symbolism," then for an emphasis upon semantics as the mean between thought and language.

His first independent volume, *Principles of Literary Criticism* (1924), asserted its modernity in its opening sentence, echoing Le Corbusier: "A book is a machine to think with." Richards would be still the technician when, publishing his first collection of essays some thirty years afterward, he entitled it *Speculative Instruments* (1955). He had meanwhile conducted a famous and influential experiment, with the startling results that were announced in *Practical Criticism* (1929). Making the classroom his laboratory, he had registered the unmediated responses of his students to a sequence of unfamiliar poems. By a systematic analysis of these psychological data, he was able to pinpoint the sources of misconstruction and to formulate a set of criteria for interpreting poetic texts, based upon his own gifts of explication. This at a moment when, with Eliot in both vanguards, poets had been getting more difficult for the common reader and critics had been rediscovering the ironies and ambiguities of the Metaphysical School and the French Symbolists. Hence the Ricardian method of close reading could not have been more opportunely needed or more warmly welcomed. It had already become the basis of a spreading pedagogical movement in the United States when John Crowe Ransom brought out *The New Criticism* (1941), saluting Richards as a founding father.

Richards' experimentation with readers had been extended into the realm of prose through *Interpretation in Teaching* (1938). In *The Philosophy of Rhetoric* (1936) he had updated the classical models for such key figures of speech as metaphor. Scrutinizing the processes of communication as a whole, he had been shifting his focus from the receiving to the transmitting end. The reader's mind was more accessible, in the light of his responding "protocols" and the texts that prompted and controlled them. But how would it be possible to take soundings of the writer's imagination? Human guinea pigs would no longer have much to contribute. Richards took the unaccustomed step of consulting authorities, and none but he would have chosen two mentors so far apart. *Mencius on the Mind* (1931) reverts to the wisdom of the East, incidentally highlighting the quandaries of translation and intercultural dialogue. *Coleridge on the Imagination* (1934) refers this overwhelming question to the poet-critic whose struggles with it marked a retreat from the associationist psychology of Hartley to the transcendental idealism of Kant. Richards, who had begun his study as a self-confessed "Benthamite," seems to have moved backward with his subject from the positivistic tendency of British empiricism toward the metaphysical allure of neo-Platonism.

In 1926 *Poetry and Science* had attempted to reconcile Bentham with Arnold through the validating concept of poetic truth as "pseudo-statement." Dissatisfied before long with his original argument, Richards revised and qualified it in a second edition (1935). The third edition, appearing after a longish generation, indicated by its reversed and pluralized title how far his position had been changing: *Sciences and Poetries* (1970). Insofar as he distinguished the sciences ("what is done, or can be done") from the humanities ("what should be done") at an interdisciplinary conference, he emerged unequivocally as a humanist. In the interim his main attention had been turning from "Theory of Literary Criticism" to "Design of Instruction in Reading." He had been enlisted for the latter cause when his old collaborator, Ogden, invented Basic English. Richards, as a cosmopolitan pedagogue, had been attracted by its potentialities for reaching wider regions of verbal expression, necessarily at lower levels. As the critic of poetry who had done so much to emphasize connotation, Richards was fascinated by this arbitrary language of strict denotation. Limited and simplified to the point where there could only be one way of saying anything, it could be a tool for discriminating "plain sense" from associations, overtones, modulating contexts, and "stock responses."

Thus, though he kept moving on, he never abandoned his earlier interests. During the Twenties and the Thirties he was employed primarily as a Fellow of Magdalene College and a University Lecturer at Cambridge. For a somewhat longer stretch during the Forties and Fifties, and throughout an active retirement in the Sixties, he was a University Professor at Harvard. Though he was free to teach whatever and wherever he wished, to the regret of his colleagues in the Yard he stationed himself at the School of Education. Indeed he wryly spoke of having "backed out of literature" to settle down on the other side of the tracks. His sense of mission was intensified on transferring his base of operations. A speech by the visiting Winston Churchill in 1943 must have made Richards feel that further work on Basic English was regarded as his expatriate contribution to the war effort. Churchill's support, according to William Empson, gave "the kiss of death" to any hopes for the adoption of Basic as a world language, since it could thereafter be tagged as an agent of British imperialism. Nothing could have been farther from Richards' intentions. Cheerfully he continued with his research staff, devising manuals for foreign use and paperbacks ingeniously combining Berlitz techniques with comic strips, in the spirit of postwar decolonization.

His commitment to pedagogy drew him closer to home academically during the mid-Forties, when the Faculty of Arts and Sciences was confronted by an explicit need for curricular renewal. Richards thereupon recrossed the tracks to put his experience and his expertise at the service of the working committee and into the drafting of its celebrated report, *General Education in a Free Society.* As an educator he was interested in every stage of instruction, and the programs in great books at the University of Chicago and elsewhere had engaged his sympathies and his reservations. When their categorical publicist, Mortimer Adler, wrote a simplistic book called *How to Read a Book,* Richards maintained the priorities with an ironic yet modest caveat, *How to Read a Page,* implicitly suggesting that true literacy resided in a mental process rather than in the acquisition of a highly advertised bookshelf. Under the Harvard program he would make his effective reappearance as an undergraduate teacher, lecturing to freshmen and sophomores on Homer, Plato, and selected books of the Old Testament. As a by-product of this return to the ancient classics at an introductory level, he retranslated, adapted, and streamlined his own versions *in usum Delphinorum* of *The Iliad, The Republic,* and four Socratic dialogues.

He was approaching sixty when he proceeded, in his own description, "From Criticism to Creation." Criticism had been "comments on endeavors"; his educational undertakings had become "a new endeavor"; and then, perhaps because they had placed him at a farther remove from literature itself, he came back to it directly by writing poems and plays. Here again he found inspiration in Coleridge, even though his myriad-minded predecessor had been going in the very opposite direction. Richards' poetic voice, not unexpectedly, turns out to be gnomic if not didactic. The verse is tightly constructed and neatly turned; the diction is always simple but succinct. His accumulated reserves now enabled him to express more freely—what is increasingly manifest in his discursive prose—the interplay of emotions with ideas. He was much preoccupied, like the later Yeats, with the elegiac mood and the detaching insight of old age; accordingly the title of his first collection, published twenty-one years before his death, is *Good Bye Earth and Other Poems*. Not all of the plays that he composed, during so fruitful a reprieve, have yet been printed. Two of these cosmic comedies were tried out through amateur productions in which he enacted a characteristic part: that of The Conjuror in *A Leak in the Universe* and the title role in *Tomorrow Morning, Faustus!*

It is revealing not only that he engaged in dramatics upon occasion, but that—on those two occasions—he was type-cast. In his varying scientific curiosities, his propensity for diagrams and gadgets, his handling of the electronic media, his adjustment to the Age of Space, he differed strikingly from most of his fellow humanists. Yet he remained, in temperament and talent, not a technologist but a mage. To hear him speak in public was to be reminded of his Welsh ancestry, and to suspect a strain of wizards, bards, and preachers. Not that he was capable of indulging in declamation. Quite the contrary, as one hearer put it, "he poured on the restraint." This capacity for conveying an impression of powerful forces kept so beautifully under control, it would seem, had something to do with Richards' skill as an analyst of rhetoric. Whenever he read a poem aloud, in his precisely cadenced Cantabrigian English, it was an artistic performance; it was likewise a virtual explication in itself. His *persona* was never far removed from his more intimate personality. Gentle, sympathetic, and whimsical by nature, he had acquired the mountain-climber's virtues: patience, fortitude, and an admixture of carefulness and daring. Many American friends will be missing a vivacious host and guest, an endearing neighbor and colleague.

Of the more than sixty different books that carry Richards' name on the title page, a considerable number are textbooks and handbooks worked out with linguistic collaborators under his methodological guidance. Those that bear his unique stamp as a critic also seem to retain his stance as a lecturer, teacher, and educator. Readers who have ever listened to him will recognize the style, and may visualize the platform and the blackboard. Some of his techniques of demonstration have been transposed through a series of typographical devices. Coleridge's *Biographia Literaria*, with its leaps from quotation to formulation, its *collage* of stylistics and metaphysics, its juxtaposition of anecdotes and theories, proved to be a problematic model. The great elucidator, in his preoccupation with the subtleties and complexities of his material, may not present the most lucid reading matter himself. Richards, dealing concretely with a text, could be the most percipient and perspicuous of commentators. When he took what he termed "the Copernican step," substituting the telescope for the microscope, he was perforce an explorer rather than a guide. The wonder was that, like few other literary critics, he should so often think in planetary dimensions. No other single individual, over the past two generations, has had more impact on the teaching of English or on the interpretation of poetry.

EDMUND WILSON:
THE LAST AMERICAN
MAN OF LETTERS

This commemorative tribute, based on a friendship of some thirty-five years, frequently as neighbors, was published in the (London) Times Literary Supplement *(October 11, 1974). It was based in part on a briefer and less personal sketch, "Edmund Wilson and the Comparative Outlook," suggested by Roy Harvey Pearce and read to a meeting of the International Association of University Professors of English at the University of California (Los Angeles) in August 1974.*

•

It is a long time since anyone set out to be—let alone became—a genuine man of letters. Sartre, who would scorn that epithet, has vented a good deal of spleen in denouncing literature itself as a way of life. American writers, when they were not oracles, have tended to be roughs, readier to assume an athletic stance than to be caught at a desk in a library. Yet when Edmund Wilson died in 1972, it was widely conceded that his unique stature had been based on a lifelong and whole-hearted commitment to letters. As a proponent of the moderns in years when Modernism was still contemporary, he had sharply detached himself from the genteel or the academic tradition. Occasionally and temporarily he accepted teaching posts at universities, but he was too little of a public performer ever to be at ease on the lecture platform. From first to last he considered himself a journalist, and as such no less the practitioner of "a serious profession" than De-Quincey, Shaw, Poe, Huneker, or Mencken. Wilson was indeed "a vanishing type, the free man of letters," Van Wyck Brooks acknowledged rather wistfully; for Brooks, another estimable prototype, had found his own freedom somewhat inhibiting.

The freelance gains his independence at the price of vocational security. Wilson's ten-year failure to pay his income tax, whether in a fit of absent-mindedness or a protest à la Thoreau, publicized the question of his earnings. His financial existence had been hand-to-mouth until he arrived at his sixties, when it was eased by an inheritance, plus increasing royalties from his books. He had incidentally acquired a toughness and shrewdness in professional dealings which could outmatch publishers and editors. The rejection slips he mailed to those who solicited his participation in their projects are now collectors' items. What he protected so warily was the right to choose his own subjects and to follow them at his dogged pace, wherever they led. The myriad-mindedness of his interests unfolded through the single-minded pursuit of one investigation after another. He was a professional, not a dilettante, precisely because he did not seek to cultivate too many things at once. He pursued his self-imposed assignments as an investigative reporter, working toward the highest intellectual level. But from his apprentice labor-reporting to his interviews with Santayana, Malraux, Silone, and Mirsky, it was the human aspect that he conveyed.

It was his biggest scoop to cover the Dead Sea Scrolls. He pulled it off by working up Hebrew and Biblical archaeology, seeking out and interviewing the rival schools of experts, and thereby elucidating for laymen the problems of Higher Criticism. His journalistic sense of timing was matched by a seismographic feeling for controversy and a flair for restating the basic issues. He attained his wide horizons through extensive legwork. He had rounded out and registered the grand tour of Europe at thirteen. He was at the hot gates of the two World Wars largely in a spectatorial capacity. Tours of duty as a correspondent took him to Russia, Hungary, Israel, and to ethnic enclaves nearer home: the Iroquois and Zuñi Indians, the Francophone blacks of Haiti and the two cultures of Canada. With *Travels in Two Democracies, Europe without Baedeker,* and *Red, Black, Blond, and Olive* he established himself among the most interesting travel writers of his era. Shortly before his death, when—as it happened—I returned from a brief trip to Mayan sites in Central America, he was eager in his questioning and sad in his repeated lament: "I shall never see them."

Stephen Spender has recently formulated a catchphrase which could be applied to Wilson's prickly attitudes toward the United Kingdom: *Love-Hate Relations.* His love for English literature was unabated from childhood; his resentment of certain English literati was provoked by their unthinking habits of condescension. Paradoxically, his reservations about postwar England began with hating to see it Americanized, though there may have been some *Schadenfreude* in his conception of it as "a failing organism." Descended from a pre-Revolutionary line of Anglo-Scottish lawyers, doctors, and Presbyterian ministers, he remained an early American, a proudly independent ex-colonial internationalist in the mood of Franklin and Jefferson and other ghosts of the Enlightenment. His boldest paradox was the invidious comparison elaborated in *A Piece of My Mind:* "I have had a good many more uplifting thoughts, creative and expansive visions . . . in well-equipped American bathrooms than I ever had in any cathedral." This is not the stock philistinism of Mark Twain or George F. Babbitt. Rather it is a pawky retort to the famous plaint of Henry James on the absence of Old World monuments from the native scene. As a matter of fact, its targets are not snobbish Europeans but sentimental Americans.

Wilson took a special pleasure in welcoming refugee intellectuals from abroad, who seemed to be fulfilling Gibbon's prophecy that a war-torn civilization might be reborn in the New World. He took further satisfaction in the polyglot elements of American life: "we are culturally almost as close to the other European countries as to England." Unlike so many of his contemporaries, he had never undergone an expatriate period; he had lived in Greenwich Village, worked for a newspaper, then edited and contributed to magazines. But the Continent was no more than a backdrop for Yankee antics in the fiction and career of Scott Fitzgerald, who had taken Wilson as his mentor from their Princeton days. European vistas, on the other hand, shadowed Wilson's pictures of the homeland. In *The Undertaker's Garland,* a doleful miscellany put together in 1922 with his college friend, the poet John Peale Bishop, he expressed a romantic disenchantment on returning from Paris after the War. "At home, the humanities had little chance against the Anti-Vice Society and the commercialism and the industrialism which had caught up the very professors from the great universities." Yet if Mencken could fight back such forces, Wilson could introduce more sophisticated values.

Nineteen-twenty-two was, of course, an *annus mirabilis* for world literature: the year of *The Waste Land, Ulysses,* and the death of Proust midway through the publication of his prodigious novel. Wilson was soon to emerge as "a critical synoptic eye" by interpreting these masterworks in close relation to selected others, in both English and French. But he was likewise ready to meet on their own ground—in *Vanity Fair, The Dial,* and *The New Republic*—those emergent writers who were creating something of a twentieth-century renascence in the United States: Hemingway, Anderson, Lardner, O'Neill, Stevens, Cummings, the Fugitives. It would not have flattered him to be called a pioneer in American Studies. When the Modern Language Association belatedly undertook to sponsor the series of major texts that he had long campaigned for, he voiced his dissatisfaction with their editorial procedures in a testy pamphlet. He had meanwhile edited that seminal anthology, *The Shock of Recognition,* which documents the course of American literature through the firsthand reactions of authors to authors. His most substantial book, and the one he came to regard as his best, was his literary inquiry into the experience of the American Civil War, *Patriotic Gore.*

No one would be able to vie with Wilson himself as his biographer. The detailed journal he kept for more than sixty years might well be an American counterpart of the cultural record left in France by the brothers Goncourt or André Gide. He printed snippets from these notebooks, along with reminiscent comments, in *A Prelude* and *Upstate.* It would have pleased him to learn of the arrangements lately concluded to bring out the manuscript as a whole, under the skillful editorship of Leon Edel. There will also be an important collection of letters, which is currently being gathered by his widow, Elena Wilson. More problematically, and yet inevitably, he will become an inviting subject for theses and monographs, for a kind of Research and Development far removed from the criticism he practiced. Though he was amused by the give-and-take of being reviewed or debated, he was consistently deprecatory about the formal studies that had already begun to come out in his lifetime. The irony is that most of these have been written by naïve and hasty Americanists, who—in spite of the opportunities provided by Senator Fulbright—have had no perspective upon the cosmopolitan dimensions of Wilson's work.

As for professors of English, he liked to say they were lazy. "They rarely know anything but English Lit." And that, he would agree with Ezra Pound, could not be adequately comprehended without a broad command of other literatures. In "A Modest Self-Tribute," Wilson advances the truly modest claim "that I have tried to contribute a little to the general cross-fertilization, to make it possible for our literate public to appreciate and understand both our Anglo-American culture and those of the European countries in relation to one another." Unlike Pound, he retained some piety for his educational background.

He retained his ties with Princeton through Christian Gauss, whose undergraduate courses in Dante and in the French Romantics had opened up the possibilities of comparative literature. Since Gauss would become a dean and put little in print beyond the usual jetsam of administration and pedagogy, his contribution must stand on the achievement of his sometime pupil. It was a distinguished one if it imparted, as Wilson writes in the dedication to *Axel's Castle*, "my idea of what literary criticism ought to be—a history of man's ideas and imaginings in the setting of the conditions which have shaped them."

He was generous in his tributes to former teachers, and he took the trouble to set down pedagogical suggestions for English, Latin, and Judaic studies. Nothing really delighted him so much as to show up the professors at their own game. "There are few things I enjoy so much as talking to people about books which I have read but they haven't," he disarmingly confided, "preferably a book that is hard to get or in a language they do not know." I can remember how his face would fall, if it chanced, when he mentioned such a book, that I had happened to read it. One was luckier to be ignorant of it, for then one would be treated to an admirable private lecture. Though he had laid a groundwork in Classics and Romance Languages at college, he continued to increase his stock of tongues. He was almost forty when he took up Russian; he was in his fifties when he studied Hebrew; at seventy he was being tutored in Hungarian. His accent stayed intrepidly American—to judge him wherever I could—and his syntax gropingly impressionistic. Yet one could not but be impressed by the resolution that armed him for each of these ventures in the enlargement of consciousness.

His linguistic one-upmanship reached the point of hybris, perhaps, in his polemical interchange with Vladimir Nabokov over the latter's translation of *Evgeni Onegin*. If the gods have laughed in recent times, they had occasion to do so when Wilson claimed to know Russian better than Nabokov and Nabokov claimed to know English better than Wilson. Wilson must be given credit, however, for his earlier part in introducing both Pushkin and Nabokov to American readers. The professional reception of Wilson's forays into Hebrew has scarcely been less controversial, though conflict seems to be inherent in the problem he attacked. What we can admire is the way he girded himself in responding to such a challenge: "Ah, the pleasure of approaching a new language!" Dictionaries and grammars always held a promise and a

delight: the sound of strange words, the pattern of unfamiliar para-
digms, the turning of a key to another culture. The critic's quest for
origins cannot have been pushed farther than his essay "On First
Reading Genesis." His own style met those criteria—Lucidity, Force,
and Ease—which had been laid down for him at the Hill School by
the benign John Lester, a Quaker Englishman from Haverford and
Harvard.

Wilson could fuss like the Fowlers over correctness of usage in
other writers, even though the very speed and range of his own writing made for occasional imprecisions in phrasing or detail. He might
have been characterizing himself when he spoke of Voltaire as "a fast-
producing journalist, with a style based on conversation." Half apolo-
getically, he attributed its "personal emphasis" to the self-assertiveness
of its formative decade, the Twenties. No apology was needed for a
directness which often shifts from first to second person, or for a spon-
taneity which is sometimes rendered breathless by the amount of observation packed into limited space. The recording observer developed, predictably, through a *persona* into a personality. We recognize
the tone of voice in the first-person narrator of the novel he published
in 1929, *I Thought of Daisy*. There he plays a generic young American
intellectual, all too allegorically submitting to a sequence of moral influences, among which the earthy heroine proves to be most elusive.
The other three are literary types in whom, despite the standard novelistic disclaimer of identifications *à clef*, we can discern some traits of
John Dos Passos, Edna St. Vincent Millay, and Alfred North Whitehead.

Wilson's other volume of fiction, *Memoirs of Hecate County*, also
consists of semi-imaginary portraits fastened together loosely if dia-
grammatically. If it had not been singled out for censorship in the
chaste year 1946, it would have created a dimmer impression. His
plays, in suffocating drama with dialogue, surpass those of his prime
model, Bernard Shaw. It was toward observed reality that Wilson
learned to look for dramatic scenes and convincing characters. The
chapter headings of *To the Finland Station* might have been stage
captions for an Epic Drama by Brecht: "Marx and Engels Take a
Hand at Making History." Wilson's first collection of verse, including
some prose, was significantly entitled *Poets, Farewell!* Nonetheless he
went on poetizing through insomniac nights in the country, evoking
absent friends or other places and moments; his second and third collections, reprinting selectively, were *Notebooks of Night* and *Wilson's*

Night Thoughts. The intonation is movingly personal in his memories of Fitzgerald or the elegiacs addressed to his wife Elena. But for the most part the poet-critic exercised his skill in imitations, metrical experiments, "Scurrilous Clerihews," satirical ballads, and parodies—notably and notoriously the poisonous "Omelet of A. MacLeish."

It is the same interlocutor who speaks throughout Wilson's work, with more and more consistency and firmness, a seasoned individual confronting the varied manifestations of human individuality. And no array of talents can have seemed so protean, so dazzling and difficult, so esoteric and idiosyncratic as the generation that flourished during the first thirty years of our century. With *Axel's Castle* Wilson came forward as their authoritative interpreter. He presented six contemporary writers: two Irishmen, two Frenchmen, two American expatriates. His pellucid common sense dispelled those difficulties which then were thought to put off readers from Yeats, Valéry, Eliot, Proust, Joyce, and Gertrude Stein. Moreover, by his framing chapters and suggestive cross-references, he managed to signalize these seemingly unrelated figures as "the culmination of a self-conscious and very important literary movement." It is doubtful whether a French or English critic would have perceived or admitted or traced the connections. Eliot had sounded a cue by acknowledging his particular debt to the *Symbolistes,* who in turn derived through Baudelaire from Poe. Proust might have offered a stumbling block to a narrower historian, inasmuch as his maiden article had been an attack on *Le Symbolisme.*

Wilson broadened the concept to extend it not only from French to English, but from poetry to prose fiction. His chapters on the novelists go deeper than those on the poets, and he would afterward be propounding the thesis that the Virgilian poet had been outdated by the Flaubertian novelist ("Is Verse a Dying Technique?"). Symbolism, in rough historical outline, was a second wave of Romanticism, a more intensive reaction against trade and technology. Yet, instead of reacting against science like many belletrists, Wilson pointed to analogies in the organicism of Whitehead and the relativity of Einstein. In his choice of latter-day Symbolists, there was one strategic weakness: Gertrude Stein. This is probably more obvious today, when she is clearly less meaningful than she may have seemed, while the others mean so much more. Wilson sensed the deficiency, allotting her his shortest and thinnest chapter, eked out with a barely relevant section on Dadaism, and frankly conceding the boredom induced by her pretentious prattle. But the book would have been greatly strengthened, in both scope and substance, if in place of that dubious example Wilson had chosen a German contemporary, a Rilke or a Thomas Mann to stand among his peers.

It throws some light upon Wilson himself, as a guide and master of ceremonies, to recall his penchant for sleight of hand. He could wax nostalgic over such heroes as Maskelyne and Houdini. He had a way of fascinating children by creating a mouse out of his handkerchief. Because I showed no interest in his card tricks, he once accused me of lacking intellectual curiosity. There was an element of this concern in his critical approach, as it were, to the masters of literary legerdemain: a resolve that the eye should be as quick as the hand, and undistracted by patter, in discerning how the effects of magic are produced. Thus a parlor magician is the very opposite of a guru; he lives in a rationalistic, not a mystical, world; his mysteries exist in order to be demythologized. So it was with Yeats's bards, with M. Teste, with the fabulous artificer Daedalus, when they became the subjects of Wilsonian elucidation. Those who complained of too much plot-synopsis and summarizing failed to appreciate how much decoding and unriddling had been involved—in a process which ultimately carried Wilson back to the original hunting ground of exegesis, the Bible.

It is a method which, in dealing with less complex materials, tends to overcomplicate them, as Wilson would do with the symbols in *Dr. Zhivago* or the hallucinations in *The Turn of the Screw*. At the hands of many subsequent critics, it would be no method at all, but a pretext for subjective overreading. Yet the impact of *Axel's Castle* was a monumental clarification for the works it discussed and the movement they constituted. The title has become identified with both, though the connotations of the silly play by Villiers de l'Isle Adam now seem extremely farfetched. Nor does the case of Rimbaud still seem so exemplary, as an alternate mode of escape from reality. Wilson, though he was enlarging the definition of Symbolism, still associated it with the last refinements and rarefactions of *fin-de-siècle* estheticism. It did not occur to him that Dante, whom he cited frequently, was the Symbolist *par excellence;* while Kafka, who was just beginning to appear posthumously, never held much attraction for Wilson. Retrospectively, he seems to have underestimated the humanistic ethos of his writers and the universality of their myths. Yet, if we apprehend them more fully today, we are beholden to Wilson's insights.

After the *ne plus ultra,* what next? The Symbolists had come to a dead end; for all their art and intellect, they had revealed themselves the spokesmen of a decadent society. Writing at the outset of the Thirties, he was prepared to bid farewell to all that, as he had defined it and illustrated it richly, and to welcome a return to Naturalism on some simpler plane. The closing paragraph of the essay on Proust is elegiac in its receding view of "the Heartbreak House of capitalist culture." Like other honest minds disturbed by such outrages as the Sacco-Vanzetti trial, Wilson was increasingly caught up in the social urgencies of the new decade. But unlike certain other critics, who found the shift easy because their artistic principles were lax, he refused to confound esthetics with politics. He did less reviewing; he traveled and reported on farms and factories, strikes and elections; he chronicled the Depression and the New Deal. Describing himself as "a progressive," he voted for Communist candidates in 1932. In 1935 he made his pilgrimage to the Soviet Union. There, to his later embarrassment, he stood at Lenin's tomb and recited Proust's ethical discourse on the death of Bergotte.

This attests, at any rate, the fund of good will and sympathetic responsiveness that Wilson had brought with him. He had also brought along his observant eyes and, since he had picked up the language, inquiring ears. He was bound to notice features of Russian life which impaired the hopes and ideals of fellow-travelers, and therefore bound—in all candor and honesty—to produce a qualified report. His position was similar to Gide's, in that both came back from Russia to face a second disillusionment: the blind hostility of local party hacks, predetermined to condemn and blacklist all accounts but the most uncritical glorifications of their promised land. *To the Finland Station,* with its titular image of Lenin arriving at Petrograd in his sealed train to take over the Revolution, had been conceived as an affirmative sequel to the study of Axel in his solitary retreat. Its compelling theme was nothing less than ideas transposed into actions, "man's reading of, and possible control over, history," the use of knowledge to "change the world." But had it been changed, after all or had the god failed? The book was disappointing because it frankly mirrored the poignant disappointment of 1940 over the train of events that had run amok after 1917.

Wilson measured his own far-ranging perspectives by being "incurably history-minded." Because of the number and variety of his *portraits littéraires,* he has repeatedly been compared to the biographical miniaturist Sainte-Beuve. Actually, he felt a closer kinship with the more comprehensive historian Taine, whose *History of English Literature* had been a landmark in adolescent reading. Taine's environmentalism must have fostered a preoccupation with *milieux,* with the conditions that shape the writer. But Marxism had promised to reveal how a writer could reshape conditions. Unfortunately its formula, the so-called Dialectic, turned out to be less a scientific technique than it was another religious mystique. In retracing the revolutionary traditions, Wilson proved better versed in Michelet than in Herder, more inspired by French historiography than by German *Geistesgeschichte.* Marx was the dominating protagonist, and he was saluted as iconoclast and prophet, as Swiftian satirist and "Poet of Commodities." Yet, with the ebbing of the author's socialist convictions, the panorama seemed confining rather than liberating. His point of view, withdrawing from ideology, fell back on psychology. Marx's carbuncles assumed the sort of influence that Pascal had attributed to Cleopatra's nose.

Since the historical climax of the Finland Station pointed toward the terrible anticlimax of Stalinism, Wilson announced his recoil in *The Triple Thinkers*—echoing the announcement of Flaubert that the serious writer should be triply disengaged from religion, fatherland, and social conviction. One of these essays, possibly Wilson's unhappiest, rushes from the Marxian orbit to a Freudian extreme by reducing the opulent dramaturgy of Ben Jonson to a case history in anal eroticism. Wilson himself had been briefly exposed to psychoanalysis during a transitory breakdown; he had gone on writing steadily, productively, and characteristically through his few weeks in a sanatorium. His psychoanalytic viewpoint was enunciated and exemplified in *The Wound and the Bow.* It envisaged a parable of the artist in the myth of Philoctetes, the Sophoclean hero, banished by his fellow warriors for his suppurating trauma only to be recalled and honored for his transcendant gift. Dickens was the principal exemplar, and Wilson's penetrating psychograph, "The Two Scrooges," coincided with George Orwell's revaluation in focusing upon a great novelist whose very popularity had caused him to be critically neglected. Wilson, as a decipherer of enigmas, was as much attracted to *The Mystery of Edwin Drood* as to *Finnegans Wake.*

Though he was always interested in tracing and testing doctrines, he was quite incapable of becoming doctrinaire. Marxism and Freudianism offered aids to social and psychological understanding, which he drew upon eclectically. The Cold War of the Fifties confirmed the outlook of Social Darwinism articulated in the Shavian diatribe that serves as an introduction to *Patriotic Gore*. Lincoln there is coupled with Lenin and Bismarck as the successful mouthpiece of an imperialistic myth. In the national ordeal men and women suffered on both sides with heroic idealism—so Wilson demonstrated in circumstantial depth, tending slightly to favor the chivalric mythos of the Confederate losers. *Patriotic Gore* may now be supplemented and balanced by Daniel Aaron's well-ordered survey, *The Unwritten War,* which presses the speculation as to why the Civil War produced no literary masterpieces. Wilson holds up no esthetic canon; he takes his evidence where he finds his witnesses. Making some rediscoveries in his re-reading along the way, he pays less attention to Whitman and Melville than to Sidney Lanier and F. G. Tuckerman. For all his introductory reservations, he seems more at home in the tragic past of *Patriotic Gore* than in the utopian future projected by *To the Finland Station*.

His deliberate strategy, in building up his books, was to get himself assigned reviews of other books which might conduce to his subject matter. But while he was gradually putting together these central achievements, and making intermittent excursions into near and distant fields of cultural reportage, he was also lightly bearing the reviewer's burden of holding forth each week upon some new and regularly different publication. His miscellaneous reviews and shorter articles form a continuous "literary chronicle," running from the early Twenties through the middle Sixties. Edited with considerable revision and afterthought, as well as paste and scissors, they comprise a trilogy whose titles seem to reflect the critic's varying responses to the changing objects of his scrutiny. The earliest and largest, *The Shores of Light,* recalls the Twenties and Thirties in classically nostalgic retrospect: "a period that is very much livelier and had a much more exciting development than the war-darkened years of the forties." This is followed chronologically (though it was published second) by the compilation devoted to the Forties, *Classics and Commercials*—admittedly a mixed bag. *The Bit between My Teeth,* the concluding volume, sags with the strain of living in "our ghastly time."

It is evident that, during the last three decades, in pieces written mainly for *The New Yorker,* Wilson dug into remoter themes, played old-fashioned hobbies, and avoided most of his younger contemporaries: Bellow, Mailer, Updike, Barth. The explanation, *tout court,* is that nearly all of them bored him. It should be said that he was easily bored, and that "boring" had those overtones of dismissal which we associate with the French *ennuyeux* or the British "tiresome." He was similarly confident and emphatic in his use of such adjectives as "trashy," "overrated," and "second-rate." Consequently he seldom gave out blurbs, and his "first-rate" was a rare and authentic accolade. While keeping up his Classics—see his speakeasy meditation on Persius or his discussion of Housman's scholarship—he could do a neat hatchet job on commercials: on Somerset Maugham's betrayal of talents and standards, on the "professorial amateurishness" of Tolkien's pseudo-folklore, or the detective story ("Who Cares Who Killed Roger Ackroyd?"). The publishing market, during the long half-century he had closely watched and actively taken part in, had become flooded with "imitation books." But how to tell the real thing from the imitation? Who can tell us, if not our literary critics, and what is it that qualifies them?

But how, you will ask, can we identify this élite who know what they are talking about? Well, it can only be said of them that they are self-appointed and self-perpetuating, and that they will compel you to accept their authority. Impostors may try to put themselves over, but these quacks will not last. The implied position of the people who know about literature (as is also the case in every other art) is simply that they know what they know, and that they are determined to impose their opinions by main force of eloquence or assertion on the people who do not know.

Such determination is more common than such authority, as he was well aware. There are all too many criticasters who think they know what they do not know. The rules of the ultimate game, like the laws of Proust's *patrie perdue,* are invisible to fools—who are usually in the majority, and whom Wilson never suffered gladly. He once wrote a letter inviting me to join him in the annual award of a "booby prize for literary criticism—to be announced perhaps by the *Partisan Review.*" I shall not repeat the names of his candidates, but it is worth recollecting that one of his prizes was to be "a copy of *Bouvard et Pécuchet.*" Picking up a volume by the knowledgeable Saintsbury, he noted that it would hardly be understood by the "New York critics," and still less by "the 'explicating' New Critics and the academic myth-and-symbol men." His low threshold of patience has its positive side in his restless curiosity, admittedly his "main motive," an intellectual appetite as voracious as Saintsbury's. He was not without his blind spots (everything connected with Spain), not to mention his soft spots (Edna Millay). I suspect that his journals may disclose a certain cold-bloodedness: that of the reporter living his life for "the story in it."

Having been the literary conscience—according to Fitzgerald—of the brilliant generation he outlived, Wilson became "increasingly detached" from the pressures of the passing moment and from a bureaucratized society which he viewed with mounting distaste. There was nothing plaintive in this opinion; he had had his world as in his time; and if it implies a negative judgment upon the present, it cannot easily be brushed aside. Delving into history more deeply, he was more concerned with revivals than with discoveries, and his late discoveries were encountered afield: S. Y. Agnón, Marie-Claire Blais, the brothers Marcelin. He looked upon himself as "a survivor," "a man of the twenties"—if not of the eighteenth century. "Old fogeyism is comfortably setting in." No longer the leg-man or traveler, now sedentary and housebound, he shuttled back and forth between his two old country homes on Cape Cod and in upstate New York. He cultivated "a sense of my continuity" by turning over family albums and setting down youthful reminiscences. Overtaken in his hearty elder years by gout, *angina pectoris*, and various other ailments, he might well be alive today if he had not typically rejected an operation which would have paced his heart with an electronic device.

His childish nickname, "Bunny," may have been apt for a slight, shy, sensitive, and very nervous young man. He would take on weight with middle age, physically and temperamentally, and behave gruffly with strangers. A short and stocky figure, whose russet hair had thinned and grayed, he had a splendid head: a Roman nose and a stubborn chin, animated by a wheezing voice and a booming laugh. He collected puppets and put on Punch-and-Judy shows. I had the privilege of witnessing one of these, performed with his daughter's help for his step-grandchildren, where he had great fun in flaying about him and taking on all comers. So did we, as we did with his performance in the larger sphere. This became a continuous yet variegated monologue, in which the critic ended by eclipsing the criticized. He interviewed himself; in another letter he wrote me, "I've developed a new literary genre: reporting my own table talk." The results were Johnsonian rather than

Coleridgean. One of his Christmas—or rather, New Year's—pamphlets sent out to friends offers this poetic counsel:

> Beware of dogmas backed by faith;
> Steer clear of conflicts unto death.
>
> Keep going; never stoop; sit tight;
> Read something luminous at night.

Ever since the epoch of the Dead Sea Scrolls the children of light have been fighting the children of darkness. As a poet, Wilson courted the nocturnal muse; in the daytime he stood for beleaguered enlightenment; he gravitated toward the shores of light (*in luminis oras*), however they may have receded since the heyday of the Latin poets. Above all, he sat tight, he never stooped, he kept going in the wry hope that civilization would be doing so likewise. He had a vein of Hebraism, in the Arnoldian sense, which he must have inherited through his Calvinist ancestors. His tombstone, in the Wellfleet cemetery, bears a Hebrew inscription echoing the words of God to Joshua after the death of Moses, and traditionally recited when the reading of a book of the Torah has been completed: "Be strong, and of good courage." It is hard to imagine a more appropriate epitaph for a great critic.

BEING STRONG:
EDMUND WILSON'S CORRESPONDENCE

As the publication of Wilsoniana has continued, I have had to revise my expectations for the notebooks (at least for The Twenties; The Thirties *is still forthcoming as I write). It is the* Letters on Literature and Politics: 1912–1972 *(New York: Farrar, Straus & Giroux) that more richly embody the intellectual record of Wilson's activities and associations. This was well understood by the late Mrs. Wilson, who was consequently so expeditious in bringing them out. I reviewed them for* The New York Review of Books *(October 27, 1977). Brendan Gill's exception and my reply appear in the issue of December 8.*

•

The blurb on the jacket that characterizes the author as "this era's greatest man of letters" echoes an assumption which will not be challenged here. But what does that really mean? Most likely, an all-round competence in the various genres of literature. However, if he had been more successful than he was as a novelist, a dramatist, or a poet, he might have been saluted first under one of those categories. (On some occasions he wistfully declared that *Memoirs of Hecate County* was his best book, but any writer may be forgiven for viewing his latest or least appreciated effort as his masterpiece.) Indeed his versatility was such that he once planned a choreography for the Swedish Ballet which would have starred Charlie Chaplin. Voltaire was for many years regarded as a greater playwright than Racine; Johnson wrote a mildly interesting novel and a terrible play; both of them achieved their central positions as "men of letters." Edmund Wilson has been their worthiest successor in our time.

There can be little question, when it comes down to letters in their more literal sense. Correspondence has become a losing—if not a lost—art during our century of dictaphones and long-distance telephone calls. Wilson was enough the child of his natal century (b. 1895) to have kept the art under cultivation, and much of what is printed in these pages was transcribed from holograph. It represents a salient part of a much larger totality, which should all be published at some future date, when matters of privacy can be ignored. Presumably it will be; and this should mean that ellipses will be filled in, correspondents' letters will be printed, and what is now monologue will become dialectic. Wilson, though a great talker, was also—being an experienced reporter—a shrewd questioner and a sympathetic listener. When he describes a visit from Isaiah Berlin, he reports tongue-in-cheek that "We [not *he*, the manuscript has been checked] spent all the time talking brilliantly, covering rapidly, but with astonishing knowledge, sure intelligence, and breathtaking wit, an incredible variety of subjects."

If Wilson is to be categorized as a critic, it must be as a critic at large, a critic of everything. The balance between literature and politics in the title of this liberal selection turns out to be closer than it might have initially appeared. Some of his incidental commentary, on the two World Wars, the Depression, the Sacco-Vanzetti case, the impact of socialism in the Soviet Union and elsewhere, let alone the cataclysmic changes in the American way of life (titularly referred to as *Jitters* and then *Earthquake*), may well prove to be more penetrating in the long run than the comments of his stuffier colleagues on *The New Republic*, Herbert Croly or Walter Lippmann. His pamphlet on the income tax and the Cold War may not have been "the hottest thing since Tom Paine," but significantly he turned its royalties over to A. J. Muste's peace movement. Though his ultimate concern was with the individual expression that lay "behind politics," he consistently refused to station himself *au dessus de la mêlée*.

Indeed it was his engagement in so many of the cultural struggles of his long era that has given this testimony its enormous breadth and continuous vitality. Within one early sentence he couples Heine's enlistment (as "a soldier in the war for human liberation") with Ibsen's announcement (that "the younger generation is knocking at the door"). His best-known book, *Axel's Castle*, for all its elucidation of Post-Symbolist subtleties, is a valedictory to the "resignationism" of Proust, Joyce, and Eliot. His other two major works, *To the Finland Station* and *Patriotic Gore*, deal respectively with Communism and with the Civil War. Truly he could say that his "single aim [had] been literature." Yet, as he tells James Branch Cabell, of all people, "everything of mine . . . is rather heavily social-historical." Hence he detested the rarefactions of New Criticism, deprecated a study of Yeats for seeming to take place in a political void, and even suggested that Max Beerbohm's dandyism should be examined from "a social slant."

One of these letters is a kind of socialist manifesto, written after his experience with the miners' strikes at Harlan County, Kentucky, in collaboration with Lewis Mumford, Sherwood Anderson, and others, though evidently unpublished. Moving leftward from the wartime idealism of his presidential namesake, through the ideological infighting of the Stalinists and the Trotskyites, he preserved his Yankee common sense and radical independence. He was never so directly involved as John Dos Passos; neither did he recoil to the right, like his disillusioned friend. That friendship must have been severely tested by the series of letters criticizing Dos Passos for his apostasy (calling him "a hot-air artist" who sounded, on the subject of Senator Goldwater, "like a teenager squealing over the Beatles"). Since Wilson also presented more reasoned arguments, it is too bad that this important dialogue must stand incomplete; but one looks in vain for some of the counterarguments in Townsend Ludington's inadequate collection of Dos Passos' letters and diaries.

Since Wilson was himself a veteran editor, who had shored up Scott Fitzgerald's fragments with *The Crack-Up*, and taken on the vested cohorts of the M.L.A. in a controversy over editing, we have some notion of the treatment he would have preferred for himself. Elena Mumm Wilson has brought to her editorial task those qualities of understanding devotion which gave him twenty-five years of happy marriage. Annotation is reduced to a minimum, and most correspondents are identified by quoting Wilson's references to them elsewhere. The sequence is roughly chronological, decade by decade, with occasional rearrangements for thematic continuity. On the whole, it is remarkable that so rich and copious an accumulation could be gathered and selected within five years of the author's death. Naturally, there are lacunae: surely the correspondences with Mary McCarthy and Edna St. Vincent Millay must have had literary and political, as well as personal, aspects. It would have been enlightening to recover some of the many letters to Biblical scholars, such as the late W. F. Albright. And there might have been written communication with Svetlana Allelulieva.

But here is God's plenty, as Dryden said of *The Canterbury Tales*. And if Mrs. Wilson has had to be highly selective in representing such fascinating interlocutors as Vladimir Nabokov, it is good news that all of Wilson's one hundred and forty letters to him, together with Nabokov's reciprocal part in the exchange, will be published in a separate volume to be edited by Simon Karlinsky. This should help to dispel some of the numerous inaccuracies currently being circulated by Andrew Field's glib and capricious biography. Moreover, it should bring out much that was delightful and stimulating—not only to the two individuals, but to those of us who had the privilege of being friends with both—which has been overclouded by later polemics. Another clouded record is set straight by the reference—albeit not by title—to Matthew Josephson's *Life Among the Surrealists.* In this attempt to work up a set of memoirs by dropping the names of more talented contemporaries with whom the author had marginally associated, Wilson felt himself traduced. Lawyers agreed to corrections in further printings, for which there seems to have been little opportunity.

More serious is the clarification of his role in bringing out Fitzgerald posthumously. Therein Wilson's admitted toughness with publishers served his deep loyalty to his friend's work. For putting *The Last Tycoon* into publishable shape, he received an honorarium of five hundred dollars, which he donated to the Fitzgerald estate. Extraordinary as it may seem today, Scribner's was allowing Fitzgerald's books to go out of print, and Wilson had great difficulties in finding a publisher for *The Crack-Up.* In a gossipy book which reflects the corporate superciliousness of its theme, *Here at The New Yorker,* Brendan Gill has insinuated that Wilson sought financial advantage for himself in the arrangements he finally made with the more receptive firm of New Directions. The correspondence with Fitzgerald's executor makes clear that Wilson received the modest fee of two hundred dollars for the whole thing, and shared half of it with other contributors. The fact that one hundred dollars should be the compensation for a labor of love by an outstanding talent, carried out over months of intermittent endeavor, merits more than malicious anecdote.

Mrs. Wilson's edition is enhanced with an apt and amusing *montage* of illustrations. Daniel Aaron's lucid and thoughtful introduction is worthy of Wilson himself, in relating his development to the sociocultural currents of his times. There is an additional one-page foreword by Leon Edel, the General Editor of the Edmund Wilson Papers now in the Beinecke Library at Yale. He gives his imprimatur to this project, and acknowledges the sponsorship of his own contribution by the National Endowment for the Humanities; but he does not tell us what we would like to know about the extent and character of the papers or his plans for putting the rest of them into print. It should be remembered that the sixty years of the letters are also covered by intimate journals. Wilson had begun to publish these in *A Prelude,* which conveyed him from juvenilia through the First World War. He had likewise dipped into fairly recent notebooks to eke out his celebration of ancestral terrain, particularly his reoccupation of the old stone house at Talcotville, New York, in *Upstate.*

But the main installment to appear thus far has been *The Twenties,* edited largely by Wilson at the end of his life and completed by Professor Edel, whom we trust to follow it with volumes out of the successive decades. I should very strongly like to agree with him that it constitutes "perhaps the largest authentic document of the time." Furthermore, in a brief memoir for *The Times Literary Supplement,* I actually voiced an expectation that the Wilson diaries might turn out to be an American counterpart for what Gide and the Goncourts had recorded about French literature. It is therefore saddening to admit, though there are others who have reacted similarly, that this particular volume has left me with an anticlimactic impression. Much of it is devoted to what Professor Aaron, in a tactful phrase, has termed "disciplined dissipation." Though there were bound to be valid insights and suggestive jottings, a good deal of the narration seems preoccupied with psychological tensions, erotic experiments, and the search for identity that was to be resolved in the Thirties.

The Twenties were, of course, by no means so ebullient as the image they present in popular legend, and Wilson's letters about both *The Great Gatsby* and *The Big Money* emphasize their tragic view of human nature. Professor Edel's "portrait" in *The Twenties* applied to Wilson his own formula of *The Wound and the Bow,* and counterpoised his private anxieties with his professional accomplishments. Lacking the fuller information that we may hope for from subsequent volumes, we may question the General Editor's relegation of these letters to "the margin of [Wilson's] posthumous publications." Given his long-range commitment to the life of the mind, as contrasted with his frenetic strivings and strayings during the Twenties, there is substantial reason to infer that the emphasis should be placed on his letters, and that his diaries may belong in the background. He was not, after all, a highly creative writer, so that the wound-bow problem applies to him in a limited degree. Living within the hoopla of Greenwich

Village, he remained a lonely man, whose relations best expressed themselves in his intellectual correspondence.

Though he spent his working hours on his public writing, his epistolary habits were confirmed by his first marriage, inasmuch as his wife's schedule was regulated by her theatrical engagements (several of them in O'Neill's earlier plays). "Having, as a rule, no one to talk to at the cocktail hour," he wrote a school-and-college friend in 1925, "I have formed the habit of pouring it all into my correspondence to avoid the necessity of talking to myself." Another precondition for the letter writer is the itinerary of his career. Though Wilson never underwent an expatriate phase, his horizons were always widely cosmopolitan. Even when he presages "a shifting of the capital of the world's culture from Paris to New York," he warns Fitzgerald against the limitations of American provinciality. Nor did he ever feel quite at home in New York, where publishers were turning literature into a "cloak and suit business," fellow critics like Burton Rascoe and Gilbert Seldes were succumbing to the marketplace, and levels of taste were being set by "the Van Doren trust."

Regular jobs with *Vanity Fair, The Dial,* and *The New Republic* seem to have kept him somewhat unwillingly in the metropolis. He was in his late thirties when he detached himself to become a freelance; he was not to be free from financial insecurities until his late sixties. Making his base of operations in an early nineteenth-century farmhouse just off the Mid-Cape Highway at Wellfleet, he lived from one roving assignment to another: occasionally a reluctant term at a college or university, often an exploratory tour of cultures ranging from Iroquois to Israeli. This semiperipatetic mode of existence, besides providing much occasion to correspond, helped him to maintain his broad perspective and his critical distancing. For several years he sent out printed holiday letters in humorous verse to his widely scattered circle of friends. These were termed New Year—rather than Christmas—greetings; for, though he was deeply interested in the origins of Christianity, he personally rejected it as "the worst imposture in history." (Old Voltairean that he was, he needled Allen Tate and W. H. Auden about their religious conversions.)

Wilson was frustrated in what he could have fulfilled superbly: his desire to edit a first-rate highbrow general magazine, such as has not existed in the United States since *The Dial.* Curiously enough, it was his approach to Harold Ross, seeking practical advice in this matter, which brought about his appointment to "Clifton Fadiman's job reviewing books on *The New Yorker.*" He commenced with misgivings, expecting it to last no longer than a year. In fact, the connection lasted for almost thirty years; and though he now and then chafed against editorial conformities, the editors allowed him a free hand in sponsoring his cultural explorations afield, and allowed them plenty of space amidst the fall advertising. Having wielded the blue pencil himself, he was twice-trained professionally, and his relations with publishers' editors—notably Maxwell Perkins of Scribner's—show both astuteness and adaptability. He had been helpful with his own contributors, and adept at recruiting talents. It is too bad he could not persuade Hemingway to do a piece on Mussolini for *The New Republic.*

His principles of reviewing come out in letters to R. P. Blackmur, whose stylistic prolixities he gently but firmly emends. Blackmur's doubtful access to Dante or the *Symbolistes* in their own languages prompts Wilson's patient correction. His literary standards put to shame the scholarship of latter-day academics. Thus he can point out omissions, in acknowledging Gilbert Highet's survey, *The Classical Tradition.* He discusses the niceties of translation from Latin with Rolfe Humphries and Erich Segal, and delivers a damaging report to a publisher on Lionel Abel's versions of Rimbaud. Characteristically, the opening letter, addressed to a schoolmate who would become a classical scholar, Alfred Bellinger, puts down the latest Kipling by holding up the model of Homer. With his principal mentors at Princeton, Dean Christian Gauss and the Scottish philosopher, Norman Kemp Smith, Wilson stayed in touch throughout their lives. But, on later encounters, he has surpassed them: he cannot interest Gauss in Joyce or Hemingway, and he fears that Kemp Smith's rationalism is deliquescing into mysticism.

His acquaintance with the ancients and with continental culture lent a special authority to his reception of the modernists, at a moment when they were shocking most other readers who happened to be well versed in the classics. The countershock of recognition was electrically registered when he reviewed *Ulysses* at its quasi-surreptitious publication and *The Waste Land* from proofs in the same year. Writing to John Peale Bishop about Eliot's poem, he labels it "the greatest knockout up to date," and he uses a similar epithet five years later in congratulating Hemingway upon *The Sun Also Rises.* There are frequent expressions of acknowledgment to the leading writers of the period for copies of their books. Few of these do not mingle hard-headed counsel—not to say instruction—with perceptive appreciation, and some of them contain lists of detailed errata. While accepting an early accolade from H. L. Mencken, which must have meant a lot to him, he cannot desist from a postscript questioning one of that amateur linguist's solecisms: the habitual misuse of the adjective *jejune*.

For all his curiosity and catholicity, Wilson did not aspire to be a universal mind: on such grounds, he was suspicious of Albert Schweitzer; and he deliberately left out certain interests in order to be conversant with many others. Not reading Spanish, though he mastered more difficult tongues, on principle he never read *Don Quixote*. He avoided Thomas Mann, and had little feeling for the Germans. Certain of his judgments may strike us as wrongheaded: e.g., Housman as a poet of higher stature than Eliot. In *Vanity Fair* he started the game of listing the overrated, which has lately been played in the pages of *Esquire* and *The Times Literary Supplement*. Certainly he was far-sighted in derogating Aldous Huxley at the height of his vogue. In declaring Frost "flat and uninteresting," he has yet to convince most readers, and he seems to have gone up and down about Stevens, Pound, Cummings, and Marianne Moore. But it is refreshing when he recalls the forgotten felicities of poets like Elinor Wylie or Phelps Putnam. And it was discerning of him to discover so soon that Sartre was more of a journalist than an artist.

The tone of these epistles varies appreciably with the given addressee. Even the salutations and signatures are variously nuanced. Yet anyone who might have been put off by Wilson's published *persona*, finding it alternatively elusive or overbearing, may now enjoy the uninhibited flow of his candid conversation: responsive, crusty, hortatory, elegiac, jocular, and invariably poised for argument. He drops into parody and hoax, along with ingenious verse; his prevailing insistence upon the highest standards in all fields is alleviated by a sporadic note of ribaldry. The table of contents includes a letter in elementary Hungarian (translated and reproduced in facsimile), a better-known letter to the editors of *The New York Review of Books* proposing an American equivalent to the Bibliothèque de la Pléiade, and a characteristic response to John Wain's request for an interview in *The Observer*, counterposing questions for Mr. Wain to answer. The scope of interests and initiatives manifested here, or throughout his listed *oeuvre*, justified Wilson in demurring when he came to be conventionally characterized as "a mediator between artist and public."

He came an unforeseeable distance since he had professed himself, when he started out, a journalistic middleman. Professor Aaron's concluding assessment, that "he was the moral and intellectual conscience of his generation," broadens the testimonial of Fitzgerald which is fully documented here. "Brace up your artistic conscience, which was always the weakest part of your talent!" Bunny admonishes, on the eve of Scott's first success. "Be strong" is likewise his repeated watchword for their poetic classmate Bishop. Both of them needed, and insufficiently heeded, this admonition. Wilson, surviving both by a robustious generation, went from strength to strength. When he studied Hebrew, he learned that his motto signified an avowal of reinvigoration for the reader turning from one book of the Pentateuch to the next. He had it engraved on a plaque "tacked up over the oxygen tank in my bedroom-study." Shortly afterward it was inscribed on his gravestone. He had lived up to his own prognosis, after he had told the psychiatrists during a three-week hospitalization in 1929, "I had always thought I was a strong personality."

What the terse injunction meant to him is spelled out in a letter to Louise Bogan, whom he thought of "as fundamentally such a strong and wise individual," but who found herself in the same mental situation two years later:

These are times of pretty severe strain for anybody, to lapse into a vein of editorial generalization. Everything is changing so fast and we are all more or less in a position of having been brought up in one kind of world and having to adjust muscles, socially, sexually, morally, etc., to another which is itself in a state of flux. Still, we have to carry on, and people like you with remarkable abilities, even though they're more highly organized nervously than other people, are under a peculiar obligation not to let this sick society down. We have to take life—society and human relations—more or less as we find them—and there is no doubt that they leave much to be desired. The only thing that we can really make is our work. And deliberate work of the mind, imagination, and hand, done, as Nietzsche said, "notwithstanding," in the long run remakes the world.

It is a credo for that endangered species, the autonomous individual. Writing within a month or so to Tate, Wilson still affirmed a qualified faith in human progress, to be attained through the gradual collaboration of art and science. This belief grew harder to sustain through the post-Depression years, when it would seem more *à propos* to read Gibbon and note contemporary analogies. As Wilson's personal retrospect lengthened, he was amused to watch "one's own day before yesterday turning up as literary history." He objected when reviewers called him "mellow," yet admitted to Dos Passos that he now saw himself "as a probably moldering and mellow old codger from the frivolous twenties," whose own world was as remote to his juniors as the Civil War had been to him in youth. That he survives such a world so energetically, conveying its dedications and dissidences to ours, and preserving its dynamic impetus in these letters, makes him an exemplar and this book a monument.

A CONTEST
BETWEEN CONJURORS:
NÀBOKOV AND WILSON

I must have met Vladimir Nabokov—as Edmund Wilson did—very shortly after his migration to the United States. Having no occasion to cross swords in public, our friendship lasted until his recent death. It was particularly close during the Forties when he resided in Cambridge, teaching Russian at Wellesley College in the mornings, conducting his research on lepidoptera at the Agassiz Museum in the afternoons, and devoting most of his evenings in the cramped apartment on Craigie Street to his earlier English writings. He kept in touch with Wilson mainly through correspondence; but their occasional reunions were galas, at which my Russian wife and I often had the privilege of being present. Some of The Nabokov-Wilson Letters: Correspondence Between Vladimir Nabokov and Edmund Wilson, 1940–1971, *ed. Simon Karlinsky (New York: Harper and Row) seem to catch the sparks that their joint presence struck off. Sadly, they also reflect the lengthening shadows of misunderstanding. I reviewed them for* The New York Review of Books *(July 19, 1979). Since publication, it appears that some twenty-five further letters from Nabokov to Wilson have turned up in the Beinecke collection. These should be included in the next edition, and may add some interesting details, though Professor Karlinsky has informed me that they do not change the general picture.*

•

In the nostalgic evocations of his "autobiography revisited," *Speak, Memory*, Vladimir Nabokov neatly characterized the external pattern of his uprooted career as a Hegelian triad. Its thesis comprised the first two decades, indelibly Russian. Its antithesis, during a little more than the next twenty years, had been his post-Revolutionary expatriation in Western Europe. His roughly equal period in the United States (1940–60), where he became not only a citizen but a writer in English, would be a synthesis as yet unchronicled. Toward the end of his last seventeen years, passed mainly in Switzerland, he envisaged a dialectical sequel, *Speak On, Memory*, which would cover his American sojourn, including his friendship with Edmund Wilson. It may well serve the best interests of equity that, while lacking such a personal deposition, we now have the full two-sided documentation (with a few occasional gaps) for this quickening and pungent episode of our recent literary history. In that area Wilson's central position has long been established by his own writings, and is being reinforced by the posthumous publication of his letters and diaries and notebooks. Nabokov's course, by contrast, has been meteoric and unpredictable, an elusive presence between engagements with other worlds.

Monuments are being erected to him in his adopted country, however, more hastily and indiscriminately than he might have preferred—to judge from his own review of a farfetched monograph on his use of symbols.[1] He did have gracious words for contributors to a *Festschrift* on the occasion of his seventieth birthday.[2] He not only welcomed interviewers to his retreat at Montreux; he firmly set the tone and substance of those interviews, and considered them worthy of reprinting in *Strong Opinions* (1973). To his subsequent regret, he encouraged the biographical lucubrations of Andrew Field, repudiated by his son at a memorial symposium.[3] At the latest meeting of the Modern Language Association, inevitably, a special section was devoted to "New Directions in Nabokov Criticism." And we may now subscribe to *The Vladimir Nabokov Research Newsletter*, whose first issue informs us that there are already some twenty books and nearly forty doctoral dissertations, along with the scores of essays and articles pertaining to his works.[4] More and more these activities are coming to resemble the academic cult of Ezra Pound, and tending to parody the master they study. Even as brashness raises the pitch of the Poundians, so archness tinges the inflection of the Nabokovians.

Yet such reservations by no means apply to the present editor, Simon Karlinsky. He has validated his credentials as an articulate and knowledgeable interpreter of Russian literature at the University of California (Berkeley), and is jointly responsible for the best collection in English of Chekhov's letters. Since this new correspondence bristles with Cyrillic quotations, involving frequent mistakes by Wilson and corrections by Nabokov, it is important that the editing should be in expert professional hands, and Professor Karlinsky's purview is broad enough to provide informative and helpful annotation for the numerous other matters that were bound to arise. It is not his fault if he misses one or two private jokes between the pair of correspondents and their intimate friends: e.g., the allusions to a basket of fruit naïvely and crassly sent to Mary McCarthy (then Mrs. Wilson) by another emigré writer, Mark Aldanov, in the hope of eliciting a grateful review from her intransigent husband. And it is too bad that neither Nabokov nor Karlinsky sets Wilson straight, when he attributes "I do not like thee, Dr. Fell" to *Tom Brown's School Days*. With what glee Wilson would have put down anyone who had forgotten that the slightly misquoted line had been paraphrased from Martial by Thomas Brown, the Restoration wit!

Though a certain number of excisions are indicated, out of due respect for living personalities, the text remains well seasoned with literary gossip. The editor has introduced it with a suggestive essay, "Dear Volodya, Dear Bunny; or, Affinities and Disagreements." (Curiously, neither writer ever signs his nickname, and Bunny seems reluctant in addressing Volodya as such.) Mr. Karlinsky has taken pains to be tactful and evenhanded, and of course he is entirely justified in the assumption that readers need to be told more about the Russian background than about the American. Moreover, although Wilson's far-ranging curiosity even extended to Nabokov's avocation for butterflies, Russian culture is the theme to which both writers from their divergent angles most commonly animadvert—and not simply to its literature, but to its traditional dueling code or its technique of fornication in taxicabs. Mr. Karlinsky dispels the widespread misconception, shared by Wilson, that Nabokov was an apolitical esthete, and points to the remarkable chapter on the ideologue Chernyshevsky in *The Gift*, perhaps the finest of his Russian novels and the least appreciated in English. Wilson never really read it; nor did he read the totalitarian nightmare, *Invitation to a Beheading*; and he disliked the latter's English counterpart, *Bend Sinister*.

The interchange had been tested at its very beginning, since *To the Finland Station* had just appeared; Nabokov's responding opinions about it, while politely dissenting, were historically and socially informed. His adherence to a tradition of old-fashioned constitutional liberalism, for which his public-spirited father had met with assassination, together with a scorn for reactionary White Russians and an amused fondness for his fellow Americans, is explicitly voiced in Nabokov's letters. One of them expresses his mixed emotions, decidedly more anti-Nazi than anti-Soviet, at the point when Russia entered the Second World War. On the other hand, Mr. Karlinsky, who did not

share the Western experience of the Twenties and Thirties, is somewhat doctrinaire in reproaching Wilson for his fellow-traveling radical
phase, minimizing the Sacco-Vanzetti case in the retrospective light
of the Gulag archipelago. If the Soviet Union was the god that failed
for so many left-wing intellectuals, Wilson was both early and candid
in expressing his firsthand disillusionment, and—like André Gide under similar circumstances—he soon became a target for party-liners.
Though the disagreements would overshadow the affinities, Mr. Karlinsky could have likened Wilson to Nabokov in their parallel records
of prickly integrity.

The span of dates in the title may prove misleading. The volume
contains two hundred and sixty-four entries, well over half of them
from the first seven years of their literary dialogue.[5] By the time Nabokov would be moving from Cambridge to Ithaca, and Wilson would
be inheriting a house in upstate New York, they would be drifting
apart. Wilson could describe Nabokov as "one of my closest friends"
to his old Princeton mentor, Dean Gauss, and could say directly: "Our
conversations have been among the few consolations of my literary life
through these last years—when my old friends have been dying, peter-
ing out or getting more and more neurotic, and the general state of
the world has been so discouraging for what used to be called the humanities." In his turn, Nabokov could foresee "that we will have many
a pleasant tussle and that neither will ever yield a thumb (inch) of
terrain (ground)." He had arrived as a wartime refugee, destitute and
virtually unknown, fearing he was "too old to change Conradically,"
though he had started to compose in English. Wilson saw this process
of transposition as "one of the strangest cases on record"—stranger
than Conrad's, inasmuch as the Polish novelist had not previously
written fiction in his native language.

Wilson was still facing his own problems of financial insecurity; but
he had an influential network of literary connections; and he was
temporarily back at *The New Republic*, where he could assign reviews.
With immediate generosity he became Nabokov's patron, agent, and
editorial adviser, setting up initial contacts with the magazines that
would sponsor his stories and sketches, chiefly *The Atlantic Monthly*
and *The New Yorker*. As it happened—in spite of Mr. Karlinsky's account—it was not Wilson who put Nabokov into contact with James
Laughlin of New Directions, the publisher of his first American books.[6]
Later on Wilson would play an advisory part in disengaging Nabokov

from Laughlin's list. He did contribute a sympathetic blurb which warmed up the tepid critical reception of *The Real Life of Sebastian Knight,* as well as a short but favorable review of the little book on Gogol. But though he kept promising an article on Nabokov, he published nothing else until his *Onegin* polemic. Words of appreciation in his letters are always balanced by criticisms and suggested corrections. Yet he continued to further Nabokov's fortunes, seeking other reviewers where he himself entertained doubts, and putting his hard-won wisdom of the marketplace at the disposal of his less worldly friend.

It seems then a significant aberration that, having done so much to aid Nabokov personally and professionally, Wilson never quite wholeheartedly waxed enthusiastic about his writing, especially in view of the bypaths and sideshows upon which he himself was sometimes willing to focus attention. The author of *Memoirs of Hecate County* seems to have been frankly put off by the manuscript of *Lolita,* whose author regarded it as his "best thing in English," albeit Wilson liked it "less than anything of yours I have read." As for the pyrotechnical *Pale Fire,* it gets no mention whatsoever, and Wilson would confess that he could not finish *Ada.* No one could have foreseen how a *succès de scandale* would precipitate Nabokov's recognition, but to Wilson that turning point must have seemed peculiarly ironic. His reciprocal interest, and it was keen, had been of the kind he took in his informants as a reporter. What better tutor could there have been than Nabokov for his own persistent forays into the Russian language and its literature? As a student, Wilson was intrepid; he was not too embarrassed to ask the most elementary questions, to make his fastidious interlocutor wince at solecisms, to theorize prematurely, or to toss up "a salad of mistakes" in quasi-Russian doggerel, which evoked "a nasty letter" now fortunately lost.

Nonetheless, original acquaintance had been sealed by collaboration, when Wilson prefaced and polished Nabokov's translation of Pushkin's playlet, *Mozart and Salieri,* and it was brought out as a joint undertaking. A book produced by the same division of labor, illustrating and discussing various Russian writers, was likewise contemplated. Indeed Nabokov once proposed, as he gravitated toward *Evgeni Onegin,* that he and Wilson should "write together a scholarly prose translation . . . with copious notes." Wilson had done a free translation into rhythmic prose of Pushkin's "Bronze Horseman," which

Nabokov approved. Nabokov translated three stanzas of *Onegin*, observing both rhyme and meter; Wilson praised them, and advised him against continuing a project of such length; but Nabokov felt increasingly preoccupied and ultimately obsessed by the challenge to his unprecedented situation. No single writer had ever been so adept in both Russian and English as himself. Naturally he was impatient with the ineptitudes of such precursors as Oliver Elton and the Yarmolinskys. Yet his own perceptive grasp of Russia's great novel in verse, along with his conscious ambivalence as a poet between two worlds, consecrated his monumental commitment to an attitude of the utmost austerity—as if to confirm the occlusion of the linguistic barriers.

Wilson would be warranted in accusing Nabokov of condemning himself to wear a hair shirt. Obviously balking at the dictatorship of rhyme, which is more stringent in English because of its relative scarcity and which therefore fosters jingling interpolations, he proclaimed "a new method" based on "scientific thinking." His highest aspirations, he would admit at other times, were merely to supply a student's pony, compromising less and less between an iambic lilt and the Russian word-order. In his quest for literalism he ransacked the dictionaries, intermingling slang with archaisms, and was so concerned with lexical approximations that he sacrificed the sense of context and continuity. We are reminded of Ben Jonson's comment that the synthetic diction of Spenser's *Faerie Queene* was not a recognizable language. The pity of it was that Walter Arndt had preceded Nabokov by a year or so with a readable and reasonably faithful version of *Evgeni Onegin* which nimbly preserved the verse-forms, and that Nabokov—instead of drawing upon his stylistic skills to eclipse his predecessor—sought to crush him with a highhanded review.[7] The irony becomes all the sharper if one has noticed that the concluding paragraph of *The Gift* accords with a perfect *Onegin* stanza, and that it has been formally and precisely translated in the English rendering.

Pasternak, since he had been working from English to Russian, was admittedly faced with an easier task. Yet Pushkin calls, like Shakespeare, for supple mediation rather than a rigid interposition in the name of some unattainable equivalence:

As much as the author, the translator must confine himself to a vocabulary which is natural to him and avoid the literary artifice involved in stylization. Like the original text, the translation must create an impression of life and not of verbiage.[8]

Conversely and perversely, Nabokov kept pressing further in the opposite direction, bringing out a flatter new edition a decade afterward,
where revision meant "defowlerization" plus a "correlative lexicon" of
key-words. The lavish set of four volumes, sponsored by the Bollingen
Foundation, includes—besides a Russian text in facsimile—more than
a thousand pages of commentary and appendices, both prosodic and
genealogical. These belong among the curiosities of scholarship as
well as literature, not unlike Burton's *Anatomy of Melancholy*. Nabokov was "at heart a pedant," he had confided to Wilson; after all, he
had spent most of his American years on university campuses; and his
Pushkinian commentator is, *inter alia*, a *persona* in the satiric vein of
Kinbote and Pnin. One of the stubbornest bees in his scholarly bonnet
is the repeated insistence that, despite much evidence to the contrary,
Pushkin was unfamiliar with English and consequently dependent on
French translations—which Nabokov dug for with the dedicated drudg-
ery of an M.L.A. researcher. Wilson would explain this quirk in terms
of psychological rivalry: Pushkin might surpass Nabokov on the home
ground of Russian poetry, but not in the mastery of a second tongue.

"The best account . . . of Nabokov's *Onegin*" to emerge from its
controversial reception, Wilson acknowledged, was a review-article by
the late Alexander Gerschenkron of Harvard, a learned economic historian who was furthermore an impassioned devotee of poetry in
many languages. Picking his well-informed way between the brilliant
intuitions and the crotchety preconceptions of Nabokov's criticism,
Gerschenkron gave him ample credit for "a mass of solid learning."
His conclusion was that the "translation can and should be studied,
but . . . it cannot be read."[9] Thus he lent authority to the judgment
that Wilson was, in any case, fully qualified to make for himself on
the question of the poem's readability. But Wilson, when he broached
the issue of prosody, went out on a limb which had too often been
shaken by the gusts of earlier exchanges. Coming to it via the quanti-
tative cadences of the Greco-Latin classics, he had overemphasized
the conventional regularity of Russian verse, and invidiously contrasted this with English versification in its substitutions and varia-
tions. Nabokov had argued for flexibility by scanning, tabulating, and
diagramming selected passages. But it had taken nine years for Wilson
to learn, from his wife's cousin Gleb Struve, the principle of one-
stress-per-word in Russian metrics.

In a letter addressed to me from Montreux on November 1, 1963,

Nabokov wrote that his forthcoming "work on Eugene Onegin . . . crackles with contempt for mediocrity and stupidity." This made it clear that, while he was reconstructing a masterpiece according to his lights, he was incidentally resolved to flail about him—and not solely at other interpreters. The letters to Wilson crackle with such *obiter* put-downs. T. S. Eliot is "a fraud and a fake," Thomas Mann "that quack," Dostoevsky third-rate, Stendhal worthless, Gorki worth C$^+$, Goethe a vulgarian, while D. H. Lawrence and Sherwood Anderson are "both complete mediocrities artistically." These disparagements may have helped to buoy up Nabokov's spirits in the days of obscure endeavor, but they reverberate harshly when broadcast by his worldwide fame. Wilson vainly tried to attract him to Henry James, who was charming but impotent, to André Malraux, whose French he criticized, to William Faulkner, whose stale romanticism blended Victor Hugo with Harriet Beecher Stowe; and the novels of Pasternak and Solzenitsyn were barely mentionable. Wilson's one success was to convert Nabokov, for all his prejudice against women writers, to an admiration for Jane Austen. Both swore by Flaubert and Dickens, and were strongly interested in Proust, Joyce, and Jean Genet. Nabokov was more open to newer talents: Beckett, Robbe-Grillet, Raymond Queneau.

The differences in taste were between a brisk humanist, whose interests ranged from Biblical exegesis to Indian tribal dances, and a mandarin artist, who inserted chess problems into his elegant volume of English poems. A mutual propensity for wordplay stimulated the two to some of their liveliest interactions. From his first letter, Wilson tried to curb Nabokov's "lamentable weakness for punning"; but Nabokov had a better ear for languages and poetry in general; and Wilson scored a triumph by demonstrating that the French adjective, *fastidieux*, is a *faux ami* of the English "fastidious." Both delighted in puzzles, hoaxes, and leg-pulls of all sorts. Wilson performed his parlor magic for young Dmitri Nabokov, and earned Vladimir's salute as a "fellow magician." One of Nabokov's earliest Russian stories was called "The Magician," and he movingly compares himself—exiled from his native language—to a vagrant conjuror in "An Evening of Russian Poetry" and again in "On a Book Entitled *Lolita*." If Wilson found Sebastian Knight "absolutely enchanting," that was more than a cliché; for, to Nabokov, "the great writer is first of all an enchanter." Again, on a more ominously competitive note: "I loved your article on magic though I think you might have mentioned the leading Russian Wizard who so completely mystified the Cape Cod Enchanter."

In their game of words and wits the tension mounted between the rival prestidigitators. Forced to put on his tricks in a foreign land, it had seemed fortunate for Nabokov that the leading critic there knew Russian as well as Wilson did. Reading his remark about Nabokov in an interview—"He and I disagree on everything in literature except Pushkin"—we are retrospectively confounded by the precariousness of the link.[10] Eight years before the controversy erupted, after an argumentative visit to Ithaca, Wilson thanked his host by warning him that he would be reviewing the *Onegin*. In the same letter he testily rallied Nabokov over his newly won popularity:

> I hope that *Lolita*, as a study of amorous paternity and delinquent girlhood, will touch the American public to the point of making your fortune. If you can get her married to Pnin in Alaska and bring them home to life tenure and the American way of life in some comfortable Middle Western university, you may be able to compete in popularity with *Marjorie Morningstar* and be lecturing on young people's problems from Bangor to San Diego.

Genus irritabile vatum! For his part, Nabokov had made no secret of their increasing divergence. He was stirred to serious reflections (though not without a pun) by some of Wilson's brief and hasty comments introducing a paperback selection of Chekhov's tales:

> You can well imagine how strongly I disapprove of your preface. Do you really think that Chekov is Chekov because he wrote about "social phenomena," "readjustments of a new industrial middle class," "kulaks" and "rising serfs" (which sounds like the seas)? I thought he wrote of things that gentle King Lear proposed to discuss in prison with his daughter.

After the break and six following years of silence, on learning of what was to be Wilson's long terminal illness, Nabokov was moved to recall their meeting of minds with a friendly note. Wilson's reply, though not unfriendly, was as pugnacious as ever. He served notice that he was revising and reprinting the *Onegin* review, and also urged his correspondent not to take offense at a passage from his diary appearing in *Upstate*, which related to the Ithaca visit.[11] Predictably Nabokov would flare up at what he deemed an invasion of privacy, and fire off a haughty protest to *The New York Times*, thereby publicly declaring an end to communication.[12] Wilson's last word had been a postscript to his final letter, characteristically questioning a date in

Speak, Memory. It was a faltering gesture of one-upmanship, since the point was readily explainable by the discrepancy between the Julian and Gregorian calendars—a symbolic discrepancy, in this unique conjunction.

N O T E S

1 Vladimir Nabokov, "Rowe's Symbols," *The New York Review of Books,* XVII, 5 (October 7, 1971), p. 8.
2 *For Vladimir Nabokov on His Seventieth Birthday,* ed. Alfred Appel, Jr. and Charles Newman, *TriQuarterly,* 17 (Winter 1970).
3 *In Memoriam: Vladimir Nabokov, 1899-1977* (New York: McGraw-Hill, 1977), p. 41.
4 *The Vladimir Nabokov Research News Letter,* 1 (Fall 1978), published at the University of Kansas, p. 3.
5 Edmund Wilson, *Letters on Literature and Politics,* ed. Elena Wilson (New York: Farrar, Straus & Giroux, 1977). Contains texts of, or excerpts from, about a dozen letters from Wilson to Nabokov. (London: Routledge & Kegan Paul, 1977.)
6 See "Prospero's Progress," *Time,* XCIII, 21 (May 23, 1969), p. 91.
7 Vladimir Nabokov, "Pounding the Clavichord," *The New York Review of Books,* II, 6 (April 30, 1964), pp. 14–16, followed by Professor Arndt's response, "Goading the Pony," pp. 16–18. An admirable translation, somewhat indebted to Nabokov's but observing the prosodic scheme, has recently been published by the British poet-diplomat, Charles Johnston (New York: The Viking Press, 1978).
8 Boris Pasternak, *I Remember: Sketches for an Autobiography,* with an essay on "Translating Shakespeare," trans. Manya Harari (New York: Pantheon, 1959), p. 125.
9 Alexander Gerschenkron, "A Manufactured Monument?" *Modern Philology,* LXIII, 4 (May 1966), pp. 247, 340.
10 See "Lolita's Creator—Author Nabokov, a 'Cosmic Joker,'" *Newsweek,* LIX, 26 (June 25, 1962), p. 54.
11 Wilson's original review-article, "The Strange Case of Pushkin and Nabokov," *The New York Review of Books,* IV, 12 (July 15, 1965), pp. 3–6, was followed by two exchanges of letters between Nabokov and Wilson, *ibid.* (August 26, 1965, pp. 25–26; January 29, 1966, p. 30; and February 17, 1966, p. 29), plus Nabokov's "Reply to My Critics" in *Encounter,* XXVI, 2 (February, 1966), pp. 80–89.
12 "Letters," *The New York Times Book Review* (November 7, 1971).

THE PRIVATE LIFE OF
F. O. MATTHIESSEN

Having ventured to append a postscript, I need not interpose a headnote here, except to mention that Rat and The Devil: Journal Letters of F. O. Matthiessen and Russell Cheney, *ed. Louis K. Hyde (Hambden: Archon Books), received this notice in* The New York Review of Books *(July 20, 1978).*

•

When F. O. Matthiessen jumped to his death from a twelfth-story window of a Boston hotel on April 1, 1950, the shock reverberated far beyond his established orbit as a literary critic and Harvard professor. At the time there were other dramatic refusals to enter the second half of the twentieth century: notably that of Klaus, the eldest son of Thomas Mann, who gave up striving to find his own identity as a writer, and that of the gifted Cesare Pavese, who had begun by translating *Moby-Dick* into Italian and was scheduled to translate Matthiessen's most important book, *American Renaissance.* Officious voices were immediately raised to interpret the latter's suicide as an episode in the Cold War. His latest book, *From the Heart of Europe,* had been one man's honest if ineffectual testimony for communicating across the Iron Curtain even as it was coming down. Active more and more as a Christian Socialist, starting from undergraduate activities at Yale, he had seconded the nomination of Henry Wallace for President in 1948. He had been in friendly touch with Bronson Cutting, Jerry Voorhis, Harry Bridges, and the Trotskyist labor leader Ray Dunne. He had reported on the miners' strike at Gallup, New Mexico, presided over the Harvard Teachers' Union, participated in fellow-traveling committees, and had freely signed many a left-wing petition.

During his forty-eight years he had thus become a public figure, as well as a remarkably productive and innovative scholar-teacher. Insofar as literature was concerned, *American Renaissance* became the monument of the movement toward American studies that had developed in the United States before the Second World War and spread to Europe shortly afterward. Thoroughly committed to his teaching and taken up for a while in academic administration, with increasingly frequent leaves of absence, he was able to produce a richly substantial body of writing, and his contributions to the revival of Henry James were second only to those of Leon Edel. He had absorbed and broadened the inspirations and instigations of Van Wyck Brooks and Lewis Mumford, V. L. Parrington and D. H. Lawrence, and—more generally—of T. S. Eliot, I. A. Richards, and Edmund Wilson. His approach was "adhesive," to use a Whitmanesque word; while concentrating on the texts of major writers, it set them into context by synthesizing esthetic and social considerations. Influence was creative; he drew upon it and passed it on; and he generously acknowledged the interactions that affected all his books. Chapter by chapter, some of them were read aloud to his friends; and, since he was more interested in other styles than in his own, he utilized assistance when revising his manuscripts.

Spokesmen for the Communist Party, to which he had never belonged, loudly signalized his suicide as a political gesture. It could also be remarked that the manner of it paralleled the recent defenestration of Jan Masaryk, whose acquaintance in Prague he had cherished as a last point of contact with the hope for a free postwar Europe. But he himself was careful to write in a note, which he left in the hotel room along with his keys, his glasses, and his fraternity emblem: "How much the state of the world has to do with my state of mind I do not know." Louis Hyde, his Yale classmate, close friend, literary executor, and the editor of the present collection, opens his introduction by recalling that Matthiessen had experienced a similar impulse in December 1938, when a nervous breakdown intervened to block his work on *American Renaissance*. In the reflective and retrospective journal he briefly kept at the mental hospital, he mentioned more than once the recurrent fantasy "that it would be better if I jumped out the window." His physician, he wrote, "talks of the aggression that I am turning against myself." This would be the purport of the reply he gave my wife at dinner eleven years later, a week or so before he acted out that fantasy, when she had attempted to rally his low spirits by telling him that he was not being as aggressive as usual.

I must frankly say that it came with an emotional repercussion for me to encounter, in the proof sheets of this book, a letter addressed to myself—but unfinished and unsent—during Matthiessen's period of hospitalization forty years ago. There he expresses his perplexity over "what accounts for a slip of nerve." He had an innately powerful will, and would need it to carry through his fatal resolution. Meanwhile, he continues in his aborted communication, "there remains that damnable death-wish that I haven't yet been able to shake off." Happily, he managed to shake it off, to complete his major work, and to establish himself as a dominant force in a burgeoning field. The difference between that earlier crisis and the final one lay in the presence and absence of the painter Russell Cheney, who would die in 1945. So Mr. Hyde suggests in his opening observation, and those who knew the two men intimately will agree. Other pressures were then building up in Matthiessen's complex and sensitive mind, and he found his contacts less humanly rewarding both within the university and in the world at large. But the personal foundation on which his career depended was his relationship with Cheney: a love affair which lasted twenty years, a *ménage* for fifteen years centered in the little house they shared at Kittery, Maine (now the residence of Mr. Hyde).

A friend of Matthiessen's who has been both his student and his colleague is bound to read these letters with mixed feelings, one of which is the question whether they should have been published. Matthiessen himself, after all, brought out a splendid monograph on Cheney's life and work, with numerous illustrations and a text interwoven from his correspondence.[1] (One of those letters, not reprinted here, is revealing enough to contain the phrase: "you who are such a man's man.") Matthiessen was soon commemorated by a special issue of *The Monthly Review*, a socialist periodical in which he took great interest, subsequently republished in hard covers.[2] George White, who has been preparing a full-length biography, has already contributed a long informal revaluation to a symposium which first appeared in *Tri-Quarterly*.[3] Richard Ruland has devoted a central chapter to Matthiessen in his useful study of our literary historiography, *The Rediscovery of American Literature*.[4] An entire volume on the subject, Giles Gunn's *F. O. Matthiessen: The Critical Achievement*, is both systematic and suggestive.[5] A short but interesting memoir by Kenneth Lynn, one of his later students, has recently figured in *The American Scholar*.[6] So far as Matthiessen's "achievement" is involved—and the word was stressed by his book on Eliot—it has received and will long be receiving the attention it so well deserves, notwithstanding the backhanded afterthoughts in Alfred Kazin's latest autobiography.[7]

As for the violation of his privacy, I have little doubt that he would have hated it, and Cheney was even more self-conscious about the stigmata of homosexuality. Of course it may well be argued that a new generation has become more sympathetic, or at least more tolerant, and that this example of two fine individuals thus attaining mutual fulfillment may exercise a liberating effect upon others subjected to conventional suspicions or constraints. Yet Matthiessen had a strong sense of cultural contexts, and was intensely aware of all the risks he was courting, of the double life he was taking pains to lead. A casual comment on his soft voice by a fatuous professor of public speaking set him to wondering: "Am I just like any fairy?" Attributing to Watteau the sentiment "Let's be gay," he could scarcely have realized what the adjective would come to connote; nor could he, in his inherent seriousness, ever have accepted that connotation. Unquestionably these revelations bring out the disingenuousness of May Sarton's effort to center a novel upon his person while ignoring the basic psychological facts.[8] But Auden, who observed far less discretion in his *modus vivendi,* enjoined his correspondents to burn his letters. Eliot, however, who wanted no biography, has latterly been the victim of some rather farfetched endeavors to reinterpret his poetry in a homosexual light.

Though the letters of distinguished persons ought to be preserved and made available to biographers and qualified researchers, I am old-fashioned enough to believe that they should be classified when they were so clearly not intended for the eyes of outside readers, and that the secrets of lovers should be respected as such. Here their private pet-names, which could have little meaning for others, are not only emblematized in their signatures but flaunted together in the title. Since the executor-editor has chosen to present this material to the reading public, something must be said about his technique of presentation. As an editorial job it is not very competent. Several holograph facsimiles, included among the illustrations, make it possible to test the reliability of the transcriptions against the manuscript copy. There are occasional errors, not many, but the sampling is small; a proportionate number for the whole would be damaging. We have lost a significant detail when the word "Sung" is dropped from Cheney's description of a "piece of pottery." There are few footnotes, and some of these go astray, as with the quotation attributed to Baudelaire (via Eliot), which is actually from Villon: "*Quand* [it should have been *Que] toutes mes hontes j'ai bu."* Names and identifications, as listed in a "Cast of Characters" at the end, have been all too frequently garbled.

Mr. Hyde informs us that the correspondence mounts up to about 3,100 letters: 1,400 from Matthiessen, 1,700 from Cheney. By his word count he has given us one sixteenth of the total wordage. Almost from their first meeting they had decided to keep some account for one another of every day they spent apart, so that the sequence constitutes a pair of journals, in which the interruptions stand for their sojourns together. Mr. Hyde's selection leans heavily toward the earliest stages. The longest section covers the first year of their companionship, 1924–25; the second section deals substantially with 1929–30, when Matthiessen was beginning to teach at Harvard and Cheney was painting in the Southwest; the third is focused on the brief and painful interlude when Matthiessen was hospitalized, 1938–39; and the fourth falls within a year of Cheney's death, 1944–45. Hence the interstices in the record are overwhelming, and they are inadequately bridged by the editor's sketchy transitions and excerpted quotations. Cheney, though his settings were varied, and though his descriptions are vividly pictorial, pursued a retiring pattern of daily activity, and was uninterested in politics. Whereas Matthiessen was widely and dynamically engaged, and functioned as a kind of percipient conscience for a good many others—an "ethicist" as opposed to "artist," in his own formulation.

Presumably there should be much in the full collection, not put into print, which would have illuminated his intellectual development, his educational views, his critical principles, and his critique of society. One is curious to learn more about his firsthand reaction to his chief graduate mentors, Irving Babbitt and John Livingston Lowes (regarded then as polar opposites), or his encouragement of such younger talents as Delmore Schwartz, Charles Olson, or Richard Wilbur. Above all, students of American culture would like to trace his course of rediscovery, after his eighteenth-century immersion at Yale and Oxford and his Harvard thesis on Elizabethan prose. He describes his own epistolary prose as "A jumble of half-thoughts, events, and ideas." But Mr. Hyde has preferred to stress the personal relationship, as it is highlighted by love letters. His candor in exposing sexual intimacy is ironically counterweighed by his discretion in veiling a certain institutional commitment. That Matthiessen was an extremely loyal member of the senior honor society, Skull and Bones, had a formative impact on his character, and made him a lifelong party to an old-boy network which reached high in the establishment. Faithfully observing its code of secrecy, Mr. Hyde deletes all references to it, and substitutes such bracketed euphemisms as "[a little group of intimate friends]."

The uninitiated should not be tempted into speculation over the particular effects of this cult of brotherhood on a disposition like Matthiessen's. To the reader of Proust it might suggest his running analogy between homosexual circles and the mysterious confraternity of the Jews. Yet it seems evident that the bonding ritual prompted Matthiessen into some sort of confession, which must have been agonizing for him and embarrassing for his clubmates. To their credit—in the era when the norms of masculinity were set by Percy Haughton and the shade of Dink Stover—they were not unsympathetic. But their sympathy must have taken the form of encouraging a conversion to heterosexuality, and apparently he acceded to the extent of hoping to be happily married some day. The ambiguities of that situation were unexpectedly resolved a year or two later, after his decisive encounter with Cheney on a transatlantic liner, which led to his realization that he was what he was *by nature*," and that he could accept his nature by working out a way of living with Cheney. Characteristically, the "prologue" that informs us of the decision is an excerpt from a letter to his "[close friend]," Russell Davenport, a college poet who would edit *Fortune* and celebrate the American Century. Matthiessen's arrangement with Cheney had to be confirmed by secretly announcing it to their brethren.

For a unique human being, Matthiessen had a classic case history. Slight in stature, delicate in feature, anxious to avoid his somewhat bisexual forename (Francis), he was the youngest child of a broken family. His immigrating German-Danish grandfather had made a fortune by manufacturing Big Ben alarm clocks. Matty had little from it until his last years; indeed he had to borrow a thousand dollars to subsidize the publication of *American Renaissance*. He abhorred the callous playboy father he scarcely knew, and adored his New England mother, by whose grave he is buried in execution of his request. His psychosexual inclinations came out in his prep-school days, and tended to fix upon older men. He would not fully relate this need to "the empty space where my father should have been" until his therapeutic sessions at the McLean Hospital. That he could feel "no female sexual attraction" he had tested on an unlikely occasion when, of all people, Rudy Vallee—the crooning bandmaster, a Yale alumnus, though not likely to have been a Bones man—had rushed him into an evening at "the toughest dive in Europe." There he had felt "half ashamed" at not responding to a London whore, he confessed to Cheney, who sympathized. Yet Matthiessen had several affectionate friendships with women, two of the closest with former wives divorced from his male friends.

Cheney was his senior by more than twenty years. He too was a youngest child (with ten siblings), the wayward son in a silk-manufacturing dynasty solidly located at South Manchester, Connecticut. He too had adored his mother, and sealed his pact by setting Matthiessen's photograph in the frame where he carried hers. A handsome man at his prime, he was never robust; having recovered from tuberculosis, he was troubled by other ills, not least by alcohol; the rhythms of his artistic career were punctuated by stays in sanatoriums. He had studied art in Paris and traveled widely to practice it, living on an independent income. Confessing that he was "not an arrived character," he might have dallied into dilettantism, if his talent had not been reinforced by Matthiessen's will power. He evolved his own distinctive—if not highly original—vein of Post-Impressionism, characterized by pastel shadings and heavy outlines. His style is always graceful and decorative, though it shows a tendency to convert portraits and landscapes into still lifes. Obviously, he could never have lived by his painting, but he exhibited professionally at regular intervals, and his work is represented in various museums. If he was an amateur, it was in the most positive sense: he really loved and cultivated the beautiful, and had a genuine flair for helping others to discern it.

The initiative was Matthiessen's. When they met on the boat he was completing his Oxford B. Litt., while Cheney was heading toward the Continent. Their rendezvous at Christmas-time in Italy was a honeymoon, and Matthiessen would be disciplined at New College for overstaying his vacation. It was likewise he who proposed that they set up a household. Cheney had his misgivings and hesitations, especially over Matthiessen's firm condition that the bonded brothers be notified; and Cheney's family would disapprove. "You can't admit the situation openly," he worried. It was he who sacrificed his freedom to attain comparative stability, but he was compelled by Matthiessen's arguments. The alternatives, "Promiscuity and self-abuse are impure and ugly." And the worst alternative was the unbearable loneliness: "here is our God-given chance not to be alone." Other men have wives; and though there may be "other unions like ours," we cannot draw upon them. "We must create everything for ourselves." It would be "a marriage that was never seen on land or sea." Therefore it should have no name or label; it is "beyond society." Previous sexuality had been "lust," from which he now disgustedly withdrew. Moreover, he maintained a punctilious line between friendship and pedagogy, on the one hand, and sex on the other. Doubtless there was sublimated eros in his teaching, as there has been from Socrates to Pater.

This was their opportunity to combine "mind, body, and soul" in a single union. Most marriages profess such an ideal; few of them achieve it perfectly; and theirs, beset with impediments, bravely overcame them so far as it could under the circumstances. Cheney's drinking was already a problem, and Matthiessen helped him to fight it by chiding, pleading, and warning, which probably did much to postpone an inevitable surrender. Both of them felt occasionally tempted into lapses that ultimately strengthened their fidelity. Russell was a gentle, modest, and charming individual, whose cultivation came naturally to him while Matty exerted himself—and that very exertion played its part in his success as a pedagogue. Yet he often drew upon an awareness which had been sensitized and enlarged by the contributions of Cheney. These were most perceptibly exemplified in the synesthetic linkages between literature and the arts. But Cheney was also the cicerone to Europe and to languages, where Matthiessen was admittedly his pupil, and where Baudelaire's French would have to be confronted. It was Cheney who first set Matthiessen to rereading Whitman, even while the young Rhodes scholar was visiting Eton and Windsor, and who suggested and illustrated Matthiessen's first book: a study of Sarah Orne Jewett, his mother's relative, the accomplished storyteller of that region into which they had just settled down.

It was Cheney who expressly enacted the wifely role, in a manner which might not be called liberated today. He was an excellent cook, and often supplemented the pleasant meals of their black houseman, Nelson, on our visits to the cottage at Kittery, where a succession of fat and pampered cats enjoyed the freedom of the dinner table. Whenever Matty talked shop with a visiting colleague, it was Russell's habit to converse with that colleague's wife. All would join together for a view of the latest paintings in his studio, a long walk by the seashore or across the countryside, or a guided tour of historic Portsmouth across the harbor. Sometimes there would be a game or two of deck tennis, dominated by Matty's driving spirit. "He is a fierce competitor," as a familiar neighbor put it. "He usually wins—at whatever it is." Roles changed when he underwent his failure of nerve, and Russell temporarily became the protective partner. But he could not be so for long, since the fear of his death was "the obscure demon" that Matty was fighting: "whether I could face life without Russell." During the five-year respite the two lived together in Boston more openly than before. Their apartment on Pinckney Street (Mr. Hyde skips over their previous domicile on Mount Vernon Street) would be the scene of literary gatherings and of their warmly remembered Christmas parties.

Living there alone for five years after the loss he had feared, Matthiessen could not escape from an extended feeling of isolation. He took less and less satisfaction in his Harvard ties, criticized himself for wasting his energies in criticizing an unsympathetic administration, and seemed to be losing those resources of empathy which had met and captivated the minds of prior generations of students. He was on leave of absence during his final year, immersed in the rebarbative and cheerless fiction of Theodore Dreiser, who would be the subject of a posthumous book. He saw many people who were fond of, and concerned for, him; but they could hardly reconstitute his domestic partnership. At its inception he had written Cheney: "You'll give me balance, a touch with life. And instead of being an energetic accurate little machine, I may be a personality." He became one indeed, most abundantly; wholeheartedly he realized the precept that he had quoted from *Piers Plowman: "Disce, doce, dilige* (Learn, teach, love)"; and yet his shifting equilibrium had rested on the assurance of Cheney's continued devotion. Prodding him for more letters in their earliest interchange, Matthiessen had jocularly asked: "how else am I going to write your biography in the year 1970?" Yet I have heard Matty remark—and not in a moment of stress—that he never expected to live beyond the age of fifty.

Many of those who may have shared his unhappiness over the state of the world at mid-century, having been more securely insulated by more fortunate circumstance, still survive to be no happier about the current state of affairs. But Matthiessen was not an ideologue, not political by temperament, as Eliot justly surmised. He was in truth a devoutly religious man, temperamentally if not theologically or liturgically, with an increasing adherence to the Anglican faith. He could not be a Marxist because he was a Christian, as he often told his leftist friends, while he told his more conservative friends that, if he were not a Christian, he would become a Marxist. His final act was certainly not a statement for either Christianity or Marxism. Yet, when so well-defined an identity opts for the Stoic alternative of self-destruction, he leaves the rest of us feeling some sense of guilt for our mere survival. This I think he understood and intended to convey, as an unwritten message far more searching than these indiscreetly published letters. Thus his death reopened the existential question raised by the first two sentences of Albert Camus' *Myth of Sisyphus:* "There is only one philosophical problem which is truly serious; it is suicide. To judge whether life itself is or is not worth the trouble of being lived—that is the basic question of philosophy."

Any answer would be far from pointing toward the conclusion that Matthiessen's own life had not been richly rewarding, to himself as well as to untold others. For him the judgment was a matter of timing, of weighing the rewards against the troubles. In the words he especially valued from *Hamlet:* "The readiness is all." As an epigraph to *The Achievement of T. S. Eliot* he had cited a farsighted maxim of Yeats: "We begin to live when we have conceived life as a tragedy." The framing paradox in his interpretation of American literature is that this conception had been balanced, seemingly overbalanced, by all the optimistic imperatives—"the smiling aspects," in the byword of Howells, who once consoled Edith Wharton for a theatrical fiasco by telling her that what the audience expected was "a tragedy with a happy ending." Matthiessen was as much committed to the Party of Hope as to the Party of Memory in their Emersonian conflict. But his preoccupation with the common man seems, like Whitman's, to have been the *mystique* of an uncommon man. Consciousness of belonging to a harassed minority may have aided him to identify with unpopular causes, to transfigure a psychic alienation by standing "out in left field." At the same time he was drawn ambivalently, through his Yale associations and his early recognition at Harvard (under the Lowell régime), into what he rather too seriously regarded as an élite.

Though the opposition between the academic establishment and the ideological left was not nearly so extreme as he conceived it, he came to hold an almost schizoid image of his existence. Alternatively an outsider on the inside or an insider on the outside, he consistently stood near the edge of the action. Individual experience, confirmed by social observation, deepened what he termed in *American Renaissance* "a profound comprehension of the mixed nature of life." This made a striking drama out of his dialectical treatment of our greatest literary imaginations: the American dreams of Emerson and Whitman pitted against the darkening visions of Hawthorne and Melville. Thesis was countered by antithesis; but, though the book speaks hopefully of synthesis, there was none for its author; the buoyant particularities were outmatched by the tragic universals. That impulsion to leap from a precipice, which Poe has so dizzyingly detailed, had long been tantalizing Matthiessen. He was fascinated by the fall from the yardarm in *White-Jacket,* and from the Tarpeian Rock in *The Marble Faun,* as he was by the concept of the Fall of Man in Judeo-Christian theology, occasioned by the angels' primordial tragedy. In his ultimate choice he literally dramatized a response to the criticism of Walter Rathenau: "America has no soul and will not deserve to have one until it consents to plunge into the abyss of human sin and suffering."

●

Wishing to end—as I think F. O. Matthiessen would have wished—on more of an equipoise, I turn back to the paragraph I wrote for the memorial issue of The Monthly Review, II, 6 (*October 1950*):

Matty was starting to teach at Harvard in 1929 when I was a freshman, and it was my great good luck to be in his first class. The twenty years that have elapsed since then have witnessed revolutionary changes in the study of literature, which owe as much to his efforts as to anyone's. What he particularly represented, for those of us who studied and later taught with him, was a shift from the philological to the critical approach and from a historical to a contemporary emphasis. The movement of his energetic and comprehensive mind, which was richly associative rather than strictly logical, gave him a special feeling for the relations between the arts and above all for the interrelationship between social problems and cultural developments. Insofar as we who basked in his light or followed paths he had broken were able to escape from the besetting triviality and mediocrity of academic scholarship, it was owing to his deep concern for fundamentals. His healthy impatience with minor works, which clutter the curriculum and scarcely survive beyond doctoral dissertations, came as the corollary to his intensive preoccupation with masterpieces. It is not without significance that the adjective "major" figured so often in his lectures and writings. Style, in the elegant sense, was something he disdained to cultivate; but there is another sense in which every paragraph bears his stylistic signature. Certain words, which Ted Spencer used to call "Mattyisms," were the recurrent touchstones of his vocabulary. Not only "major" but "impact," "achievement," "focus," and "crystallize," attest his habit of fixing on what was genuinely important and projecting a clearer awareness of it. "To come to grips with"—his friends will always associate this expression with him, and it will always remind them of his sincere determination to meet issues squarely and vigorously. Perhaps it is also worth remembering that, whenever he spoke, his characteristic gesture was an exploratory motion of the right hand and sometimes the left, as if he were groping through the darkness toward what Melville would have called "the usable truth." But if we seek a characterizing phrase from the literary tradition that he interpreted in *American Renaissance,* and to which *From the Heart of Europe* itself belongs, we find it in Emerson's "Society and Solitude." In Matty's lively companionship and in his tragic loneliness, in his strong convictions and his delicate sensibilities, he lived that paradox intensely. Hence he has spoken, and will continue to speak, as one of the most authoritative voices of our culture, its achievements, and its conflicts.

N O T E S

1 F. O. Matthiessen, ed., *Russell Cheney (1881–1945): A Record of His Work* (Published for the Memorial Exhibition, 1946-1947).

2 Paul M. Sweezy and Leo Huberman, ed., *F. O. Matthiessen (1902–1950): A Collective Portrait* (Henry Schuman, 1950).

3 George Abbott White, "Ideology and Literature: *American Renaissance* and F. O. Matthiessen," in *Literature and Revolution,* ed. George Abbott White and Charles Newman (New York: Holt, Rinehart and Winston, 1972), pp. 430–500.

4 Richard Ruland, *The Rediscovery of American Literature* (Cambridge, Mass.: Harvard University Press, 1967), pp. 209–273.

5 Giles B. Gunn, *F. O. Matthiessen: The Critical Achievement* (Seattle: University of Washington Press, 1975).

6 Kenneth S. Lynn, "Teaching: F. O. Matthiessen," *The American Scholar,* XLVI, 1 (Winter 1976–77), pp. 86–93.

7 In *New York Jew* (New York: Knopf, 1978) Mr. Kazin writes: "I have never known another teacher whose influence on students had so many harsh personal and political consequences." In *F. O. Matthiessen (1902– 1950): A Collective Portrait* (Henry Schuman, 1950) Mr. Kazin wrote, of the same lectures at Salzburg: "he gave us all something that will always live in my mind as an example of the reconciliatory spirit at its most instinctive, its most truthful, its most loving."

8 May Sarton, *Faithful Are the Wounds* (New York: Rhinehart, 1955).

APPENDIX:
A LETTER TO F. O. MATTHIESSEN
(ABOUT T. S. ELIOT)

Here is an afterthought, written forty-five years ago and certainly never intended for publication. I print it with the awereness that an appendix is a gratuitous sort of organ, which can be irritating on occasion. Recently, while the foregoing papers were being put together, Matthiessen's biographer, George Abbott White, unearthed this letter, which I had entirely forgotten about. I am publishing it at his indulgent suggestion, and with the perhaps too kind permission of the Beinecke Library at Yale University, repository of the Matthiessen correspondence. My excuse is that it seemed to round out a cycle by moving back from a generation of retrospect to a firsthand situation in medias res: *how it happened to strike a callow contemporary.*

Eliot was then in mid-career. He had spent the previous year at Harvard College, where he had delivered those Charles Eliot Norton Lectures which became The Use of Poetry and the Use of Criticism. *Matthiessen was then an assistant professor, fourteen years his junior; I was in the graduating class, ten years younger than Matthiessen. He very early, I somewhat later, had come to the realm of literature as Eliot was rediscovering and reshaping it. His poetry to date was still regarded as* Kulturbolschewismus *by most of our academic elders, though his critical prose had already been genuflecting toward traditionalism. And some of us, who had just begun to worry about the state of the world in 1934, balked at* After Strange Gods (*which he subsequently all but repudiated*).

Matthiessen wrote his book in 1933–34, while I was in Europe on a traveling fellowship. (Eliot, in London, had received me benignly, and had accepted the mentioned article on John Cleveland for his Criterion.) *Matty was in the habit of showing or reading sections of his books to friends; by the time he had completed this manuscript, I was home recovering from an illness; hence I read it through as a whole, and it stimulated these epistolary thoughts. I should add that my more specific comments were penciled on the text, and that he was always very receptive and patient in considering such queries or suggestions. His own pencilings on the margins of my letter consist mainly of numerous checks and question marks and exclamation points.*

231

It is with much diffidence that I release this item, and rather as a document than as a critique. Indeed its very lack of diffidence—the temerity, the severity, the asperity—toward my closest teacher and the living writer we both most admired should now become a source of embarrassment to me. I might have saved my face by numerous cuts and careful revisions; but that would have deprived the piece of what may be its sole merit, documentary authenticity; and so, except for the usual mechanics of copy-editing, I have exposed it completely, stylistic excrescences and all. It would salve the author's feelings if at least it demonstrated that he is no longer quite so precious, so pedantic, or so dogmatic as he was at the age of twenty-two.

●

2631 E. Lake of the Isles Boulevard,
Minneapolis, Minnesota.
31 July 1934.

Dear Matty:

My greatest difficulty, in getting a letter to you started at this point, is to find some explanation for my unpardonable dalliance with your manuscript. It would be morally, if not literally, true to say I have clung to it deliberately, as tangible evidence of the existence of interests that are not cultivated and values that have never been recognized hereabouts, or as the only experience of the summer that I should like to remember. The basic literal fact is that it arrived while I was elsewhere (engaged in the tedious, but presumably successful business of convalescence), and that I have actually had a little more than two weeks to contemplate it. When I consider how much merely following—at a respectful distance to the rear—your considerations on Eliot, has done to dispel the effects of three months of laziness and lethargy, and to reintegrate the fragments of my summer, I am almost tempted to keep the manuscript a little longer, even though at my back I always hear the stern daughter of the voice of God shouting, "Hurry up, please, it's time!"

Here, then, is your manuscript, and here are a few speculations it has suggested to my mind. They are not likely to be of much value to you, but they will perhaps demonstrate of what value your essay was to me—and hence could be to the interested reader. Such as they are, they tend to be long-winded, and so I have shelved the letter I had previously begun, in the hope that the other matters might be resolved in future conversation. There is one question, however, which cannot abide that long, and that is the matter of your associate professorship. The moment I first read about it, in Dan Boorstin's letter, seemed to be one of those excessively rare occasions on which one's private ideals and the standards of those in authority are in absolute harmony, and I felt very hopeful and pleased with things in general.

In turning to what you wrote about Eliot, I should like, before all else, to tell you how pleased I was by the many things you did not write about him. Of course I hardly expected you to be either captious or obsequious, but I was not quite prepared to find, behind such complete control of Eliot's background and expression, so successfully impersonal a point of view. When I summon up remembrance of the literary demagogues who take Eliot's poetry as the starting-point for an indictment of contemporary culture or the official spokesmen who employ it as a ritual of esthetic initiation, I begin to appreciate the rigors of your task. Your book has roots of its own. To be without general prepossessions or special theory, so that one constructs his critique neither by cataloguing the divergences between the author's works and his own *a priori* conceptions nor by attempting to "explain" his author in terms of psychoanalysis, mysticism, or dialectical materialism, is as rare today as honest critical writing.

I am glad you adopted no artificial scheme to determine the presentation of your ideas. A ready-made approach—be it biographical or generic—is all too apt to introduce false clarity and irrelevant emphasis, to exhaust itself in quibbles upon limitations and terminology, and to convert a thoughtful inquiry into a mechanical exercise. Every subject, to rehearse a favorite prejudice of mine, has its unique, innate arrangement. The *mot juste* cannot, I believe, be considered as an absolute or divorced from its context. If one is anxious to express his meaning as exactly as possible, succession of ideas is quite as important as choice of words, and a great deal more troublesome. In this case, by following the associative logic of Eliot's ideas, by insisting on the intrinsic relationship of his influences and his imagery, his thought and his style, and by letting his own preoccupations, as you have discovered and related them, form a series of focal points for your study, you seem to have found the *ordonnance juste*.

You have also found it convenient not to discriminate formally between Eliot's precept and example, but to illuminate the verse by the prose and again to illustrate his literary ideals by his practice as a poet. Strictly speaking, this method involves a possible fallacy, in the form of a difficulty which invariably presents itself when one is attempting to deal critically with any of the subjective writers of the post-Romantic period. Eliot's work is its own definition, *sui generis*. He has no direct answer to *"Was hat sich der Autor vorgesetzt?"* Instead, he leads you immediately to Goethe's question, *"Und inwiefern ist es gelungen, ihn auszuführen?"* Until it is done, it is impossible to find out what this author is trying to do; unless he is successful, his original intentions are forever lost. It follows either that Eliot's poetry is the perfect embodiment of his literary ideals or that his criticism is a mere accessory after the fact to his poetry. Your own criticism of Eliot, then, is necessarily inductive, for your author has deliberately cut you off from objective criteria and external standards. The spectacle of a Dr. Johnson deciding that *The Waste Land* would be a better poem if it rhymed more regularly, or of a Coleridge suggesting a number of minor changes in the imagery and phrasing, is absurdly unthinkable. So intimate is Eliot's idiom that, like the peculiar tone of Joyce, it has taken on a semblance of inevitability. To suggest that anything in it be otherwise is to intrude upon the poet's privacy. Since he does not allow his critic to distinguish between intention and achievement, Eliot allows himself no margin of failure. Within his finished work there can be no room for discrepancy or possibility of miscarriage in the carrying out of his plans; as with Joyce, we must judge it by the success of the whole.

I have not been speaking of Eliot as if he were a very orthodox poet. Paul Elmer More, one of the recognized authorities on the subject of orthodoxy, has already discovered in Eliot that spiritual dichotomy which all well-conducted subjects of *Shelburne Essays* are required to present as a prerequisite, and it is only Eliot's prose which has won Mr. More's *nihil obstat*. The fact that Eliot acknowledges actuality as the substance of poetry, stresses the historical unity of human values, and calls our attention to the importance of those other poets—of various schools and periods—who have been most concerned with these recurring issues, almost persuades us to forget that, like them, he is an innovator and has evolved a new technique for successfully dramatizing some of the more elusive phases of experience. An epigraph from Charles Maurras is not, in my opinion, sufficient recompense for the half-dozen pages you might have devoted to a concrete technical analysis of Eliot's style. You have penetrated the subject incidentally, in connection with music and the *Symbolistes,* or particularly the "objective correlative"; you have displayed fine tact in ignoring Eliot's snob appeal and the attitude that would view his work as an arcanum to be withheld from the profane. You have put before us enough of Eliot's mind to make his symbols appear vivid and cogent. I wonder if it would not be possible to formulate an exact description of the structure he employs for his poetic effects, of that method which I can only adumbrate as a process of turning the facets of the mind against one another by a system of intellectual *Leitmotiv* and producing an emotional response. Eliot, after all, does not merely ask us to fill in allusions and follow up references. He imposes upon us tasks of collation, comparison, and criticism. He is not simply freighting the ordinary figures of speech with recondite imagery; evocation, quotation, juxtaposition, and association are his tropes. Context is to him what the conceit was to the Metaphysicals. His climaxes come not in the lines, but between them.

The contextual method, if I may call it that, depends on the highest degree of self-consciousness, on a feeling for the contrast between the literary and the actual. This feeling is present in Sterne and Byron, who treated it as a broad joke; in Tieck and Heine, who developed it into romantic irony; and, most significantly for Eliot, in Laforgue, who imposed upon the broken-down particles of literary convention an arbitrary symbolic significance and found that, by playing upon them, he could appeal directly in lyric snatches to the individual emotional experience. What Eliot has taken from and added to this series of attempts to make poetry more flexible would, I think, be worth treating in detail. The habit of literary reminiscence that is Eliot's most characteristic and, in a sense, most original trait, sets him apart from the other symbolists by giving him a definite status—intellectually, if not technically—in relation to tradition, and by enabling him to draw on a wider and more complex range of material than his own experience could have provided. Sitting in the attic of his rented house where the dusty and discarded litter of Western civilization is stored, he has somehow been able, in sifting over this confusion of dead rubbish, to explore the interior arrangement and the furniture of the human mind further than any poet, beyond Dante and Racine, has done.

You have doubtless seen Edmund Wilson's recent article on "The Canons of Poetry," in which he seems to make an able, if somewhat rough-and-ready, approach to Eliot's contextual method. Wilson accuses Eliot of anthologizing, both in his verse and in his prose. A high poetic level, if I understand his argument, cannot be sustained; any poetry written in. the traditional forms must contain long pedestrian stretches. Eliot is found guilty of trying to evade this nemesis by writing entirely in purple passages and initiating a cult of the fragmentary. The charges, as reported, are substantially true; but Wilson seems unnecessarily obtuse in regard to Eliot's aims. Eliot obviously is seeking a formula for heightening and for cultivating those rare moments of immediacy which used to be called ὕψος and are now referred to as the *nouveau frisson.* He has found something like this in that peculiar form of metonymy which he designates the "objective correlative." Eliot's technique, when you think of it, is not unlike Pavlov's; the relation of his "set of objects" to an original situation has been established by associative means, and we respond to their impulse as the dog to the bell. Thus, by concentrating on psychological crises and situating his activating circumstances within the realm of the intellect, he occasionally succeeds in doing what writers do rarely: in communicating emotion directly, rather than vicariously.

Before we leave the subject of Eliot's poetic technique, I must confess to a persistent doubt which still occasionally besets me. I took this particular misgiving to you a couple of years ago, whereupon you performed a remarkable exegesis on "A Cooking Egg," and I came away breathlessly convinced that there was no seeming obscurity in Eliot's work which did not mask a definite and necessary connotation, that Eliot foresaw and was bent upon communicating all the possibilities of a phrase, a *nuance,* or a situation, and that here was a poet who—being at the same time sensitive, erudite, and precise to a very high degree—was able to keep this range of suggestion completely under control. All I had to do was to try to be as sensitive, as erudite, as precise as Eliot, and the veil would be lifted from my eyes. Until that devoutly-to-be-wished consummation, I have been proceeding cautiously, deepening my pleasure in his poems by gradually unraveling the various strands of connotation. Your book, by pointing out correspondences, implications, and retwined traditions, has manifestly enriched their significance for me, and will for others. This is a legitimate critical procedure, although, considering all the apparatus you must have acquired, I am glad you have resisted the temptation to expound, and have saved your essay from becoming—like Gilbert's book on Joyce, or Damon's on Blake, or Seurat's on Milton—a mere collection of scholia.

But let me dramatize my doubt. Seeking a characteristic passage of interpretative criticism, I turn at random to your discussion of the state poems on which Eliot is now engaged. You tell us the series is ultimately to be grouped together and called "Coriolan." This piece of information enables you to illuminate these poems by referring them to the special complex of philosophical and social ideas for which Eliot has found an archetype in the broken Roman hero. You think it suggestive to add that this collective title serves to evoke Beethoven's overture, as well as Shakespeare's character. One might go farther and argue that, by choosing the name in its attenuated form, Eliot has deliberately committed himself to Beethoven's conception of his protagonist; but this conception is almost antithetical to that of Shakespeare, as the writers of program notes seldom fail to point out; and to approach the one by means of the other is to become very much confused. Now Eliot, with his sensitive perceptions, must surely have foreseen the consequences of his decision to leave off the second-declension-masculine-nominative-singular termination. It would be impertinent to remind so erudite a poet that Beethoven based his overture upon a court play of his own time, an abstract and stilted piece of humanitarian wrangling by Hofrat Heinrich Joseph von Collin. Yet "Coriolan," to be utterly precise, is less redolent of Shakespeare than of Grillparzer, the "poet of intellectual thralldom," or of Kotzebue, melodramatic symbol of the loss of academic liberties.

My first thought was that possibly, in this case, Eliot had overreached himself and hit off a few more connotations than he had bargained for. I felt for a moment that he might be embarrassed to realize that he had crowned his poetic reflections on the nature of the hero with a title suggesting Metternich, taking Vienna rather than Rome for its setting, tainted with the suspicion of intrigue, reaction, and pensioned poetry. My second thought was that, by his own confession, his admirers have discovered unexpected significances in Eliot's writing ere now, and that he has a reserve of surprising *savoir faire* for these occasions. I could even imagine him coolly incorporating into his original design the obtrusive associations that—as I have pointed out—cluster about the name "Coriolan," and discovering in the Viennese tinge, after all, an authentic, if somewhat stiff and debilitated, assertion of the Monarchic, as opposed to the Napoleonic, principle. And the matter might be clarified for all time and given the status of doctrine by a few casually trenchant paragraphs dropped somewhere into the corpus of Eliot's critical prose, ending perhaps with a sudden intimation of Kotzebue's manifest ethical and artistic superiority to Goethe!

However, one might pursue the same exegetical methods elsewhere in Eliot and not emerge so happily for everyone concerned. For example, the juxtaposition of the words "watchful" and "waiting" in the description of the Leader from the same poem might, even to a delicate ear, suggest a recent leader in whose eyes it could hardly be said that there was "no interrogation." The name of the old companion-in-arms whom the poet encountered on King William Street, could, by an ingenious turn of argument, be established as an appropriate symbol for the American abroad. Yet, since we are now speaking of *The Waste Land,* it would be harder to explain the wanton misreading of Ovid on which Eliot claims to have hinged a crucial passage in his poem (Milman Parry is my authority). What, in short, is the sufficient reason that compels the reader of Eliot to keep up with the reactionary French press in such demanding detail, and at the same time to forget that Prufrock is actually the cognomen of a successful Saint Louis manufacturer? Clearly, it is not impossible to catch Eliot napping or to find, in his text, an occasional *crux* from which no amount of enthusiastic higher criticism can extricate him.

All this is mere caviling, of course, and the petty discrepancies I have uncovered may, at most, be only tactical errors; but my point is that if, by the application of processes no more farfetched than those normally involved in the digestion of Eliot's poems, they can be made to yield inferences obviously alien to the poet's purpose, his whole system may thereby be reduced to absurdity. In calling his recent verses "Coriolan," he is possibly only adding another impressionistic touch to his accumulation of atmosphere by suggesting the background of a concert room; but, if such is the case, he errs by expecting the reader's interest in his reference to be as shallow as his own. Is Eliot justified in arbitrarily delimiting the connotations he has conjured up? Can he control an inference, once he has touched it off? Is any single poet, working outside a fixed set of conventions, wise and farseeing enough to avoid all the pitfalls of associative anarchy that Richards has explored and of which he has given us so terrifying an account? If the system of poetic suggestion that Eliot employs is to be regulated by anything stronger and more universal than personal caprice, the poet must not only be sensitive, erudite, and precise; he must be omniscient.

Your essay is a measured and authoritative demonstration of the vitality of tradition. By incidentally segregating and appraising so many varying strands of thought, by affirming the continuity of literature as well as life, and by recording the very impact of ideas from the past on an acute contemporary consciousness, you have given the book a critical purport that is almost independent of its subject. In narrowing the focus to Eliot himself, I am tempted to ask whether you have not kept your survey of his background too exclusively in the abode where the Eternal are. Eliot, no doubt, will be pleased with the austere and discriminating taste you have shown in selecting his influences. Latterly he has revealed an increasing disposition to cover his tracks, to make some of his more advanced critical discoveries retroactive. But Eliot has few indiscretions to account for and no retractions to offer. Surely there is nothing abnormal in the development of his interests and views; possibly, to the critic, there is something significant. A man cannot choose his own ancestors, after all: and if we ignore Eliot's immediate literary environment in favor of more remote ones, we put him in the awkward situation of a rich costermonger who leases a place in Surrey and fills it with spurious portraits. One can no sooner understand Eliot without taking into consideration the literary movements of the past half-century than appreciate Donne without knowing the Elizabethan sonneteers. Albert Friend, whom you may have known, confronted Eliot with a series of parallel passages from his own work and that of Morris, Swinburne, *et al.*, and to most of them he owned up. One may too readily assume that Eliot's critical favorites have been his most constant models, and here again I must regret that you have not seen fit to distinguish style from thought.

Eliot the critic, and the critic of Eliot as well, would doubtless prefer to contemplate Dante and the *Symbolistes*. Yet in order to trace the progress of Eliot as a poet, one must also face the less attractive task of treating Pound and the Imagists—not to mention Browning and the Pre-Raphaelites. The other evening, when I picked up an early volume of Ezra Pound, I had a sudden realization of the literary outlook from which he and, in a slightly lesser degree, Eliot had started. It was Pound the *Rive Gauche* Browning in his full repertory of poses—half Villon, half Kipling, with a dash of bitters—flaunting his absurd Wardour Street vocabulary and his erudition borrowed from the booksellers on the *quais*. But the genesis of such a poetic achievement as "Gerontion" could clearly be discerned in an experimental echo like "La Fraisne." This poem and "Marvoil" and perhaps a few more, unlike the rest of the verse then being written in English, were not mere still lifes or, at best, landscapes. Under the masquerade there existed a robust and genuine personality, and his archaic trappings seemed the more unreal by contrast.

Pound exercised his talent for self-dramatization to rescue the lyric from the pointless prettiness and the unexploited observation of the Edwardians and others. He would substitute "for dreams—men," as he proclaimed in his manifesto "Against the Crepuscular Spirit in Modern Poetry." More than one of his collections is significantly entitled *Personae*. Here we must acknowledge his debt, and the debt of all who follow, to Robert Browning, who—at a time when poetry had been almost entirely emasculated—was able to isolate the most flexible and characteristic genre of English verse, the soliloquy, and to preserve it in aromatic spirits. But Browning's sense of the past was, in general, the kind one experiences in walking through the Victoria and Albert Museum. What was really lacking was a sense of the present, and Pound's early "Piccadilly" revealed as passionate a contemporaneity as anything in *The Waste Land*. The romantic medievalists of the nineteenth century were trying to manipulate lay figures before painted backdrops; Pound and Eliot, in their various disguises, spoke for themselves, and became—like Shakespeare's Romans—timeless.

But Pound and Eliot have gone in opposite directions since the day their paths crossed in the *selva oscura* of Imagism. Pound's career, unlike Eliot's, will never be reckoned as one of his artistic achievements; it has been too haphazard, too undisciplined, too peripheral. While Eliot has become increasingly intent upon his *rapports* with society, Pound has gone into retreat and hoisted his drawbridge. Like a retired tragedian a little mad but harmless, he continues to strut and fret and rehearse his favorite roles. Now he is Guido Cavalcanti, now Peire Vidal, now Lao T'ze; but most of the time these days he plays over his greatest success, Malatesta, a loftier and less self-conscious pose than the others—but still a pose. And when we come upon him muttering strangely and grimacing fearfully and gesturing a little ridiculously, we endeavor to give him our polite attention and not to smile. The hegira from Idaho to Rapallo seems exotic and farfetched; the pilgrimage from Saint Louis to Russell Square is, in the light of the criticism and comment with which Eliot has consolidated his position, not only plausible but inevitable.

To the growth of a historical consciousness in literature, Pound and Eliot furnish an appropriate climax, when poetry and criticism become complementary, if not interchangeable, and both are occasionally mistaken for an anthology. Ever since the heroes of Henry James—Baedeker in hand—began to haunt the capitals of Europe, we Americans in particular have taken ourselves rather seriously as heirs of all the ages. We sent out painters, professors, and *parvenus* to admire, report, and exclaim. Like the Oriental visitor of the eighteenth century, the American, under this eclectic discipline at best, was able to view the past more steadily and completely than the European, because its institutional survivals had not intruded so far into his own life. Thus his American origins were a source of strength to Eliot, when he became an English literary critic. Tillyard told me that, in his opinion, the chief quality Eliot brought to the criticism of English literature was intolerance. When we envisage the state of uncontrolled astigmatic catholicity which was being genially promoted by Gosse and Saintsbury, as well as by Squire and McCarthy, and by a whole crew of blind mouths with their appreciations and reviews, we must admit that it was up to someone to cross the Atlantic with this alien contribution.

The forces of tradition, in their present confused and adulterated state, could not have been so acutely apprehended by anyone on whose training they had operated directly. And yet, since the circumstances of Eliot's life had at no time cut him off completely from tradition, he has been able to make his way back to it in steady, logical steps. But why should Eliot, having originally perceived the subject with such *finesse*, now be so willing to embrace its impure and desiccated concrete embodiment, modern orthodoxy? *Que diable allait-il faire dans cette galère?* As one who does from theoretical motives what others do from use and wont, he is likely to be regarded within the fold as a doctrinaire. His tract on the Lambeth Conference is indeed a curiosity in the annals of theology. If a proselyte may censure a synod, why need he have joined the church at all—unless, perchance, to make the most of an anomalous situation? Eliot has been converted by the persistent intelligence, the measured doctrine, and the cogent

sonority of a number of seventeenth-century divines; but he must gen-
uflect to the decretals of a conclave of stout, gaitered old gentlemen
whose talents are expended in district visiting, wireless talks, and
Consols. It is a supreme test of faith. His religion, one might almost
venture to say, and to cite Dean and Chapter for it, is a more serene
and purer conception than that held by the ordained clergy of the
Church of England. It is, in short, a literary conception.

Arnold has been found wanting by this generation because he
brought a purely literary training to bear on modern life, because he
presented the spectacle of a school inspector attempting to settle the
problems of church and state. A knowledge of "the best that has been
thought and said" somehow did not seem to prepare a person for the
moral shock of reading that "Wragg is in custody." Although Eliot has
not been afraid to face and to criticize modern life, he has not been
able to take his last stand on any firmer ground than that hypothetical
and highly selective reconstruction of the past which generally comes
to be the mental climate of the professional man of letters. He has recently attacked, with much justification, any theory of economic de-
terminism for the future; but, if one as insufficiently acquainted with
economics as Eliot is may say so, he cannot retract the economic developments of the past century; and it is these developments, unfortunately, which have made obsolescent any program his authorities have
to offer. Having arrived at his present position by sound abstract rea-
soning, he has contracted, of late, a habit of giving out endorsements
to various recent manifestations which seem to offer a temporary illustration of his views: witness his sanction of the English distributists,
the Nashville agrarians in this country, and other groups who seek to
evade economic difficulties by reversion to a more primitive scheme of
social organization. Their naïveté, and his, is reminiscent of Shelley's:
"If England were divided into forty republics, . . . each would produce philosophers and poets . . ." Today there is particular danger
that the purity of Eliot's motives will be misunderstood, and that, as
in the case of the late Stefan George, it will be taken for granted that
he has given his benediction to an atavistic and obscurantist political
movement.

Eliot's most ambitious literary creation is the world about which he
writes. Whenever he discusses religion, society, politics, or economics,
he has reference not to actuality but to some non-Euclidean realm devised for the convenience of critics and professors, where causation

is strict and behavior logical, where generalizations are rigidly enforced and material factors kept in their place. Eliot is a Platonist *malgré lui,* for his world is naught but a pale reflection of the world of ideas. Perhaps it would be more accurate to say that he has created a kind of mirage by projecting his own private system on the world without, by a process of teleology or what the psychologists call wishful thinking. His verse and prose, taken together, constitute a cosmic comedy, with his personal preoccupations as the *dramatis personae;* Dante, Coriolanus, Baudelaire, and I. A. Richards—all equally real— are among the heroes of the piece, and the villains, for whom he has doubtless reserved some writhing torment, include Sweeney, Hobbes, Shelley, and Sir Ferdinand Klein. Strictly speaking, Eliot's church never existed, and that is why it is such a satisfactory haven. Perfect orthodoxy today can be attained only in a library—and in a library only of certain books, as Eliot well might add.

To return, then, to the library, where a more comfortable discussion awaits us, I have often thought it might prove illuminating to codify Eliot's scattered appraisals of English literature. Richards privately suspects Eliot of carrying a little notebook, like a schoolmaster, in which there is a definite mark after the name of every writer. The result of such a codification as I propose would be a hierarchy, presided over by a fastidious and autocratic pope who could canonize and excommunicate at will, unless, of course, one were unprepared to acknowledge the source of Eliot's authority, in which case the whole arrangement would shrink to an ignominiously protestant stature. As editor and publisher, Eliot understands the traffic in influence, the arts of propaganda, the contingencies on which reputations hinge (turn to his most recent discussion of classicism and romanticism for a cold-blooded admission in this regard). His critical task has been to present academic concepts to an artistic audience, to bridge the distance between Oxford and the two Cambridges on the one hand and Bloomsbury, Greenwich Village, and Montparnasse on the other, so that his Jacobeans now enjoy a vogue not dissimilar to the kind of success contemporary literary movements command. In the latter case, Eliot is only following a direction pointed out by Barrett Wendell, when, as the first American to lecture at a French university, he found the seventeenth century a subject peculiarly germane to the intellectual development of both cultures.

Eliot's attempts to depreciate have been, on the whole, less happy than his discoveries. In sniping at Swinburne, Shelley, and others, he is performing a work of supererogation; for has not the very appearance of Eliot's own verse constituted a sufficiently sharp repudiation of the lyricism of the nineteenth century? Without sneering, he has taught the rest to sneer at Milton, a poet whom, in his attitude toward his time and toward his work, Eliot curiously resembles. But I should not speak of Milton, for I do not understand what a "dazzling disregard of the soul" means in this connection, although it might mean that both Milton and Dryden wrote before the Romantic Movement and do not invite a cult of sensibility. In my essay on Cleveland I tried to suggest that Eliot, followed by George Williamson and the rest, has been responsible for the sentimentalization of Donne and the Metaphysicals, who were really an intellectually hard-boiled lot. As for the issue to which Eliot has consecrated the most splenetic passage in his criticism, it is sheer iconoclasm to proclaim Bramhall right and Hobbes wrong in a day when Hobbes is represented by a formidable tradition and the traditions to which Eliot attaches himself have become fragile and tenuous. If Eliot is right, he is now able to play Athanasius, and to maintain his orthodoxy against the whole world. But Athanasius was upheld by posterity; Bramhall was not. The only thing that could have told him, and Eliot after him, that he was right was the Inner Light, of which "it may be said that probably every man knows when he has it, but that any man is likely to think he has it when he has it not; . . . no one, in short, can be the sole judge of whence his inspiration comes." The seeker for authority, in selecting his principles from the tangle of conflicting traditions we have on hand, is governed in his choices by—what? Only his innate sensibility and the flickering guidance of the Inner Light.

In the last analysis, Eliot's critical technique is impressionistic, his dogma based on nothing less ephemeral than good taste, and his authority a personal authority. By his "intuitive precision" I take it you do not imply a theory of criticism through revelation, which would be open to the same objections as the Inner Light. Perhaps you refer to those exhilarating moments when he is able to throw a neglected half-truth into epigrammatic relief, to effect—if I may import a phrase of Valéry's—a sudden economy of thought. Again it is the craftsman's sensibility that has operated, not the critic's principles. His perception of the relationship between Babbitt and Pound will, after a preliminary shock, be conceded; but it is only begging the question, after all; for the two men are related through Eliot, and he himself is their middle term. This subjective logic is characteristic of Eliot's criticism. Nearly half the time he is occupied in the exhibition and degustation of passages, as one savors the bouquet of a sound vintage. " 'Mobled queen' is good." The limitations of sensibility, however, come out rather sharply when it is made the sole apparatus for textual emendation. It is significant that, whenever he discusses the drama, Eliot is chiefly concerned with the problems of dramatic versification. His taste is the more precise and definitive when he is dealing with those genres he habitually employs, reflective poetry and critical prose; in other forms, he is more likely to be led astray by the second-rate, by a Rostand or a Wilkie Collins. Eliot's criticism is most successful when he speaks as a poet.

What drives Eliot afield as a critic is his desire to formulate. Often, particularly in the lectures on the *Use of Poetry*, one has the feeling that he is making a supreme effort, only to achieve the obvious. His penchant for citing the titles of books approved by himself I find a trifle irritating, although I am sure he does it solely in the interests of conscientiously documenting his argument, just as the reader of one of Eliot's reviews is generally given to understand at some point or other that the notions incidental to the article ultimately rest upon the ontological principles which a devout communicant of the Church of England may be expected to maintain. One becomes suspicious, therefore, when Eliot takes a thing for granted. With the employment of the term "autotelic," for example, he seems to have got around the painful duty of expounding a naïve and uncritical esthetic concept. Yet this concept, by leading him to insist on the personality of the writer rather than the conventions under which he wrote, clouds his interpretation of a number of important works—most notably *Hamlet*, where he is still at one with Dowden (a fact which does not impair the value of the generalizations in his essay). It is questionable whether a theory of poetry as the sublimation of the poet's private sufferings, or as a substitute for the confessional, can be reconciled with Eliot's deepening consciousness of the poet's social responsibilities.

As one takes a receding view of Eliot, one is impressed by his ruthless ability to limit himself by the narrow shelves of his library, the very few books from which he has formed his individual frame of reference. Yet it would hardly be exact to call him a traditional poet; the sources of the fragments he has shored up are too widespread and their texture is too variegated. His eclectism comprises European culture from 1300 to 1850. Although Christianity is the only milieu broad enough to envelop both Dante and Baudelaire, a background stretched out so thin loses its uniformity and continuity, and becomes too vague for critical purposes. Eliot points out that Baudelaire was able to blaspheme; it is also worth noting, and a lamentable testimony to the heterodoxy of his day, that he was able to blaspheme and not suffer *auto-da-fé*. But the point is nugatory. A more compelling reason than his eclecticism for not recognizing in Eliot a traditional poet is his failure to discern the significance of convention, as the stylistic means of realizing tradition. The conventions of many dead poets figure in his work; but, for reasons beyond his control, he himself writes in none. And, in the place of convention, the symbolist poet can only present the shifting pattern of his own thoughts. The sole living form in which a system of poetic convention is still enforced is the lyric to the popular song.

My inability to share your enthusiasm for Eliot's recent syllabus of errors may be partially traced to the circumstance under which I approached it. The bookseller sent out *After Strange Gods* and Rivera's *Portrait of America* in the same package. After this devastating comment, any generalization I could make would be an impertinence. I might add, however, that the *volo episcopari* tendencies one previously perceived in Eliot have reached a climax, or that, having enriched the critical vocabulary with such dubious acquisitions as *heresy, error, diabolic, safe,* and *right,* he will be expected in the future to give the less colorful *deplorable* a much-needed rest. Eliot's is an exclusive Inferno, for he condescends to damn few except members in good standing of the Bloomsbury group. But it requires no extraordinary penetration to discover that D. H. Lawrence's characters do not conduct themselves properly; John N. Sumner has often made that particular *trouvaille* in the course of his daily routine. What I had hoped for was a thoughtful affirmation of the dependence of literary characterization upon a definite moral background, and not—despite one or two interesting remarks on Original Sin—an *index expurgatorius.* Nor can I believe that the way to discredit Irving Babbitt's intelligent eclecticism is for Eliot to make a confession of his own ineptitude in the study of Oriental thought, although this naïve enthymeme affords a good illustration of what might be called Eliot's *argumentum ad seipsum.* When I turned away from the book, with Eliot's plaint—"I confess I do not know what to make of a generation which ignores these considerations"—still droning in my ears, I thought of what a long distance it has been between the time when a poet devoted his efforts to shocking the bourgeoisie and a time when the poet devotes his efforts to being shocked by the bourgeoisie.

Eliot has so contrived his career that his position, after every step he has taken, seemed final. Thus, while there is life, there is hope that he will not remain in a state of permanent bafflement. You have profoundly and conclusively explored his relations with the past; dare you chart his relations to the future? The present, at any rate, is distinctly the moment for a careful and detailed consideration of him in his own terms, such as you have given us, before we turn him over to the determinists—psychological and economic—into whose hands our literary history has fallen. His crew of more expansive admirers, such as the Leavises, is already dwindling away. Spender has publicly consigned him to his chapel among the ruins. Richards does not see any indication of more major poetry in the offing. Since his year in this country, one occasionally glimpses an unexpected trait which might almost be characterized as flippancy in Eliot. Whether this is due to the fact that he has transferred his intellectual burdens to the church, or to his decision to put the Clarence Gardens phase of his life definitely behind him, I do not know. In either case, the problem is a private one. Perhaps Auden's brilliant political satire, *The Dance of Death*, conveys some idea of the direction his influence is taking. By repudiating the art-for-art's-sake and Bohemianism of the previous generation, his criticism helped to reclaim the intellectual as a member of society, and, in a sense, to lead the next generation toward communism. Eliot's views and those of the socialist critics—though the distinction must not be blurred—differ less in their positive program, than in the philosophical principles on which they are based.

My notes have run out at last. It was my original thought that I could best tell you how much I liked your essay by swooping down on it here and there from some unaccustomed vantage point. Now, as I read what I have written, I see that this letter could not possibly be useful to anyone beyond myself, and furthermore I am by no means certain that I have managed to make clear to you what a fine job I think you have done. I cannot tell you how deeply touched I was by the thought that you should send your manuscript to me, and I only wish we had been able to discuss these matters together. In such cases, I have not too much confidence in the power of written words or, perhaps I should say, in my power over them; they are too forward, too vain, too intrusive, too anxious to bring their friends. After some hesitation, I have decided to mention, before concluding, the passage in which you allude to my impressions of *Coriolanus* at the Comédie Française. The letter you have quoted is, of course, your property, and if anything in it is of any use to you, you are at perfect liberty to incorporate it into what you have to say. But I feel, in all seriousness, that, by interrupting the rhythm of your essay to introduce my name, you have allowed a kindly instinct to blemish what is in all other respects a well-proportioned and mature achievement.

As ever,

Harry

INDEX